A GAZETTEER OF ILLINOIS

IN
THREE PARTS

CONTAINING A GENERAL VIEW OF THE STATE, A GENERAL VIEW OF EACH COUNTY, AND A PARTICULAR DESCRIPTION OF EACH TOWN, SETTLEMENT, STREAM, PRAIRIE, BOTTOM, BLUFF, ETC.; ALPHABETICALLY ARRANGED

By J. M. Peck, A. M.
AUTHOR OF A NEW GUIDE FOR EMIGRANTS, ETC.

Second Edition
ENTIRELY REVISED, CORRECTED, AND ENLARGED

HERITAGE BOOKS
2007

HERITAGE BOOKS
AN IMPRINT OF HERITAGE BOOKS, INC.

Books, CDs, and more—Worldwide

For our listing of thousands of titles see our website
at
www.HeritageBooks.com

A Facsimile Reprint
Published 2007 by
HERITAGE BOOKS, INC.
Publishing Division
65 East Main Street
Westminster, Maryland 21157-5026

Copyright © 1993 Heritage Books, Inc.

Entered according to the act of congress, in the year 1834, by
J. M. Peck, in the clerk's office of the district court of Illinois

— Publisher's Notice —
In reprints such as this, it is often not possible to remove blemishes from the original. We feel the contents of this book warrant its reissue despite these blemishes and hope you will agree and read it with pleasure.

International Standard Book Number: 978-1-55613-782-2

INTRODUCTION.

The utility and importance of an accurate Gazetteer of Illinois to every class of citizens within the state, and to all other persons who desire full and particular information, are too obvious to need proof.

The first edition of this work was undertaken by the author more than four years since, at the suggestion and request of many of his fellow citizens, some of whom filled distinguished posts of honor in the state and nation. Four thousand two hundred copies of it were published by R. Goudy of Jacksonville, Illinois, a due proportion of which were sent to other states, and have been extensively circulated.

In complying with the call for a new edition, it became necessary to make an entire revision of the work and add much new matter—so rapid had been the changes and the progress of this state in three years. Ten new counties have been organised—

Boone, Cass, Kane, Livingston, McHenry, Ogle, Stephenson, Whiteside, Will, and Winnebago—and a large addition to the descriptive list of names in part third.

No state in the "Great West" has attracted so much attention, and elicited so many enquiries from those who desire to avail themselves of the advantages of a settlement in a new and rising country, as that of Illinois; and none is filling up so rapidly with an emigrating population from all parts of the United States, and several kingdoms of Europe. Consequently, the call for correct information of all portions of the state has become pressing.

In preparing this work with special reference to to this call, the author has kept one point constantly in view. Accuracy of description, or a registry of facts and things as they actually exist in every part of the state, has been a paramount object. How far he has succeeded will be submitted to the judgment of his fellow citizens in each county. That no imperfections or inaccuracies exist in the work, the author is not vain enough to imagine; but that as a whole, or as to its parts, it is sufficiently accurate for all useful purposes, will appear on reference to the labor bestowed to obtain correct information of every spot he attempts to describe.

To the facts and observations of many years' residence in the state, and traveling in all the older settlements, of which record was made for his own use, and that of his immediate friends, may be added the following facilities for gaining correct topographical and historical information.

In the winter of 1832, '33, the author spent several weeks at Vandalia, during the session of the legislature, where the principal part of the work was written. Access was had through the polite attention of the governor, secretary of state, auditor, and other public officers, to all the public documents, state records, and journals. Both houses of the legislature, with equal liberality, granted a copy of the laws and journals of that body, and likewise, (if duplicates existed,) copies of all preceding laws, journals, and printed documents, of the territorial and state governments. These were carefully examined, and from them much valuable information obtained.

Personal intercourse was also had with the members of the legislature and other gentlemen, from each county, and from that source many of the facts in the general description of the counties in Part Second, and the particulars of each place in Part Third, were obtained. The course of the author was, to spend two or three hours each evening with gentlemen from a county, who were well acquainted with every part, and write a brief sketch of the same.

These were drawn off in proper order the next day, and, in many instances, submitted to the same persons for inspection and revision. All the items for one county were thus finished before entering upon a survey of another.

By this method, no creek, prairie, or settlement, known by name amongst the people, would escape notice, and accuracy of description would be attained.

These accounts were then collated with the statements received from other sources, and from the author's own notes of observation.

The same mode, including a more extensive correspondence with postmasters, and other gentlemen of intelligence in every county, has been pursued, together with a large stock of information gained while compiling with another gentleman, a "*New Sectional Map of Illinois*," published in New-York by J. H. Colton.

No small pains have been taken to obtain the latest information, especially from the recently organised counties in the north, where new settlements are made every month, and villages spring up as the growth of a summer. Still, some settlements, planted within the present year, may not have come to the author's knowledge.

It would be rather invidious to name individuals from whom the author has received aid in this work, and to whom he is desirous of returning his humble and grateful acknowledgements. To the officers of state, the members of the legislature, postmasters, and other citizens, his thanks are due. Much of the real value of the work is from information they imparted, or from documents and records over which they had legal control.

The Appendix of the former volume containing a brief Gazetteer of the Wisconsin Territory has been left out of this work. That territory, having an organised government, and a great increase of its population, counties, settlements, etc. should have a Gazetteer of its own. For this purpose the author is aiming to collect materials.

It has caused the author no small trouble to decide upon the orthography of proper names. Many of those found in this work have never been published to any extent, so as to become settled in orthography. In offering new names to the public it is desirable the spelling should conform to the pronunciation. While the author does not feel authorised to make innovations upon established usages, he is willing to contribute his humble mite to improve the orthography of the language, where custom has not fixed it.

Many aboriginal names in the west were first written in French, and after by persons of very inferior literary attainments. Some of these have already undergone changes. Thus we have Wabash for Oubache,—Washitau for Ouchitta; and for similar reasons we ought to write Wisconsin for Ouisconsin,—Mackinau for Michilimacinac,—Merodosia for Marais d'Ogee, etc.

Such aboriginal names as have not been printed, the

author has spelled according to the pronunciation, and for the correctness of this he has relied upon information of persons accustomed to hear the sounds expressed by natives.

After all, several discrepancies will be discovered in different parts of the work.

In such names as have the French or broad sound of *a*, he has preferred the termination of *au* to *aw*. The exceptions are in Wabash and a few others, where the *a* is sanctioned by custom, and the sound generally understood.

Rock Spring, (*Illinois*,) *May*, 1837.

PART FIRST.

GENERAL VIEW OF THE STATE OF ILLINOIS.

Situation, Boundaries and Extent.—Face of the Country, and Qualities of Soil.—Rivers and Lakes.—Mineral, Animal, and Vegetable Productions.—Manufactures.—Natural Curiosities, and Antiquities.—Climate and Health.—Civil Divisions.—Government.—Education.—Religious Denominations.—Public Lands.—Plans of Internal Improvement.—History.—Miscellaneous Remarks.

SITUATION, BOUNDARIES, AND EXTENT.

THE State of Illinois is situated between 37 and 42 degrees, 30 minutes, north latitude, and between 10 degrees, 25 minutes, and 14 degrees, 30 minutes, west longitude from Washington city. It is bounded on the north by Wisconsin territory, north east by Lake Michigan, east by Indiana, south east and south by Kentucky, and west by the state of Missouri, and Territory of Wisconsin.

Its extreme length is 380 miles, and its extreme width, 220 miles;—its average width, 150 miles. The area of the whole state, including the portion of lake Michigan within its boundaries, is 59,300 square miles.

This result has been obtained after a careful estimate of the surveyed portions in the land districts, and calculating the remainder by its medium length and breadth.

The exact length of its northern portion is now ascertained from the continuation of the fourth principal meridian, from the vicinity of Rock river to the northern boundary. The exact length of the northern boundary from the Mississippi at the northwestern corner of the state, to lake Michigan, is 144 1-3 miles. The eastern boundary leaves the Wabash river at a point about 60 miles north of Vincennes, and continues due north to the northern boundary of Indiana. The northern boundary line extends into the middle of lake Michigan.

The act of Congress authorising the people of Illinois to form a state government, and the convention in framing the constitution, described the following as the boundaries of the state.

" Beginning at the mouth of the Wabash river, thence up the same, and with the line of Indiana, to the north western corner of said state; *thence east with the line of tha same state, to the middle of lake Michigan;* thence north along the middle of said lake, to north latitude 42 degrees and 30 minutes; thence west to the middle of the Mississippi river; and thence down along the middle of that river to its confluence with the Ohio river; and thence up the latter river along its northwestern shore to the beginning."

Within these described boundaries, allowing for the curves of the rivers, are not less than 59,300 square miles or 37,952,000 acres.

The water area of the state is computed at 3,750 square miles as follows:

	Square Miles.
Lake Michigan	2,750
One half of the Mississippi, for 700 miles, including its meanderings, at the ordinary stage of water	350
Half of the Wabash river	50
Estimates for small lakes, ponds, and rivers within the state	600
	3,750

With this deduct 5,550 square miles for irreclaimable wastes, and there is left, in Illinois, 50,000 square miles or 32 millions of acres of arable land. In this estimate, inundated lands, submerged by high waters, but which may be reclaimed at a moderate expense are included.

FACE OF THE COUNTRY, AND QUALITIES OF SOIL.

THE general surface is level, or moderately undulating, the northern and southern portions are broken, and somewhat hilly, but no portion of the state is traversed with ranges of hills or mountains. At the verge of the alluvial soil on the margins of rivers, there are ranges of "bluffs" intersected with ravines. The bluffs are usually from fifty to one hundred and fifty feet high, where an extended surface of table land commences, covered with prairies and forest of various shapes and sizes.

When examined minutely, there are several varieties in the surface of this state which will be briefly specified and described.

1. *Inundated Lands.* I apply this term to all those portions, which, for some part of the year, are under water. These include portions of the river bottoms, and portions of the interior of large prairies, with the lakes and ponds which, for half the year or more, are without water. The term "bottom" is used throughout the west to denote the alluvial soil on the margin of rivers, usually called "intervals," in New England. Portions of this description of land are flowed for a longer or shorter period, when the rivers are full. Probably one tenth of the bottom lands are of this description; for though the water may not stand for any length of time, it prevents settlement and cultivation, though it does not interrupt the growth of timber and vegetation. These tracts are on the bottoms of the Wabash, Ohio, Mississippi, Illinois, and all the interior rivers.

When the rivers rise above their ordinary height, the

waters of the smaller streams which are backed up by the freshets of the former, break over their banks, and cover all the low grounds. Here they stand for a few days, or for many weeks, especially towards the bluffs; for it is a striking fact in the geology of the western country, that all the river bottoms are higher on the margins of the streams than at some distance back. Whenever increase of population shall create a demand for this species of soil, the most of it can be reclaimed at comparatively small expense. Its fertility will be inexhaustible, and if the waters from the rivers could be shut out by dykes or levees, the soil would be perfectly dry. Most of the small lakes on the American bottom disappear in the summer, and leave a deposit of vegetable matter undergoing decomposition, or a luxuriant coat of weeds and grass.

As our prairies mostly lie between the streams that drain the country, the interior of the large ones is usually level. Here are formed small ponds and lakes after the winter and spring rains, which remain to be drawn off by evaporation, or absorbed by the soil. Hence the middle of our large, level prairies are wet, and for several weeks portions of them are covered with water. To remedy this inconvenience completely, and render all this portion of soil dry and productive, only requires a ditch or drain of two or three feet deep to be cut into the nearest ravine. In many instances a single furrow with the plough, would drain many acres. At present this species of inundated land offers no inconvenience to the people, except in the production of miasm, and even that, perhaps, becomes too much diluted with the atmosphere to produce mischief before it reaches the settlements on the borders of the prairie. Hence the inference is correct that our inundated lands present fewer obstacles to the settlement and growth of the country, and can be reclaimed at much less expense, than the swamps and salt marshes of the Atlantic states.

RIVER BOTTOMS, OR ALLUVION.

The surface of our alluvial bottoms is not entirely level. In some places it resembles alternate waves of the ocean, and looks as though the waters had left their deposit in ridges, and retired.

The portion of bottom land capable of present cultivation, and on which the waters never stand, if, at an extreme freshet, it is covered, is a soil of exhaustless fertility; a soil that for ages past has been gradually deposited by the annual floods. Its average depth on the American bottom is from twenty to twenty-five feet. Logs of wood, and other indications, are found at that depth. The soil dug from wells on these bottoms, produces luxuriantly the first year.

The most extensive and fertile tract, of this description of soil, in this state, is the *American Bottom*, a name it received when it constituted the western boundary of the United States, and which it has retained ever since. It commences at the mouth of the Kaskaskia river, five miles below the town of Kaskaskia, and extends northwardly along the Mississippi to the bluffs at Alton, a distance of ninety miles. Its average width is five miles, and contains about 450 square miles, or 288,000 acres. Opposite St. Louis, in St. Clair county, the bluffs are seven miles from the river, and filled with inexhaustible beds of coal. The soil of this bottom is an argillaceous or a silicious loam, accordingly as clay or sand happens to predominate in its formation.

On the margin of the river, and of some of its lakes, is a strip of heavy timber, with a thick undergrowth, which extends from half a mile to two miles in width, but from thence to the bluffs, it is principally prairie. It is interspersed with sloughs, lakes, and ponds, the most of which become dry in the fall season.

The soil of the American bottom is inexhaustibly rich. About the French towns it has been cultivated, and produced corn in succession for more than a century, without exhausting its fertilising powers. The only objection that can be offered to this tract is its unhealthy character. This, however, has diminished considerably within eight or ten years. The geological feature noticed in the last article—that all our bottoms are higher on the margin of the stream than towards the bluffs, explains the cause why so much standing water is on the bottom land, which, during the summer stagnates and throws off noxious effluvia. These lakes are usually full of vegetable matter undergoing decomposition, and which produces large quantities of miasm. Some of the lakes are clear and of a sandy bottom, but the most are of a different character. The French settled near a lake or a river, apparently in the most unhealthy places, and yet their constitutions are little affected, and they usually enjoy good health, though dwarfish and shrivelled in their form and features.

"The villages of Kaskaskia, Prairie du Rocher, and Cahokia, were built up by their industry in places where Americans would have perished. Cultivation has, no doubt, rendered this tract more salubrious than formerly; and an increase of it, together with the construction of drains and canals, will make it one of the most eligible in the states. The old inhabitants advise the emigrants not to plant corn in the immediate vicinity of their dwellings, as its rich and massy foliage prevents the sun from dispelling the deleterious vapours."*

These lakes and ponds could be drained at a small expense, and the soil would be susceptible of cultivation. The early settlements of the Americans were either on this bottom, or the contiguous bluffs.

Beside the American bottom, there are others that resemble it in its general character, but not in extent. In Union county there is an extensive bottom on the borders of the Mississippi. Above the mouth of the Illinois, and along the borders of the counties of Calhoun, Pike, and Adams, there is a series of bottoms, with much good and

* Beck.

elevated land, but the inundated grounds around, present objections to a dense population at present.

The bottoms of Illinois, where not inundated, are equal in fertility, and the soil is less adhesive than most parts of the American bottom. This is likewise the character of the bottoms in the northern parts of the state.

The bottoms of the Kaskaskia are generally covered with a heavy growth of timber, and in many places inundated when the river is at its highest floods.

The extensive prairies adjoining will create a demand for all this timber. The bottom lands on the Wabash are of various qualities. Near the mouth, much of it is inundated. Higher up it overflows in high freshets.

These bottoms, especially the American, are the best regions in the United States for raising stock, particularly horses, cattle, and swine. Seventy-five bushels of corn to the acre is an ordinary crop. The roots and worms of the soil, the acorns and other fruits from the trees, and the fish of the lakes, accelerate the growth of swine. Horses and cattle find exhaustless supplies of grass in the prairies; and pea vines, buffalo grass, wild oats, and other herbage in the timber, for summer range; and often throughout most of the winter. In all the rush bottoms, they fatten during the severe weather on rushes. The bottom soil is not so well adapted to the production of small grain, as of maize or Indian corn, on account of its rank growth, and being more subject to blast or fall down before harvest, than on the uplands.

3. *Prairies.* A large part, probably two-thirds of the surface of the state, is covered with prairies. A common error has prevailed abroad that our prairie land is wet. Much of it is undulating and entirely dry. *Prairie* is a French word, signifying *meadow*, and is applied to any description of surface, that is destitute of timber and brushwood, and clothed with grass. Wet, dry, level, and undulating, are terms of description merely, and apply to prairies in the same sense as they do to forest lands.

Level prairie is sometimes wet, the water not running

off freely is left to be absorbed by the soil, or evaporated by the sun. Crawfish throw up their hillocks in this soil, and the farmer who cultivates it, will find his labors impeded by the water.

In the southern part, that is, south of the national road leading from Terre Haute to the Mississippi, the prairies are comparatively small, varying in size from those of several miles in width, to those which contain only a few acres. As we go northward, they widen and extend on the more elevated ground between the water courses to a vast distance, and are frequently from six to twelve miles in width. Their borders are by no means uniform. Long points of timber project into the prairies, and line the banks of the streams, and points of prairie project into the timber between these streams. In many instances are copses and groves of timber, from one hundred to two thousand acres, in the midst of prairies, like islands in the ocean. This is a common feature in the country between the Sangamon river and lake Michigan, and in the northern parts of the state. The lead mine region, both in this state and the Wisconsin territory, abounds with these groves.

The *origin* of these prairies has caused much speculation. We might as well dispute about the origin of forests, upon the assumption that the natural covering of the earth was grass. Probably one half of the earth's surface, in a state of nature, was prairies or barrens. Much of it, like our western prairies, was covered with a luxuriant coat of grass and herbage. The *steppes* of Tartary, the *pampas* of South America, the *savannas* of the southern, and the *prairies* of the western states, designate similar tracts of country. Mesopotamia, Syria, and Judea had their ancient prairies, on which the patriarchs fed their flocks. Missionaries in Burmah, and travellers in the interior of Africa, mention the same description of country. Where the tough sward of the prairie is once formed, timber will not take root. Destroy this by the plough, or by any other method, and it is soon converted into forest land. There are large tracts of country in the older settlements, where, thirty or forty years since, the farmers mowed their hay, that are now covered with a forest of young timber of rapid growth.

The fire annually sweeps over the prairies, destroying the grass and herbage, blackening the surface, and leaving a deposit of ashes to enrich the soil.

4. *Barrens.* This term, in the western dialect, does not indicate *poor land*, but a species of surface of a mixed character, uniting forest and prairie. These are called "openings" in Michigan.

The timber is generally scattering, of a rough and stunted appearance, interspersed with patches of hazle and brushwood, and where the contest between the fire and timber is kept up, each striving for the mastery.

In the early settlements of Kentucky, much of the country below and south of Green river presented a dwarfish and stunted growth of timber, scattered over the surface, or collected in clumps, with hazle and shrubbery intermixed. This appearance led the first explorers to the inference that the soil itself must necessarily be poor, to produce so scanty a growth of timber, and they gave the name of *barrens* to the whole tract of country. Long since it has been ascertained that this description of land is amongst the most productive soil in the state. The term *barren* has since received a very extensive application throughout the west. Like all other tracts of country, the barrens present a considerable diversity of soil. In general, however, the surface is more uneven or rolling than the prairies, and sooner degenerates into ravines and sink-holes. Wherever timber barely sufficient for present purposes can be found, a person need not hesitate to settle in the barrens. These tracts are almost invariably healthy; they possess a greater abundance of pure springs of water, and the soil is better adapted for all kinds of produce, and all descriptions of seasons, wet and dry, than the deeper and richer mould of the bottoms and prairies.

When the fires are stopped, these barrens produce timber, at a rate of which no northern emigrant can have any just conception. Dwarfish shrubs and small trees of oak and hickory are scattered over the surface, where for years they have contended with the fires for a precarious existence, while a mass of roots, sufficient for the support of large trees, have accumulated in the earth. Soon as they are protected from the ravages of the annual fires, the more thrifty sprouts shoot forth, and in ten years are large enough for corn cribs and stables.

As the fires on the prairies become stopped by the surrounding settlements, and the wild grass is eaten out and trodden down by the stock, they begin to assume the character of barrens; first hazle and other shrubs, and finally a thicket of young timber, covers the surface.

5. *Forest, or timbered land.* In general, Illinois is abundantly supplied with timber, and were it equally distributed through the state there would be no part wanting. The apparent scarcity of timber where the prairie predominates, is not so great an obstacle to the settlement as has been supposed. For many of the purposes to which timber is applied, substitutes are found. The rapidity with which the young growth pushes itself forward, without a single effort on the part of man to accelerate it, and the readiness with which the prairie becomes converted into thickets, and then into a forest of young timber, shows that, in another generation, timber will not be wanting in any part of Illinois.

The kinds of timber most abundant are oaks of various species, black and white walnut, ash of several kinds, elm, sugar maple, honey locust, hackberry, linden, hickory, cotton wood, pecaun, mulberry, buckeye, sycamore, wild cherry, box elder, sassafras, and persimmon. In the southern and eastern parts of the state are yellow poplar, and beech; near the Ohio are cypress, and in several counties are clumps of yellow pine and cedar. The undergrowth are redbud, papaw, sumach, plum, crab apple, grape vines, dogwood, spice bush, green brier, hazle, &c.

The alluvial soil of the rivers produces cotton wood and sycamore timber of amazing size.

For ordinary purposes there is now timber enough in

most parts of the state, to say nothing about the artificial production of timber, which may be effected with little trouble and expense. The black locust, a native of Ohio and Kentucky, may be raised from the seed, with less labour than a nursery of apple trees. It is of rapid growth, and as a valuable and lasting timber, claims the attention of our farmers. It forms one of the cleanliest and most beautiful shades, and when in blossom, gives a rich prospect, and sends abroad a delicious fragrance.

6. *Knobs, Bluffs, Ravines, and Sink-holes.* Under these heads are included tracts of uneven country found in various parts of the state.

Knobs are ridges of flint limestone, intermingled and covered with earth, and elevated one or two hundred feet above the common surface. This species of land is of little value for cultivation, and usually has a sprinkling of dwarfish, stunted timber, like the barrens.

The steep hills and natural mounds that border the alluvions have obtained the name of *bluffs.* Some are in long, parallel ridges, others are in the form of cones and pyramids. In some places precipices of limestone rock, from fifty to one or two hundred feet high, form these bluffs.

Ravines are formed amongst the bluffs, and often near the borders of prairies, which lead down to the streams.

Sink-holes are circular depressions in the surface like a basin. They are of various sizes, from ten to fifty feet deep, and from ten to one or two hundred yards in circumference. Frequently they contain an outlet for the water received by the rains. Their existence shows that the subtratum is secondary limestone, abounding in subterraneous cavities.

There are but few tracts of *stony ground* in the state; that is, where loose stones are scattered over the surface, and imbedded in the soil. Towards the northern part of the state, tracts of stony ground exist. Quarries of stone exist in the bluffs, and in the banks of the streams and ravines throughout the state.

The soil is porous, easy to cultivate, and exceedingly

productive. A strong team is required to break up the prairies, on account of the firm, grassy sward which covers them. But when subdued they become fine, arable lands.

RIVERS AND LAKES.

This state is bounded on three sides by the Mississippi, Ohio, and Wabash rivers. The Illinois, Kaskaskia, Sangamon, and many smaller streams are entirely within its boundaries. Others, as the Kankakee, Rock river, and Vermillion of the Wabash, run part of their course within the state.

The Mississippi, which, in its meanderings, runs about 700 miles along its western border, takes its rise in Itasca lake, in latitude 45 degrees north.

From this to the falls of St. Anthony, a distance of about five hundred miles, it runs a devious course, first southeast; then southwest; and, finally, southeast again; which last it continues without much deviation till it reaches the Missouri. From thence its course is a few degrees east of south to the mouth of the Ohio.

The appearance and character of the Mississippi, above and below the mouth of the Missouri, are so distinctly marked as to lead to the general opinion that the former is but a branch of the latter. The average width of the Mississippi proper, is from one half to one mile; and its current generally is from two to four miles an hour, varying according to the height and volume of the water. The mean descent of this river is about six inches per mile. Its sources are estimated by Mr. Schoolcraft to be 1,330 feet above the level of tide water at the gulf of Mexico; the distance being computed at 3,000 miles. Below the mouth of the Missouri, the water of the Mississippi has the turbid appearance of the Missouri, and was formerly obstructed with *snags* and *sawyers.* These obstructions to the navigation have been partially removed by the enterprising Captain Shreve and his snag boat, in the employment of the general government, and the trees that form these obstructions have been cut away from its banks.

The principal tributaries of the Mississippi, within the state of Illinois, are Rock, Illinois, Kaskaskia and Muddy rivers. The aboriginal name is said to signify "*Father of Waters,*" or "*Great Waters.*"

The Ohio river, which washes the southern boundary of Illinois, is formed by the junction of the Allegheny and Monongahela rivers at Pittsburgh, and after running a southwestern course 1,100 miles, unites with the Mississippi at the extreme south end of the state. At the confluence of these rivers, as is the case with most other rivers in the west, there is an extensive and recently formed alluvion. Below the mouth of the Wabash, no large streams enter the Ohio from Illinois. Saline, Big Bay, and Cash are the largest.

The Wabash river rises in the northeastern part of Indiana, and running first a southwestern, and then a south course, it enters the Ohio about 200 miles above its mouth It is a beautiful stream, and at high water is navigated by steam boats as far as Logansport in Indiana. Its head waters approach within a short distance of the waters of the Maumee of Lake Erie, with which a canal navigation is now being constructed under the authority of the state of Indiana.

About twenty miles below Vincennes, and near the junction of White river, are considerable rapids, which obstruct the navigation in low water. Funds in part have been provided and measures are in train by the two states to improve the navigation at this place. The character of the lands and soil bordering on the Wabash does not differ materially from that on the Ohio and Mississippi; only there is more sandy soil, and its bottoms are more subject to inundation. In this region, and especially in Lawrence and Crawford counties, there are some swamps, called by travellers *purgatories.*

The principal tributaries of the Wabash within the state of Illinois, are the Vermillion, Embarrass, and Little Wabash rivers.

The Illinois, Kaskaskia, Rock, and other rivers within the state will be described under their respective names in the third part of this work. *Lake Michigan* is the only lake deserving special notice. There are several other lakes in different parts of the state, but they are small and unimportant, and rather deserve the name of ponds. A portion of lake Michigan is included within the boundaries of the state, and affords a medium of communication with the northern states and Canada. It is about 280 miles long and its medium width is about 60 miles. About fifty five miles of its southwestern border is in Illinois. Its waters are cool and clear, and it affords fine navigation for schooners and steamboats for about eight months in the year. The plan of a canal to connect its commerce with the navigable waters of the Illinois will be found under the head of " *Plans of Internal Improvement.*"

PRODUCTIONS.

These are naturally classed into *mineral, animal* and *vegetable.*

Minerals. The northern portion of Illinois is inexhaustibly rich in mineral productions, while coal, secondary limestone, and sandstone, are found in every part.

Iron ore has been found in the southern parts of the state, and is said to exist in considerable quantities in the northern parts.

Native copper in small quantities has been found on Muddy river, in Jackson county, and back of Harrisonville, in the bluffs of Monroe county. One mass weighing seven pounds was found detached at the latter place. A shaft was sunk forty feet deep in 1817, in search of this metal, but without success. Red oxide of iron and oxide of copper were dug out. Crystallized gypsum has been found in small quantities in St. Clair county. Quartz crystals exist in Gallatin county.

Silver is supposed to exist in St. Clair county, two

miles from Rock Spring, from whence Silver Creek derives its name. In the early times, by the French, a shaft was sunk here, and tradition tells of large quantities of the precious metal being obtained. In 1828, many persons in this vicinity commenced digging, and began to dream of immense fortunes, which however vanished during the following winter. They dug up considerable quantities of *horne blende*, the shining specula of which were mistaken for silver.

In the southern part of the state several sections of land have been reserved from sale, on account of the silver ore they are supposed to contain. Marble of a fine quality is found in Randolph county.

Lead is found in vast quantities in the northern part of Illinois, and the adjacent territory. Here are the richest lead mines hitherto discovered on the globe. This portion of country lies principally north of Rock river south of the Wisconsin river. Dubuque's, and other rich mines, are west of the Mississippi.

Native copper, in large quantities, exists in this region, especially at the mouth of Plum creek, and on the Peekatonakee, marked on the map, above Rock river, which puts into the Mississippi. Peekatonakee is a branch of Rock river.

AMOUNT OF LEAD MANUFACTURED.

For many years the Indians, and some of the French hunters and traders, had been accustomed to dig lead in these regions. They never penetrated much below the surface but obtained considerable quantities of the ore, which they sold to the traders.

In 1823, the late Col. James Johnson, of Great Crossings, Ky. and brother to the Hon. R. M. Johnson, obtained a lease from the United States government, and made arrangements to prosecute the business of smelting, with considerable force, which he did the following season. This attracted the attention of enterprising men in Illinois, Missouri, and other states. Some went on in 1826, more followed in 1827, and in 1828 the country was almost literally filled with miners, smelters, merchants, speculators, gamblers, and every description of character. Intelligence, enterprise, and virtue, were thrown in the midst of dissipation, gaming, and every species of vice. Such was the crowd of adventurers in 1829, to this hitherto almost unknown and desolate region, that the lead business was greatly overdone, and the market for awhile nearly destroyed. Fortunes were made almost upon a turn of the spade, and lost with equal facility. The business has revived and is prosecuted to a great extent. Exhaustless quantities of mineral exist here, over a tract of county two hundred miles in extent.

The following table shows the amount of lead made annually at these diggings, from 1821, to September, 30, 1833.

Lbs. of lead made from 1821, to Sept.			1823,	335,130
Do. for the year ending Sept. 30,			1824,	175,220
Do.	do.	do.	1825,	664,530
Do.	do.	do.	1826,	958,842
Do.	do.	do.	1827,	5,182,180
Do.	do.	do.	1828,	11,105,810
Do.	do.	do.	1829,	13,344,150
Do.	do.	do.	1830,	8,323,998
Do.	do.	do.	1831,	6,381,900
Do.	do.	do.	1832,	4,281,876
Do.	do.	do.	1833,	7,941,792
Do.	do.	do.	1834,	7,971,579
Do.	do.	do.	1835,	3,754,290
Total,				70,421,297

The rent accruing to government for the same period, is a fraction short of six millions of pounds.

Formerly the government received 10 per cent. in lead for rents. Now it is 6 per cent.

A part of the Mineral land in the Wisconsin Territory

has been surveyed and brought into market, which will add greatly to the stability and prosperity of the mining business. It is expected that the Mineral lands in Illinois will soon be in market.

Coal. Bituminous coal abounds in this state and may be found in nearly every county. It is frequently perceived without excavation in the ravines and at the points of bluffs.

Exhaustless beds of this article exist in the bluffs adjacent to the American bottom in St. Clair county, of which large quantities are annually transported to St. Louis for fuel.

A Rail Road is now constructing by a private company, from the bluffs to the ferry, six miles, for the purpose of transporting coal to St. Louis.

A large vein of coal, several feet thick, and apparently exhaustless, has been struck in excavating the Illinois and Michigan canal, a few miles below Ottawa.

A bed of *Anthracite* coal, it is said, has been discovered on Muddy river in Jackson county.

Agatized Wood. A petrified tree, of black walnut, was found in the bed of the river Des Plaines, about forty rods above its junction with the Kankakee, imbedded in a horizontal position, in a stratum of sandstone. There is fifty-one and a half feet of the trunk visible—eighteen inches in diameter at its smallest end, and probably three feet at the other end.

Muriate of Soda, or common salt. This is found in various parts of the state, held in solution in the springs. The manufacture of salt by boiling and evaporation is carried on in Gallatin county, twelve miles west-north-west from Shawneetown; in Jackson county, near Brownsville; and in Vermilion county, near Danville. The springs and land are owned by the state, and the works leased.

A coarse freestone, much used in building, is dug from quarries near Alton, on the Mississippi, where large bodies exist.

Scattered over the surface of our prairies, are large masses of rock, of granitic formation, roundish in form, usually called by the people "*lost rocks.*" They will weigh from one thousand to ten or twelve thousand pounds, and are entirely detached, and frequently are found several miles distant from any quarry. Nor has there ever been a quarry of granite discovered in the state. These stones are denominated *bowlders* in mineralogy. That they exist in various parts of Illinois is an undoubted truth; and that they are of a species of granite is equally true, as I have specimens to show. They usually lie on the surface, or are partially imbedded in the soil of our prairies, which is unquestionably of diluvial formation. How they came here is a question of difficult solution.

Medicinal Waters are found in different parts of the state. These are chiefly sulphur springs and chalybeate waters. There is said to be one well in the southern part of the state strongly impregnated with the sulphate of magnesia, or Epsom salts, from which considerable quantities have been made for sale, by simply evaporating the water, in a kettle, over a common fire.

There are several sulphur springs in Jefferson county, to which persons resort for health.

Vegetable Productions. The principal trees and shrubs of Illinois have been noticed under the head of "*Forest or timbered land.*" Of oaks there are several species, as overcup, burr oak, swamp or water oak, white oak, red or spanish oak, post oak, and black oak of several varieties, with the black jack, a dwarfish, knarled looking tree, excellent for fuel, but good for nothing else.

The black walnut is much used for building materials and cabinet work, and sustains a fine polish.

In most parts of the state, grape vines, indigenous to the country, are abundant, which yield grapes that might advantageously be made into excellent wine. Foreign vines are susceptible of easy cultivation. These are cultivated to a considerable extent at Vevay, Switzerland county, Indiana, and at New Harmony on the Wabash. The indigenous vines are prolific, and produce excellent fruit. They are found in every variety of soil;

interwoven in every thicket in the prairies and barrens; and climbing to the tops of the very highest trees on the bottoms. The French in early times made so much wine as to export some to France; upon which the proper authorities prohibited the introduction of wine from Illinois, lest it might injure the sale of that staple article of the kingdom. I think the act was passed by the board of trade, in 1774.

The editor of the Illinois Magazine remarks: "We know one gentleman who made twenty-seven barrels of wine in a single season, from the grapes gathered with but little labor, in his immediate neighbourhood."

The wild plum is found in every part of the state; but in most instances the fruit is too sour for use, unless for preserves. Crab apples are equally prolific, and make fine preserves with about double their bulk of sugar. Wild cherries are equally productive. The persimmon is a delicious fruit, after the frost has destroyed its astringent properties. The black mulberry grows in most parts, and is used for the feeding of silk worms with success. They appear to thrive and spin as well as on the Italian mulberry. The gooseberry, strawberry, and blackberry grow wild and in great profusion. Of our nuts, the hickory, black walnut, and pecaun deserve notice. The last is an oblong, thin shelled, delicious nut, that grows on a large tree, a species of the hickory, (the *Carya olivæ formis* of Nuttall.) The paupaw grows in the bottoms, and rich, timbered uplands, and produces a large, pulpy, and luscious fruit. Of domestic fruits, the apple and peach are chiefly cultivated. Pears are tolerably plenty in the French settlements, and quinces are cultivated with success by some Americans. Apples are easily cultivated, and are very productive. They can be made to bear fruit to considerable advantage in seven years from the seed. Many varieties are of fine flavor, and grow to a large size. I have measured apples, the growth of St. Clair county, that exceeded thirteen inches in circumference. Some of the early American settlers provided orchards. They now reap the advantages. But a large proportion of the population of the frontiers are content without this indispensable article in the comforts of a yankee farmer. Cider is made in small quantities in the old settlements. In a few years a supply of this beverage can be had in most parts of Illinois.

Peach trees grow with great rapidity, and decay proportionably soon. From ten to fifteen years may be considered the life of this tree. Our peaches are delicious, but they sometimes fail by being destroyed in the germ by winter frosts. The bud swells prematurely.

Garden Vegetables can be produced here in vast profusion, and of excellent quality.

That we have few of the elegant and well dressed gardens of gentlemen in the old states, is admitted; which is not owing to climate, or soil, but to the want of leisure and means.

A cabbage head two or three feet in diameter including the leaves, is no wonder on this soil. Beets often exceed twelve inches in circumference. Parsnips will penetrate our light, porous soil, to the depth of two or three feet.

The *cultivated vegetable productions in the field*, are maize or Indian corn, wheat, oats, barley, buckwheat, Irish potatoes, sweet potatoes, turnips, rye for horse feed and distilleries, tobacco, cotton, hemp, flax, the castor bean, and every other production common to the middle states.

Maize is a staple production. No farmer can live without it, and hundreds raise little else. This is chiefly owing to the ease with which it is cultivated. Its average yield is fifty bushels to the acre. I have oftentimes seen it produce seventy-five bushels to the acre, and in a few instances, exceed one hundred.

Wheat yields a good and sure crop, especially in the counties bordering on the Illinois river, and through the northern parts of the state. It weighs upwards of 60 pounds per bushel; and flour from this region has preference in the New Orleans market, and passes better inspection than the same article from Ohio or Kentucky.

In 1825, the weavel, for the first time, made its appearance in St. Clair and the adjacent counties, and has occasionally renewed its visits since. Within the last two seasons, some fields have been injured by the fly.

A common but slovenly practice amongst our farmers, is, to sow wheat amongst the standing corn, in September, and cover it by running a few furrows with the plough between the rows of corn. The dry stalks are then cut down in the spring, and left on the ground. Even by this imperfect mode, fifteen or twenty bushels of wheat to the acre are produced. But where the ground is duly prepared by fallowing, and the seed put in at the proper time, a good crop, averaging from twenty-five to thirty-five bushels per acre, rarely fails to be procured.

The average price of wheat is one dollar to one dollar twenty-five cents per bushel, varying a little according to the competition of mills and facilities to market. In many instances a single crop of wheat will pay the expenses of purchasing the land, fencing, breaking the prairie, seed, putting in the crop, harvesting, threshing, and taking it to market. Wheat is now frequently sown on the prairie land as a first crop, and a good yield obtained.

Flouring mills are now in operation in many of the wheat growing counties. Steam power is getting into extensive use both for sawing and manufacturing flour.

It is to be regretted that so few of our farmers have erected barns for the security of their crops. No article is more profitable, and really more indispensable to a farmer, than a large barn.

Oats have not been much raised till lately. They are very productive, often yielding from forty to fifty bushels on the acre, and usually sell from twenty to thirty cents the bushel. The demand for the use of stage and travelers' horses is increasing.

Hemp is an indigenous plant in the southern part of this state, as it is in Missouri. It has not been extensively cultivated, but wherever tried, is found very productive, and of an excellent quality. It might be made a staple of the country.

Tobacco, though a filthy and noxious weed, which no

human being ought ever to use, can be produced in any quantity and of the first quality in Illinois.

Cotton, for many years, has been successfully cultivated in this state for domestic use, and some for exportation. Two or three spinning factories are in operation, and produce cotton yarn from the growth of the country with promising success. This branch of business admits of enlargement, and invites the attention of eastern manufacturers with small capital. Much of the cloth made in families who have emigrated from states south of the Ohio is from the cotton of the country.

Flax is produced, and of a tolerable quality, but not equal to that of the northern states. It is said to be productive and good in the northern counties. There is an oil mill to manufacture oil from the seed, in Sangamon county.

The *palma christi*, or castor oil bean, is produced in considerable quantities in Madison, Randolph, and other counties, and large quantities of oil are expressed and sent abroad.

Sweet Potatoes are a delicious root, and yield abundantly, especially on the American bottom, and rich sandy prairies.

But little has been done to introduce cultivated grasses. The prairie grass looks coarse and unsavory, and yet our horses and cattle will thrive well on it. It is already known to the reader that this grass disappears when the settlements extend round a prairie, and the cattle eat off the young growth in the spring. Consequently in a few years, the natural grass no longer exists.

It is to be regretted that so few have thought of providing themselves with natural meadows of fifty or more acres to each plantation, by a process so cheap as that of fencing in the prairie, before the cattle had subdued the natural grass, and preserving it with a very little care, in a perfectly natural state.

But this notion was entirely incorrect. To produce timothy with success, the ground must be well cultivated in the summer, either by an early crop, or by fallowing, and the seed sown about the 20th of September, at the rate of *ten or twelve quarts of clean seed to the acre*, and lightly brushed in.

If the season is in any way favourable, it will get a rapid start before winter. By the last week in June, it will produce two tons per acre, of the finest of hay. It then requires a dressing of stable or yard manure, and occasionally the turf may be scratched with a harrow, to prevent the roots from binding too hard. By this process timothy meadows may be made and preserved. There are meadows in St. Clair county, which have yielded heavy crops of hay in succession, for several years, and bid fair to continue for an indefinite period. Cattle, and especially horses, should never be permitted to run in meadows in Illinois. The fall grass may be cropped down by calves and colts. There is but a little more labour required to produce a crop of timothy than a crop of oats, and as there is not a stone or a pebble to interrupt, the soil may be turned up every third or fourth year for corn, and afterwards laid down to grass again.

A species of blue grass is cultivated by some farmers for pastures. If well set and not eaten down in summer, blue grass pastures may be kept green and fresh till late in autumn, or even in the winter. The English spire grass has been cultivated with success in the Wabash country.

Of the trefoil, or clover, there is but little cultivated. A prejudice exists against it, as it is imagined to injure horses by affecting the glands of the mouth, and causing them to slaver. It grows luxuriantly, and may be cut for hay early in June. The white clover comes in naturally, where the ground has been cultivated, and thrown by, or along the sides of old roads and paths. Clover pastures would be excellent for swine.

Animals. Of *wild animals* there are several species. The buffalo is not found on this side the Mississippi, nor within several hundred miles of St. Louis. This animal once roamed at large over the prairies of Illinois, and was found in plenty thirty years since. *Wolves, Panthers,* and *wild cats* are still numerous on the frontiers, and through the unsettled portions of the country. Wolves harbor in almost every county, and annoy the farmer by destroying his sheep and pigs. There are three species found in Illinois:

1. The large gray wolf, or *canis lupus* of Linneus, is not very plenty, and not commonly found in the older settlements.

2. The black wolf, or *canis lycaon* of Linneus, is scarce. Occasionally they are killed by our hunters.

3. The *canis latrans* of Say, or common prairie wolf, is the most common, and found in considerable numbers. This mischievous animal is but little larger than the common fox, burrows in the prairies, and comes forth in the night to attack sheep, pigs, poultry, &c. Many of the settlers keep hounds to guard against the depredations of this animal.

Panthers and wild cats are less common, but occasionally do mischief.

Deer are also very numerous, and are valuable, particularly to that class of our population which has been raised to frontier habits; the flesh affording them food, and the skins, clothing. Fresh venison hams usually sell seventy-five cents, to one dollar fifty cents a pair, and when properly cured, are a delicious article. Many of the frontier people dress their skins, and make them into pantaloons and hunting shirts. These articles are indispensable to all who have occasion to travel in viewing land, or for any other purpose beyond the settlements, as cloth garments, in the shrubs and vines, would soon be in strings.

It is a novel and pleasant sight to a stranger, to see the deer in flocks of eight, ten, or fifteen in number, feeding on the grass of the prairies, or bounding away at the sight of a traveller.

The *brown bear* is also an inhabitant of this state, although he is continually retreating before the advance of civilization.

Foxes, raccoons, opossums, gophars, and squirrels, are also numerous, as are muskrats, otters, and occasionally beaver, about our rivers and lakes. Raccoons are very common, and frequently do mischief in the fall to our corn. Opossums sometimes trouble the poultry. I have a few facts reported to me from sources entitled to great credit, that the production of the young of this singular and extraordinary animal, is different from the ordinary process of generation in viviparous animals. The fœtus is found adhering to the teat, within the false belly, at the very first stage of existence.

The *gophar* is a singular little animal, about the size of a squirrel. It burrows in the ground, is seldom seen, but its *works* make it known. It labors during the night, in digging subterranean passages in the rich soil of the prairies, and throws up hillocks of fresh earth, within a few feet distance from each other, and from twelve to eighteen inches in height. I have seen a dozen of these hillocks, the production of one night's labour, and apparently from a single gophar. The passages are formed in such a labyrinth, that it is a difficult matter to find the animal by digging.

The gray and fox squirrels often do mischief in the corn fields, and the hunting of them makes fine sport for the boys. It is a rule amongst the Kentucky riflemen to shoot a squirrel only through his eyes, and that from the tops of the highest trees of the forest. It is evidence of a bad marksman, for a hunter to hit one in any other part.

Common Rabbits exist in every thicket. These animals annoy nurseries and young orchards exceedingly. The fence around a nursery must always be so close as to shut out rabbits, and young appletrees must be secured at the approach of winter, by tying straw or corn stalks around their bodies, for two or three feet in height, or the bark will be stripped off by these mischievous animals.

Wild horses are found ranging the prairies and forests in some parts of the state. They are small in size, of the Indian or Canadian breed, and very hardy. They are caught in pens, or with ropes having nooses attached to them, and broken to the saddle and harness. The French, who monopolise the business of catching, and breaking these horses, make them an article of traffic; their common price is from twenty to thirty dollars. They are found chiefly in the lower end of the American Bottom, near the junction of the Kaskaskia and Mississippi rivers, called *the Point*. They are the offspring of the horses brought there by the first settlers, and which were suffered to run at large. The Indians of the West have many such horses, which are commonly called Indian ponies.

Domestic Animals. These are the same as are found in other portions of the United States. But little has been done to improve the breed of horses amongst us. Our common riding or working horses average about fifteen hands in height. Horses are much more used here than in the eastern states, and many a farmer keeps half a dozen or more. Much of the travelling throughout the western country, both by men and women, is performed on horseback; and a large proportion of the land carriage is by means of large wagons, with from four to six stout horses for a team. A great proportion of the ploughing is performed by horse labor. Horses are more subject to diseases in this country than in the old states, which is thought to be occasioned by bad management, rather than by the climate. A good farm horse can be purchased for fifty dollars. Riding, or carriage horses, of a superior quality, cost about sixty, eighty, or a hundred dollars. Breeding mares are profitable stock for every farmer to keep, as their annual expense in keeping is but trifling, their labor is always needed, and their colts, when grown, find a ready market. Some farmers keep a stallion, and eight or ten brood mares.

*Mule*s are raised in Missouri and are also brought from the Mexican dominions into Illinois. They are hardy animals, grow to a good size, and are used by some both for labour and riding.

Our *neat cattle* are usually inferior in size to those of the old states. This is owing entirely to bad management. Our cows are not penned up in pasture fields, but suffered to run at large over the commons. Hence *all* the calves are preserved, without respect to quality, to entice the cows homeward at evening. They are kept up through the day, and oftentimes without much pasture, and turned to the cows for a few minutes at night, and then permitted to graze through the night over the short and withered grass around the plantation.

In autumn their food is very scanty, ond during the winter they are permitted to pick up a precarious subsistence amongst fifty or a hundred head of cattle. With such management, is it surprising that our cows and steers are much inferior to those of the old states?

And yet, our beef is the finest in the world. It bears the best inspection of any in the New Orleans market. By the first of June, and often by the middle of May, our young cattle on the prairies are fit for market. They do not yield large quantities of tallow, but the fat is well proportioned throughout the carcase, and the meat tender and delicious. By inferiority, then, I mean the *size* of our cattle in general, and the quantity and quality of the milk of cows.

Common cows, if suffered to lose their milk in August, become sufficiently fat for table use by October. Farrow heifers and steers, are good beef, and fit for the knife at any period after the middle of May. Nothing is more common than for an Illinois farmer to go among his stock, select, shoot down, and dress a fine beef, whenever fresh meat is needed. This is often divided out amongst the neighbours, who, in turn, kill and share likewise. It is common at camp and other large meetings, to kill a beef and three or four hogs for the subsistence of friends from a distance.

We can hardly place limits upon the amount of beef cattle that Illinois is capable of producing. A farmer calls himself poor, with a hundred head of horned cattle around him. A cow in the spring is worth from twelve to twenty dollars. Some of the best quality will sell higher. And let it be distinctly understood, once for all, that a poor man can always purchase horses, cattle, hogs, and provisions, for labor, either by the day, month, or job.

Cows, in general, do not produce the same amount of milk, nor of as rich a quality as in older states. Something is to be attributed to the nature of our pastures, and the warmth of our climate, but more to causes already assigned. If ever a land was characterised justly as " flowing with milk and honey," it is Illinois and the adjacent states. From the springing of the grass till September, butter is made in great profusion. It sells at that season in market for about twenty cents, and in the interior of the state for twelve cents per pound. With proper care it can be preserved with tolerable sweetness for winter's use. Late in autumn and early in the winter, sometimes butter is not plenty. The feed becomes dry, the cows range further off, and do not come up readily for milking, and dry up. A very little trouble would enable a farmer to keep three or four good cows in fresh milk at the season most needed.

Cheese is made by many families, especially, in the counties bordering on the Illinois river. Good cheese sells for eight and sometimes ten cents, and finds a ready market. The most important arrangement for the dairy business in Illinois, and especially for cheese making is to persuade a few thousand families, from the dairy regions of New England, to emigrate, and continue their industrious habits after settling here.

Swine. This species of stock may be called a staple in the provision of Illinois. Thousands of hogs are raised without any expense, except a few breeders to start with, and a little attention in hunting them on the range, and keeping them tame.

This kind of pork is by no means equal to that raised and fatted on corn, and in a domestic way. It is soft, oily, and will not bear inspection at New Orleans. It usually sells for three dollars per hundred.

Pork that is made in a domestic way and fatted on corn, will sell for from four to five dollars, according to size, quality, and the time when it is delivered. With a pasture of clover or blue grass, a well filled corn crib, a dairy, and slop barrel, and the usual care that a New Englander bestows on his pigs, pork may be raised from the sow, fatted and killed, and weigh from two hundred to two hundred and fifty, within twelve months, and this method of raising pork would be profitable.

Few families in the west and south put up their pork in salt pickle. Their method is to salt it sufficiently to prepare it for smoking, and then make bacon of hams, shoulders, and middlings or broadsides. The price of bacon, taking the hog round, is about ten and twelve cents. Good hams command twelve cents in the market. Stock hogs, weighing from sixty to one hundred pounds, alive, usually sell for from two dollars to two dollars and fifty cents per head. Families consume much more meat in Illinois, in proportion to numbers, than in the old states.

Sheep do very well in this country, especially in the older settlements, where the grass has become short, and they are less molested by wolves. But few are kept. The people from the south are more accustomed to cotton for clothing, than to wool, which sells for fifty cents per pound. Little is said or done to improve the breed of sheep, or introduce the Merino, or Saxony breed. Mr. George Flower, at Albion, has a valuable flock of Saxony and Merino.

Poultry are raised in great profusion—and large numbers of fowls taken to market. It is no uncommon thing for some farmers' wives to raise three or four hundred fowls, besides geese, ducks, and turkeys, in a season. Young fowls, butter, and eggs, are the three articles usually mustered from every farm for the market. By these means many families provide their coffee, sugar, tea, and various articles of apparel.

Eggs, when plenty, as at the close of winter and spring, sell for ten and twelve cents per dozen.

In noticing poultry, I ought not to pass over some of our wild fowl.

Ducks, geese, swans, and many other aquatic birds, visit our waters in the spring. The small lakes and sloughs are often literally covered with them. Ducks, and some of the rest, frequently stay through the summer and breed.

The prairie fowl is seen in great numbers on the prairies in the summer, and about the cornfields in the winter. This is the grouse of the New York market. They are easily taken in the winter.

Partridges, (the quail of New England) are taken with nets, in the winter, by hundreds in a day, and furnish no trifling item in the luxuries of the city market.

Bees. This laborious and useful insect is to be found in the trees of every forest. Many of the frontier people make it a prominent business after the frost has killed the vegetation, to hunt them for the honey and wax, both of which find a ready market. Bees are profitable stock for the farmer, and are kept to a considerable extent.

Silkworms are raised by a few persons. They are capable of being produced to any extent, and fed on the common black mulberry of the country.

MANUFACTURES.

In the infancy of a state, little can be expected in machinery and manufactures. And in a region so much deficient in water power as some parts of Illinois are, still less may be looked for. Yet Illinois is not entirely deficient in manufacturing enterprise.

The principal salines of this state have been mentioned under the head of minerals.

Steam Mills for flouring and sawing are becoming very common, and in general are profitable. Some are now in operation with four runs of stones, and which manufacture one hundred barrels of flour in a day. Mills propelled by steam, water, and animal power, are constantly increasing. Steam mills will become numerous, particularly in the southern and middle portions of the state, and it is deserving remark that while these portions are not well supplied with durable water power, they contain, in the timber of the forest, and the inexhaustible bodies of bituminous coal, abundant supplies of fuel, while the northern portion, though deficient in fuel, has abundant water power.

A good steam saw-mill with two saws can be built for 2,000 dollars; and a steam flouring mill with two runs of stones, elevators and other apparatus complete, and of sufficient force to turn out forty or fifty barrels of flour day, may be built for 6,000 dollars.

The northern half of the state will be most abundantly supplied with water power, and ordinary mills for sawing lumber and grinding grain are now in operation on the various streams. Probably in no part of the great west does there exist the capability of such an immense water power, as is to be found naturally, and which will be created artificially along the rapids of the Illinois and F rivers, and the Illinois and Michigan canal. Incorporate companies with ample means are now constructing hydraulic works at Ottawa, Marseilles, and other points along the rapids of the Illinois. Fox river rapids have a descent of sixteen feet at Green's mills, four miles above Ottawa, with abundant supplies of water at its lowest stage; and the river itself, from thence to McHenry county, is a rapid stream with rocky banks, admirably suited for hydraulic purposes. On the Kankakee are some fine sites for water privileges. Rock river furnishes abundant facilities for hydraulic purposes, especially at Grand Detour and Rockford. A company engaged in the establishment of a large town at the mouth of Rock river, has been recently chartered by the legislature for the purpose of cutting a canal from a point on the Mississippi at the upper rapids, to Rock river, by which they expect to gain eighteen feet fall and immense hydraulic power.

It is expected that the improvement of the Kaskaskia and Little Wabash rivers, as provided for by the recent law of the state, will create valuable water privileges along these streams.

Certainly, in connection with the improvement of the Great Wabash river by the joint operations of Indiana and Illinois, hydraulic power to any desirable extent will be created. Such will be the effect, too, upon Sangamon and other rivers within the state. Des Plaines river, and also the Calumet, furnish extensive hydraulic privileges;

and the surplus water provided by the construction of the Illinois and Michigan canal, and which may be conveniently applied to manufacturing purposes, is estimated to be equal to that required for running 700 pairs of mill stones four and half feet in diameter.

Incorporations for companies for various manufacturing purposes have been granted by the legislature within the last four or five years, some of which have been organised and commenced operations. The conclusion is, that Illinois will furnish as great facilities for manufacturing purposes, as soon as the circumstances and wants of the community shall call for their operation, as can be found in any western state.

Large quantities of *castor oil* are annually manufactured in Illinois from the palma christi, or castor bean. A number of presses are in operation in Madison, Greene, Macoupen, St. Clair, Randolph, Edwards, and perhaps other counties. The most extensive establishment is at Edwardsville, owned by Mr. John Adams, where from thirty to forty thousand gallons of oil are made annually.

Cotton Goods. A few factories for spinning cotton yarn have been put into operation in several counties on a small scale of from one hundred to two hundred spindles each. They are carried by animal power on the inclined plane.

Coarse clothing from cotton is manufactured in the southern portion of the state, where the article is raised in small quantities. Woollen cloth, and jeans, a mixture of wool and cotton, is made for ordinary wear, as is cloth from flax.

Lead. In Jo Daviess county are eight or ten furnaces for smelting lead. The amount of this article made annually at the mines of the Upper Mississippi, has been given under the head of minerals.

Boat Building will soon become a branch of business in this state. Some steamboats have been constructed already within this state, along the Mississippi. It is thought that Alton and Chicago are convenient sites for this business.

There is in this state, as in all the western states, a

large amount of domestic manufactures made by families. All the trades, needful to a new country, are in existence. Carpenters, wagon makers, cabinet makers, blacksmiths, tanneries, etc., may be found in every county and town. At Mount Carmel and Springfield, there are iron foundries for castings.

There has been a considerable falling off in the manufacture of whiskey within a few years, and it is sincerely hoped by thousands of citizens that this branch of business, so decidedly injurious to the morals and happiness of the community and of individuals, will entirely decline.

Ox mills on the inclined plane, and horse mills by draught, are common throughout the middle and southern parts of the state.

With the table of the census, taken in 1835, and published by authority of the legislature the succeeding winter, the following report was made.

Manufactories,	339
Mills,	916
Machines,	87
Distilleries,	142

This report is defective and imperfect. In some counties ordinary mechanics' shops, such as tinners, coopers, wheelwrights, &c., were reported under the head of manufactories; in others no distinction was made.

NATURAL CURIOSITIES AND ANTIQUITIES.

On the banks of the Ohio and Mississippi rivers, and the bluffs that overhang the alluvions, are many singular appearances. These consist of ledges of rock, which exhibit the most fanciful forms, and in many places are penetrated by caverns of various dimensions. Of these the "*Cave in Rock*," on the Ohio will be described under its own name. The "Devil's Anvil," "Grand Tower," "Starved Rock," "Buffaloe Rock," "Mount Joliet," and many other singular appearances will be found under their respective names, in the third part of this work.

The *Fossil Tree* of the Des Plaines and to which allusion has been made already, is fully described by Mr. Schoolcraft, in a memoir read before the American Geological Society, in 1821.

It lies in a horizontal position, imbedded in a stratum if flœtz sandstone, of a gray colour and close grain. The middle portion of the trunk is fifty-one feet six inches in length, and is eighteen inches in diameter at the smallest end. It is a species of the *juglans nigra,* or black walnut, a tree common to the Illinois, and completely petrified. It lies in the bed of the Des Plaines about forty rods above its junction with the Kankakee.

Petrifications are very common in Illinois. The "lost rocks," or boulders scattered over a surface of an evident diluvial deposit, are a curiosity. They are in great numbers towards the he heads of the Kaskaskia and Sangamon rivers, and become more numerous and are found at various depths in the soil, as the traveller passes northward along the great prairies. Indeed the geological formation of the whole state, presents a rich field for investigation in that science.

The antiquities of Illinois are similar to those of other western states. Indian graves are common, especially along the bluffs. Fragments of bones and not unfrequently whole skeletons, in a tolerable state of preservation, are found deposited from two to three feet below the surface. In not a few instances they are found enclosed with stone slabs, undressed, and obtained from the neighing cliffs. There are no proofs of a *pigmy race* of aborigines in the western states. Graves are not unfrequent where the length from the head to the foot stone, does not exceed four feet, and yet contain the skeleton of an adult of full stature. In such instances it will be found upon careful examination of the position of the bones, that the leg and thigh bones lie parallel, and that the corpse was inhumed with the knees bent into that position. Some bones of unusual size have been discovered, but I am not acquainted with facts to justify a supposition of a race of giants. Bones of a huge animal, but different from the Mammoth, have been recently found in St. Clair county.

About the Gallatin and Big Muddy salines, large fragments of earthenware, are very frequently found, under the surface of the earth. They appear to have been portions of large kettles, used, probably, by the natives for obtaining salt. Small fragments of earthenware, arrow and spear heads, stone axes and mallets, and other antiquities, are found in various parts of the state. Silver coins of ancient origin have been found at Kaskaskia. They were probably brought there by the Jesuits, or the early French emigrants.

Of one thing the writer is satisfied, that very imperfect and incorrect data have been relied upon and very erroneous conclusions drawn, upon western antiquities. Whoever has time and patience, and is in other respects qualified to explore this field of science, and will use his spade and eyes together, and restrain his imagination from running riot amongst mounds, fortifications, horseshoes, medals, and whole cabinets of relics of the " olden time," will find very little more that the indications of rude savages, the ancestors of the present race of Indians.

Of ancient military works, I have long been convinced that not half a dozen such structures ever existed in the west before the visits of Europeans. Enclosures of various sizes, and perhaps for different purposes, with an embankment of earth, three or four feet high, and a trifling ditch out of which the earth was dug, undoubtedly were formed. In all probability some of these embankments enclosed their villages; others the residence of their chiefs or head men. But what people, savage, barbarous, civilised, or enlightened, ever constructed a fortification around five or six hundred acres, *with a ditch in the inside!* Or what military people made twenty or thirty such forts, within two or three miles! At any rate I am confident these immense armies of military heroes never visited Illinois.

The remains of Fort Chartres, commenced by the French in 1720, to defend their infant settlements against the Spaniards and Indians, is probably the most ancient military work within this state, of which any portion now remains.

Those who are particularly desirous of information concerning the millions of warriors, and the bloody battles in which more were slain than ever fell in all the wars of Alexander, Cæsar, or Napoleon, with a particular description of their military works, would do well to read the "*Book of Mormon*," made out of the "golden plates" of that distinguished antiquarian Joe Smith!

It is far superior to some modern productions on western antiquities, because it furnishes us with the names and biography of the principal men who were concerned in these enterprises, with many of the particulars of their wars for several centuries. But, seriously, the attention of scientific men is invited to this subject.

And as a starting question to such an investigation, it ought to be first settled how long human bones will retain their form and solidity without decomposition, when exposed to the air, earth, water, and other causes of decay, interred two or thee feet deep in the earth. Will they preserve their form and soundness over two, or at the most three hundred years? Are not the relics of the early pilgrims of New England, and the first settlers of Jamestown mouldered entirely to dust? Will any one say that human skeletons, entombed as those are in the mounds of Illinois, but two or three feet below the surface, remain in a state of preservation five or six hundred years? A sober investigation of these questions would result in an entire overthrow of the hypothesis of existing races of men prior to the Indians, founded upon such remains.

The existence of "*Mounds*" in this and other western states has been assumed as substantial proof, amounting to demonstration, of a race of men of enterprising habits, and far more civilised than the present race of aborigines. But it is now seriously questioned whether these mounds are the work of art. I know not that any writer ever ventured to attack this supposition till John Russell, Esq. sent forth his essay in the Illinois Magazine, of March,

1831. Mr. Russell is a citizen of this state, and well known as a writer of talents and literary acquirements. He has had an opportunity of examining for himself, many of those mounds, of various dimensions. He maintains they are not artificial, and offers objections to their being productions of human art, not easily obviated.*

But there are many mounds in the west, that exactly correspond in *shape* with these supposed antiquities, and yet from their *size* most evidently were not made by man.

Monk hill, in the American bottom, near the road from

---

* In the summer of 1836, Mr. Russell made a most interesting and curious discovery, pertaining to the antiquities of Illinois, in the range of bluffs that overhang Bluffdale, Greene county, the place of his residence.

At an elevation of 80 feet above the valley, in a projecting cliff, and imbedded amongst a mass of loose rocks, Mr. R. found on excavating, three shells, nearly similar, each of which exhibited the following characteristics.

1. They were univalve, and had been bisected, the edges worked off, and the inside excavated, so as to resemble somewhat in appearance the half of a slender, straight gourd with a neck tapering proportionably in size from the body.

2. Each had evidently been used as an article of furniture, and had been prepared for the purpose by some sharp instrument, and each holds about three pints.

3. They are unquestionably of salt water origin, and belong to a description of shells not found in the waters of the Atlantic, or on any part of the American Continent. Similar shells are to be found in the South Pacific Ocean and about the Feejee islands.

4. They were most unquestionably deposited in these bluffs at the period of their formation. The position in which they were found would preclude the idea of their subsequent deposition by human or other means. They are not fossil remains, in the sense of having undergone any change in their structure, being purely natural shells, fashioned into ladles by the art of man. Very limited knowledge of the science of Conchology prevents me from defining the genus and species of these interesting remains. They are highly deserving the attention of the curious, and are yet in the possession of John Russell, Esq., Postmaster at Bluffdale, Illinois.

St. Louis to Edwardsville, is of the following dimensions. The circumference of its base is about eight hundred yards—its height 90 feet—its shape that of a parallelogram.

Mr. Flint, who has written some fine romances and considerable " History and Geography of the Western States," describes one in Ohio, between thirty and forty rods in circumference, and seventy feet high. It would be well to calculate, upon the ordinary labor of excavating canals, how many hands, with spades, wheelbarrows, and other necessary implements, it would take to throw up such a mound within any given time.

Mount Joliet on the Des Plaines, is about one mile in circumference, and 150 feet high, rising like a pyramid of sand. In the northwestern part of Illinois, and in the Wisconsin territory, are mounds of much larger dimensions, and compared to which Monk hill is but a mole hill. Mount Charles, Sinsinewa, and the Blue Mounds are on a grand scale. The latter range is three or four hundred feet high, and has an area of several hundred acres of table land on its summit. Springs of water gush from its sides. Mr. Brigham has an elegant farm on one of these mounds. West of the Arkansas territory, in the Osage country, and near Clermont's village, are a number of large, regularly formed mounds, two hundred feet high, ranging with each other, and extending in a line for ten or twelve miles. They are level on the top, and contain from two to five acres of table land, and the sides are so steep as to be inaccessible excepting in one or two places. The country around is an immense prairie, nearly level.

These large mounds are of the same shape and proportions as the smaller ones. Who supposes these to be works of human art? Who will place these among the antiquities of a country?

If any one will account for the formation of these stupendous works of nature, in a country of unquestionably diluvial formation, there are men who make no pretensions to the rank of western antiquarians, who will account for the formation of the smaller ones, of a few feet elevation, without the aid of an extinguished race of men. Until further evidence of their being the work of men's hands, I shall class them among the natural curiosities of the country.

CLIMATE AND HEALTH.

The state of Illinois, extending as it does, through five and half degrees of latitude, must possess some variety in its climate. Its extensive prairies, and its level surface, give greater scope to the winds, especially in winter. Snow frequently falls, but seldom lies long, during the three winter months, in the southern portion of the state. In the northern portion, the winters are nearly as severe as in the same parallel of latitude in the Atlantic states. The Mississippi at St. Louis is frequently frozen over and passed on the ice, and occasionally for several weeks. The hot season is longer,, though not more intense, than occasionally for a day or two in New England.

During the years 1817-18-19, the Rev. Mr. Giddings, at St. Louis, made a series of observations upon Farenheit's thermometer.

	Deg.	Hund.
Mean temperature for 1817,	55	52
Do. do. from the beginning of May, 1818, to the end of April 1819	56	98
Mean temperature for 1820	56	18

The mean of these results is about fifty six degrees and a quarter.

The mean temperature of each month during the above years, is as follows:

	Deg.	Hund.
January	30	62
February	38	65
March	43	13
April	58	47

	Deg.	Hund.
May	62	66
June	74	47
July	78	66
August	72	88
September	70	10
October	59	00
November	53	13
December	34	33

The mean temperature of the different seasons is as follows:

Winter, 34. 53—Spring, 54. 74—Summer, 74.34—Autumn, 60.77.

The greatest extremes of heat and cold during my residence in the country for seventeen years, in the vicinity of St. Louis, is as follows:

Greatest heat in July 1820, and July 1833, 100 degrees. Greatest cold January 3d, 1834, 18 degrees below zero.

The foregoing facts will doubtless apply to about one half of Illinois. This climate also is subject to sudden changes from heat to cold; from wet to dry, especially from November to May. The heat of the summer below the 40th degree of latitude is more enervating, and the system becomes more easily debilitated than in the bracing atmosphere of a more northerly region.

The putting forth of vegetation in the spring, furnishes data for the most correct conclusions concerning the climate of a country. Some facts gathered from the observations of a series of seasons, will be presented in the appendix.

Winds. Southwesterly winds prevail during the spring, summer and autumn, at least south of the forty-first degree of latitude. In the spring, and during the rise of the Missouri, they are from a more westerly direction, and rains are usually more frequent. During the latter part of summer and autumn the air is dry and elastic. In the months of December and January northwest and northerly winds often prevail. Northeast storms are extremely rare, unless towards lake Michigan.

Weather. There is a great proportion of clear, pleasant days throughout the year. Dr. Beck, who resided at St. Louis during the year 1820, made observations upon the changes of the weather, and produced the following results.

Clear days, 245.—Cloudy, including all the variable days, 110.

The results of my own observations, kept for twelve years, with the exception of 1826, and with some irregularity, from travelling into different parts of Illinois and Missouri during the time, do not vary in any material degree from the above statement.

The putting forth of vegetation in the spring furnishes some evidence of the character of the climate of any country, though by no means entirely accurate. Other causes combine to advance or retard vegetation. A wet or dry season, or a few days of heat or cold at a particular crisis, will produce material changes.

The following table is constructed from memoranda made at the various dates given, near the latitude of St. Louis, which is computed at 38° 30′. The observations of 1819 were made at St. Charles and vicinity, in the state of Missouri. Those of 1820, in St. Louis county 17 miles N. W. from the city of St. Louis. The remainder at Rock Spring, Illinois, 18 miles east from St. Louis. It will be perceived, the years are not consecutive. In 1826, the writer was absent to the eastern states, and for 1828 his notes were too imperfect to answer the purpose.

In the columns showing the times of the first snows, and the first and last frosts in the season, a little explanation may be necessary, A "light" snow means merely enough to whiten the earth, and which usually disappears in a few hours.

Many of the frosts recorded "light" were not severe enough to kill ordinary vegetation.

42

Year	Peach & Red bud in blossom.	Straw-berries in blossom.	Black-berries in blossom.	Apple leaves begin to put forth.	Apple trees in blossom.	Grass green in prairies.	Oaks and other forest trees put forth leaves.	First snow on approach of winter.	Last frost in spring.	First frost in Autumn.
1819	April 4.	Not noted.	May 19.	April 15.	April 20.	April 18.	Half size May 19.	Oct. 8. few flakes	May 18. very light.	Sept. 23.
1820	Ap. 14. No peach B.	April 2.	May 10. fall off 17.	March 25.	April 15.	April 10.	April 22. full size May 7.	Oc. 24. few flakes	June 1, very light.	Sept. 20. Oct. 8, ice.
1821	Ap. 26. No peach B.	April 30.	May 21.	April 24.	May 3.	April 26.	Ap. 26 to May 3. f. grown 22.	Nov. 11 3 inches	Ap. 18. severe. May 9, light.	Oct. 8.
1822	April 5.	April 25.	May 10.	April 18.	April 22.	April 10.	April 29. full size May 14.	Nov. 8. 2 1-2 in.	Ap. 16. severe, ice.	Oct. 13.
1823	April 19.	April 26.	May 20.	April 15.	April 28.	April 10.	April 23.	Nov. 16. light.	April 24.	Sept. 21-2. Ice 23.
1824	April 20.	April 28.	May 18.	April 20.	April 29.	April 14.	April 30.	Nov. 1. light.	May 5.	Oct. 21. hrd freeze.
1825	March 25.	Ap.3. Ripe May 17.	May 8.	March 30.	April 5.	March 10.	April 3.	Nov. 7.	Feb. 22. Next. Ap. 20, ice.	Oct. 2-3. 27th, ice.
1827	April 4.	April 10.	May 15.	April 4.	April 13.	March 25.	April 10 full size. Ap. 30.	Dec. 11. 3 inches.	May 7, light.	Sept. 23, light.
1829	April 20.	April 24.	May 20.	April 20.	April 26.	April 24.	April 27.	Nov. 25, light.	Not noted.	Sept. 17.
1830	April 1.	April 5.	May 9.	April 1.	April 9.	April 1.	begin Ap. 5. f size May 1.	Nov. 12, 4 inches, sleet.		

The following observations were made at Augusta, Hancock county, and kindly furnished by S. B. Mead, M. D.

	1834	1835	1836
Gooseberries leaved out,		April 11	April 25
Crab Apple,	April 13	April 30	April 28
Thorn,	April 14	April 30	April 28
Black Hare,	April 14		April 28
Elm,			April 28
Forest green,	April 22	May 15	May 5
Prairies green	April 9, 15.	April 30	April 23, 25
First killing frost,	Sept. 11	Sept. 23	Oct. 4.
First snow,	Dec. 2	Nov. 20	Nov. 21
Gooseberry in blossom,	April 13	April 29	April 24
Crab Apple,	April 25	May 9	May 7
Wild plum,	April 13	April 29	April 29
Shadbush,	April 12	April 25	May 5
Redbud,	April 19	May 6	May 1, 15, 20

The dates are at the time Dr. M. first observed this progress of vegetation. Augusta is 108 miles, (according to the land surveys) north of St. Louis, and is nearly equidistant from the northern and southern extremities of the state.

I have before me also from Dr. Mead, a table of Meteorological observations taken during the years 1834, 1835, and 1836, a mere epitome of which I have room to give in this place, including the *mean* temperature for each month. The observations were made half an hour after sun-rise, at two o'clock, P. M., and half an hour after sunset, from Fahrenheit's Thermometer.

1834	Deg. Hund.		Deg. Hund.
January,	20 . 88	July,	77 . 59
February,	44 . 48	August,	77 . 40
March,	45 . 30	September,	64 . 03
April,	57 . 90	October,	56 . 25
May,	61 . 95	November,	48 . 09
June,	71 . 10	December,	36 . 76
		Annual mean	55 . 32

1835	Deg. Hund.		Deg. Hund.
January,	37 . 23	July,	72 . 61
February,	22 . 72	August,	70 . 87
March,	43 . 91	September,	62 . 23
April,	52 . 56	October,	57 . 97
May,	68 . 12	November,	40 . 55
June,	71 . 15	December,	36 . 37
		Annual mean	52 . 02

1836	Deg. Hund.		Deg. Hund.
January,	31 . 82	July,	75 . 03
February,	31 . 41	August,	71 . 59
March,	37 . 39	September,	66 . 00
April,	53 . 08	October,	50 . 65
May,	67 . 40	November,	44 . 89
June,	70 . 11	December,	24 . 84
		Annual mean,	51 . 01

WEATHER.

	Fair days.	Cloudy.	Rainy.	Snow.
1834	246	74	42	3
1835	250	67	43	5
1836	229	78	48	10

Diseases. The more common diseases of Illinois are intermittents, frequently accompanied with bilious symptoms. Those which prove fatal in sickly seasons are bilious remittents. More than one half of the sickness endured by the people is caused by imprudence, bad management, and the want of proper nursing. Emigrants from the northern states or from Europe, will find it advantageous to protect themselves from the cool and humid atmosphere at night, to provide close dwellings, yet, when the atmosphere is clear, to have their rooms, and especially their sleeping rooms, well ventilated, and invariably wear thin clothing in the day, and put on thicker apparel at night or when exposed to wet.

Families are seldom sick who live in comfortable houses with tight floors and well ventilated rooms, and who upon a change of weather, and especially in a time of rain, make a little fire in the chimney, though it may be in the midst of summer.

I have seen but few cases of genuine consumption. Affection of the liver is more common. Pleurisies, and other inflammatory diseases, prevail in the winter and spring. Ophthalmia prevails at some seasons. Dysentery is not uncommon. Fewer die in infancy than in the old states.

Finally, I am prepared to speak decidedly in favor of the general health of Illinois.

CIVIL DIVISIONS.

There are seventy counties within the state, in sixty of which courts are held. In the others the judge of the circuit where they lie, is authorised to organise them by appointing an election for county officers whenever in his opinion there are three hundred and fifty inhabitants within their boundaries. Their names, dates of formation, number of square miles, population of the state census of 1835, (with the estimation of certain new counties since formed,) and seats of justice are given in the appendix.

For the purpose of electing representatives to congress, the state is divided into three districts, each of which sends one representative.

The first district is composed of the counties of Gallatin, Pope, Johnson, Alexander, Union, Jackson, Franklin, Perry, Randolph, Monroe, St. Clair, Washington, Clinton, Bond, Madison, and Macoupen.

The second district includes the counties of White, Hamilton, Jefferson, Wayne, Edwards, Wabash, Lawrence, Clay, Marion, Fayette, Montgomery, Shelby, Vermilion, Champaign, Edgar, Coles, Clark, Iroquois, Crawford, Effingham and Jasper.

The third district is composed of the following counties: Greene, Morgan, Sangamon, Tazewell, Macon, McLean, La Salle, Cook, Putnam, Peoria, Henry, Jo Daviess, Rock Island, Mercer, Warren, Hancock, McDonough, Fulton, Knox, Schuyler, Adams, Pike, Calhoun, Will, McHenry, Benton, Boone, Kane, Ogle, Whiteside, Stephenson, Winnebago, Coffee, Bureau, and Livingston.

For judiciary purposes the state is divided into seven circuits, in each of which a circuit judge is appointed.

The *First Judicial Circuit* includes the counties of Sangamon, Morgan, Greene, Macoupen, Macon, McLean, Tazewell,

The *Second Judicial Circuit* includes the counties of Madison, St. Clair, Monroe, Randolph, Washington, Clinton, Bond, Shelby, Fayette, Montgomery, and Effingham.

The *Third Judicial Circuit*, includes the counties of Gallatin, Pope, Johnson, Alexander, Union, Jackson, Perry, Franklin, Marion, Jefferson, and Hamilton.

The *Fourth Judicial Circuit* includes the counties of Edgar, Vermilion, Champaign, Coles, Jasper, Clay, Wayne, White, Edwards and Wabash.

The *Fifth Judicial Circuit* embraces the counties of Calhoun, Pike, Adams, Schuyler, Hancock, Warren, Knox; McDonough and Fulton.

The *Sixth Judicial Circuit* includes the counties of Jo Daviess, Rock Island, Mercer, Henry, Putnam, Peoria Ogle, and Winnebago. Whiteside is in this circuit; but for judicial purposes attached to Ogle county, as are also the counties of Stephenson and Boone, formed at the recent session of the legislature, attached to Winnebago county. The judge of the circuit has authority by law to authorise them to be organised whenever petition and proof is offered that a county contains three hundred and fifty inhabitants.

The *Seventh Judicial Circuit* includes the counties of Iroquois, Cook, Will, La Salle, Kane, and McHenry.

Counties are not subdivided into townships as in Indiana, Ohio, and the more eastern states. For the convenience of holding elections, the county commissioner's court is required to divide the county into "*precincts*," and designate the house or place in each precinct where the polls shall be opened.

Electors throughout the county vote at which precinct they please.

GOVERNMENT.

The constitution of Illinois was formed by a convention held at Kaskaskia, in August, 1818. It provides for the distribution of the powers of government into three distinct departments.—The legislative, executive, and judiciary. The legislative authority is vested in a general assembly, consisting of a senate and house of representatives. Elections are held biennially, as are the ordinary sessions of the legislature. Senators are elected for four years.

The executive power is vested in the governor, who is chosen every fourth year by the electors for representatives, but the same person is ineligible for the next succeeding four years. The lieutenant governor is also chosen every four years.

The judicial power is vested in a supreme court, and such inferior courts as the general assembly from time to time shall establish. The supreme court consists of a chief justice and three associate judges.

The governor and judges of the supreme court constitute a council of revision, to which all bills that have passed the assembly must be submitted. If objected to by the council of revision, the same may become a law by the vote of a majority of all the members elected to both houses.

Synopsis of the Public Officers, Terms of Service, Manner of Appointment, and Compensation.

Governor—Elected by the people, for four years; Salary $1000 per annum: eligible for one term only in succession; Salary cannot be diminished during his continuance in office.

Lieutenant Governor—Elected by the people, for four years; paid per day during the session of the legislature; $6 per day during the last session. He is speaker of the senate, and becomes Governor in case of a vacancy in the latter office.

Secretary of State—Appointed by the Governor and Senate during pleasure; Salary $1100 per annum, including clerk hire; and $300 per annum, for additional clerk hire for 1837 and 1838. Office at Vandalia.

Auditor of Public Accounts—Elected by the legislature biennially; Salary $800; two clerks, $400 each; with additional for clerk hire during 1837 and 1838, $400 per annum. Office at Vandalia.

Treasurer—Elected by the legislature biennially; Salary $800; clerk hire $800 per annum. Office at Vandalia.

Adjutant General—Appointed by the Governor during pleasure; Salary $100. Office at Vandalia.

Supreme Judges—Elected by the legislature during good behaviour; Salary $800, with an extra compensation for 1837 and 1838 of $200.

Clerk of the Supreme Court—Appointed by the court during good behaviour; fees. Office at Vandalia.

Circuit Judges—Elected by the legislature during good behaviour; Salaries $750, with an additional allowance of $250, during 1837 and 1838, excepting the judge of the sixth judicial circuit.

Clerks of the Circuit Courts—Appointed by the courts, during good behaviour; fees. Offices at the respective seats of justice.

OF ILLINOIS. 49

Attorney General—Elected by the legislature biennially; Salary $350 and fees. Office to be kept at Vandalia.

Six State's Attorneys—Elected by the legislature biennially; Salaries $250, and fees.

Agent for the Sale of Saline Lands—Elected by the legislature biennially; Salary $200.

Three Canal Commissioners—Elected by the legislature biennially; Compensation $5 per diem, while engaged in actual business.

Three Fund Commissioners on Internal Improvement—Elected biennially by the legislature; pay $5 per diem while actually employed.

Seven Commissioners of the Board of Public Works—Elected biennially by the legislature; pay $5 per diem while in actual service.

Warden of the Penitentiary—Elected by the legislature biennially; Salary $800.

Three Inspectors of the Same—Elected by the legislature biennially; compensation per diem $2; but not to exceed $50 per annum.

GENERAL ASSEMBLY.

Number of Senators, 40—Elected for four years.

Number of Representatives, 91—Elected biennially; compensation regulated by law each session; $4 per day last session.

OFFICERS OF THE GENERAL ASSEMBLY.

Lieutenant Governor, (*speaker of the Senate*,) pay last session $6 per day.

Secretary of the Senate—pay at last session, $6 per day, and $350 for furnishing a copy of his Journal for the press.

Assistant Secretary of the Senate—pay at last session, $5 per day.

Enrolling and Engrossing Clerk of the Senate—pay at last session $5 per day.

Doorkeeper of the Senate—pay at last session $4 per day.

Speaker of the House of Representatives—pay at the last session, $6 per day.

Principal Clerk of the House of Representatives—pay at the last session $6 per day, and $350 for preparing his Journal for the press.

Assistant Clerk of the House of Representatives—pay at last session $5 per day.

Enrolling and Engrossing Clerk of the House of Representatives—pay at last session, $5 per day.

Doorkeeper of the House of Representatives—pay $4 per day.

There is some variation in compensation each session. From 20 to 25 per cent. was added by the late legislature to former rates, which does not equal the increased value of labor in every other branch of business within the last two years. The legislature usually sits from 70 to 90 days. Last session continued 93 days.

The amount of the pay of the legislature, with the present number of members, at a session of 90 days, at $4 per day, is $46,080.

Officers and Clerks of the legislature, $5,380.

Contingent expenses per session, for fuel, stationary, repairs, furniture, etc., $6,000.

Public printing of various kinds, including binding and distributing the laws, journals, etc., $12,000.

Making the biennial expenses for legislation, about $70,000, or $35,000 per annum.

The appropriations for the contingent fund for 1837, '38, are $4000 per annum.

Salaries of the Executive and Judiciary officers, $18,700; making the whole ordinary annual expenditures of the state about $53,700.

The revenue of the state is derived principally from land taxes. The tax on lands of residents goes into the county treasuries, for county purposes, while the tax on the lands of non-residents goes into the state treasury for state purposes.

The quantity of land subject to taxation on the first of August, 1836, was 5,335,041 acres. And the quantity subject to taxation

In 1837 will be	5,674,452
In 1838	5,902,127
In 1839	6,262,367
In 1840	6,616,380
In 1841	7,837,218
And in 1842 about	12,000,000

Lands sold by the general government are not subject to taxation under five years after purchase.

COUNTY OFFICERS.

Judges of Probate—Formerly elected by the legislature, during good behaviour; hereafter to be elected by the people; fees.

Sheriffs—Elected by the people, biennially; fees.

Coroners—Elected by the people, biennially; fees.

County Commissioners—Three in each county, to manage county concerns; Elected by the people biennially: $150 per day while employed in court. Regular sessions, first Mondays in March, June, September, and December.

County Clerk—Elected by the people; collector of taxes on non-residents' lands, fees; and per diem allowance while attending court.

County Treasurer—Hereafter elected by the people, biennially; per centage and per diem allowance, on moneys received and services performed.

County Surveyors—Elected by the people quadrennially; fees.

County Recorders—Elected by the people quadrennially; fees.

Justices of the Peace—Elected by the people quadrennially; fees.

Constables—Elected by the people quadrennially; fees.

Notaries Public—Appointed by the Governor and Senate, during good behaviour; fees.

Supervisors of Roads—Appointed by the county commissioners annually; exempt from military duty and serving on juries, but receive no other compensation.

Public Administrator—Appointed by the Governor and Senate; term indefinite; fees.

Commissioner of the school funds arising from the sale of the sections numbered sixteen; appointed by the county commissioners, who fix his compensation.

The right of suffrage is universal. All white male inhabitants, twenty-one years of age, who have resided within the state six months next preceding the elections, enjoy the right of electors.

Votes are given *viva voce.* The introduction of slavery is prohibited. The constitution can be altered only by a convention.

PLANS OF INTERNAL IMPROVEMENT.

Those undertaken by the state are embraced in two divisions. The Illinois and Michigan canal, and the internal improvement system adopted by the legislature last winter.

The project of uniting the waters of the Illinois river with Lake Michigan was conceived soon after the commencement of the grand canal of New York. It was brought before the legislature of Illinois, at its first session after the state government was organised by Governor Bond. The legislature, in February, 1823, appointed a board of commissioners to survey the route and estimate the cost, and make report to the next legislature, which was done. These commissioners employed Col. Post and Col. Paul of Missouri as engineers. They examined five different routes for a portion of the distance, and estimated the expense of each route. They varied from about $640,000, to $716,000. The estimate of the fifth route was upon the project of using lake Michigan alone for a feeder by directing a portion of its waters to the Illinois river, and was a fraction short of $690,000.

Upon the report of these surveys the legislature passed a bill to incorporate the "Illinois and Michigan Canal Company," in January, 1825. No stock having been taken, the legislature, at a special session, the next winter, repealed the law chartering the company.

The embarrassments of the state in its finances, growing out of the ruinous policy of a state bank without capital, prevented any thing further from being done until January, 1829, when the legislature passed an act to organise a board of commissioners, with power to employ agents, engineers, surveyors, draftsmen, and other persons, to explore, examine, fix, and determine the route of the canal.

The congress of the United States had made provision by an act passed March 2d, 1827, to give the state each alternate section of land, within five miles of the contemplated canal.

The commissioners were authorised to sell this land, to lay off town sites and sell lots, and apply the funds.

Accordingly they laid off Chicago near the lake; and Ottawa, at the junction of Fox river and the Illinois. Town lots and tracts of land were sold, a skilful engineer employed, surveys were made with more particularity, the surface of the earth perforated, the waters at a low stage examined, and estimates of the expense made. It was now ascertained that a supply of water in dry seasons, from the streams on its route, was doubtful, and that the rock approached so near the surface on the summit level between the Chicago, and the Des Plaines, as to present a serious obstacle to using the lake for a feeder.

The subsequent legislature authorised a re-examination to be made with a view to a railway, and to ascertain whether the waters of the Calamic could not be obtained in sufficient quantities for a feeder.

The result was in the report of the engineer to the commissioners; and by them to the legislature, decidedly in favor of a railway. To this project congress has given its assent.

Two estimates of the expense of a canal were submitted. The first was on the plan of following the summit ten feet above the level of lake Michigan and depend on streams for feeders.

Total cost of the entire line of $95\frac{3}{4}$ miles $1,601,965 83. Cost on the same location by obtaining a supply of water from lake Michigan, by cutting through the dividing ridge between the lake and the head waters of the Illinois river, much of it rock excavation, $4,043,086 50.

The estimated cost of a railway with a single track laid, distance 96 miles, is $1,052,428 19.

During the summer of 1832, the late Mr. Pugh, visited New York, to obtain information of the relative cost and value of canals and railways, and to ascertain whether funds could be obtained, and on what terms, to complete this work.

The state not having means at its disposal, and the session having drawn toward a close, the whole business was postponed, by abolishing the office of canal commissioners.

At a special session of the legislature held in the winter of 1835-6, an act was passed for the construction of the Illinois and Michigan Canal, the Governor was authorised to negociate a loan on the faith and credit of the state, not exceeding $500,000, a board of three commissioners was organised, with full power to employ engineers, let contracts, dispose of property and carry on the whole business on behalf of the state. One is styled the "acting commissioner" with a salary of twelve hundred dollars per annum; the others to be styled "President and "Treasurer," and to receive compensation for the time of their services at the rate of three dollars per day. The law specified that said "Canal shall commence at or near the town of Chicago, and terminate near the mouth of Little Vermilion in La Salle county, and on land owned by the state. The law furthermore provided that "said canal should not be less than forty-five feet wide at the surface, thirty feet at the base, and of sufficient depth to ensure a navigation of at least four feet, to be suitable for ordinary canal boat navigation, to be supplied with water from Lake Michigan, and such other sources as the canal commissioners may think proper, and to be constructed in the manner best calculated to promote the permanent interest of the country; reserving ninety feet on each side of the canal to enlarge its capacity, whenever in the opinion of the board of land commissioners, the public good shall require it."

The commissioners, after a re-examination of the route, and obtaining due information from all sources, "determined to adopt the recommendation of the chief engineer, and construct it of the following dimensions; to wit:— sixty feet wide at the top water line; thirty six feet wide at the bottom; and six feet deep. The irregular fluctuations, or tides in the lakes, occasioned by the action of high winds, rendered the depth agreed upon, indispensably necessary to insure a navigation of at least four feet."

This stupendous work commences on the North fork of the South branch of Chicago river, four miles to the southwest of the city of Chicago,, (the river itself forming a deep and natural canal from this point to the harbour,) and from thence extends to the Des Plaines river seven and half miles, at a place called "the Point of Oaks." This division presents a cutting 18 feet deep, through a substratum of stiff blue clay. From thence down the valley of the Des Plaines to the running out of the lake level, 25 miles, the cutting is from 16 to 18 feet deep, principally through stratified limestone, in strata from two to six inches thick. On section 23, T. 36 N. R. 70, E. of the third principal division, the commissioners have laid out a town on state property, one mile square, called *Lockport*. Here are to be two locks, ten feet lift each, placed in conjunction, so as to create twenty feet fall, and an immense water power from the surplus water drawn from lake Michigan. Here, also, will be constructed a basin for three fourths of a mile, and 120 feet wide. From Lockport the canal proceeds down the valley of Des Plaines, to Juliet where it crosses by a dam, its line runs past Marseilles, and crosses Fox river by an aqueduct betwixt the main bluff and Ottawa. A navigable feeder, will connect it with the rapids of Fox river, four miles above Ottawa, and extend through the town to the Illinois river, where a natural basin, of deep water, is at the mouth of Fox river. Below Ottawa, the canal passes down the right bank of the Illinois, near the bluffs, crosses the Pe-cum-saugan, and Little Vermilion, and enters the Illinois river, in the corner of fractional section 21, in township 33, N. Range one, east of the third principal meridian. To this point the Illinois is navigable for steamboats at all stages of water. A steamboat basin, or harbor, is to be constructed, and a large town laid off on section 15, near the termination of the canal.

The whole length of the canal including Fox river feeder, will be 100 miles, and 28 chains, to which add Chicago river, of 5 miles and 44 chains, gives 105 miles and 72 chains for the entire length of the navigable line.

The work has been arranged by the board of commissioners into three divisions, as given in the following

General Summary.

1. Summit Division, including Chicago river, 34 miles, 35, 78–100 chains, estimated cost by the Engineer, $ 5,871,324 97
2. Middle Division, 37 miles, 55,80–100 chains, estimated cost, 1,510,957 46
3. Western Division, and Fox river feeder, 33 miles, 61 20–100 chains, cost 1,272,055 08

Total estimated cost $ 8,654,337 51

The legislature, at its late session, authorised a survey of the Calumet, and the Sauga-nas-ke valley with the view of constructing a lateral canal, to open a navigable communication from the main canal to the Calumet, from which it is expected a water communication will be made in the state of Indiana to the Wabash and Erie canal.

Resources. The resources of the state to meet the cost of this stupendous work, which will connect the navigable waters of the Mississippi and Illinois, with the lakes of Canada, the gulf of St. Lawrence, and the canals and other lines of communication in Ohio, Pennsylvania and New York, arise from the sales of town lots and lands along the line of this work.

Each alternate section, along the line of the canal, and ten miles in width, has been granted by congress for the purpose. During last year, 375 lots were sold in Chicago, for the gross amount of one million, three hundred and fifty five thousand, seven hundred and fifty five dollars. In Ottawa, 78 lots sold for 21,358 dollars. The unsold lands for canal purposes, belonging to the state amount to 270, 182 acres, which, including the town lots laid off, are estimated equal to the expense of the canal.

Amount of sales for lands and town lots previous to 1833, $18,798 08$\frac{1}{2}$

Sale of lots at Chicago in June, 1836, after deducting forfeitures, $1,355,755.

Sale of lots in Ottawa, September, 1836, $21,358.

The estimated value of the lots in the town of Lockport, and the town laid off at the termination of the canal is one million and a-half dollars. The remainder of the canal lands may be estimated at 20 dollars per acre.

The project of this canal is a vast enterprise for so young a state, but truly national in its character, and will constitute one of the main arteries in eastern and western communication. The work is going forward, and from five to eight years is the period estimated for its completion.

Already commerce, in no small extent, is passing along that line. Merchants from St. Louis, from along the Illinois river, from Galena and the Wisconsin territory, and especially from the Wabash river as far south as Terre Haute, bring their goods that way.

Were a communication opened between the navigable waters, the distance from New York to St. Louis would be passed in from sixteen to twenty days.

The following result is founded upon information gathered by the commissioners.

From New York to Buffalo, 5 days.—From Buffalo to Chicago, by steamboats fitted for lake navigation, 8 days. —From Chicago to the foot of the rapids on the railway, estimating the speed at 3 miles an hour 33 hours.—From the foot of the rapids to St. Louis, by steamboats, 48 hours.

The whole distance can be passed over in sixteen days. but giving four days additional time, and the transportation on this route can be made in twenty days.

The shipments through Chicago in 1832, amounted to 300,000 dollars. In 1833, from April 8 to September 10, 70 schooners and 2 steamboats had discharged their cargoes.

In 1835, the arrivals were 9 steamboats, 267 schooners and brigs, with 5015 tons of merchandise, and 9400 barrels of salt, besides lumber, provisions, etc.

In 1836, from April 18th to December 1st, the arrivals at Chicago were 40 steamboats, 10 ships and barques, 26 brigs, 363 schooners, and 8 sloops equal to 60,000 tons.

The commercial and consequently the agricultural interests of the whole valley of the Mississippi, are concerned in the result of this undertaking. For whatever amount of produce is thrown off through this channel to the Canadas and New York, it increases the advantages of a market for the commerce that floats down the Mississippi. The Missouri, and the Wisconsin territory are no less interested in opening this communication. In accepting the donation of land made by the general government, the honor and credit of Illinois is really pledged for the success of this enterprise. There is then no ground for retreat.

I regret the prescribed limits of this work will not permit me to exhibit the important bearing that the success of this project will have upon the fur business, the lead manufacture, the Indian trade, the rapid settlement and improvement of all the northern portion of the state, and the adjacent territory, and upon the prosperity of the farming community throughout our whole interior.

It ought to be noticed that a project is now in progress in Michigan to construct a railway across the peninsula from Detroit to the mouth of the St. Joseph's river, which enters lake Michigan nearly opposite and east from Chicago. This would save the circuitous route by water, and greatly lessen the distance and risk.

GREAT INTERNAL IMPROVEMENT SYSTEM.

At the late session of the legislature, (1836-7) an act was passed to establish and maintain a general system of Internal Improvement.

It provides for a "*Board of Fund Commissioners,*" of three persons, and a "*Board of Commissioners of Public Works,*" of seven persons one in each judicial circuit.

The Board of Fund Commissioners are authorised to negociate all loans, authorised by the legislature, on the faith and credit of the state for objects of Internal Improvement; receive, manage, deposit, and apply all sums of money, and manage the whole fiscal concerns of the improvement system.

The Board of Public Works are authorised and required to locate, superintend, direct, and construct on behalf of the state all works of internal improvement, which are or shall be authorised to be undertaken by the state (except the Illinois and Michigan Canal, which is managed by a distinct Board.) This Board is required to hold semiannual meetings in June and December. Each member has specific charge of that portion of the works that falls within his own district. They are required to execute the works by letting out contracts, except in special cases.

The Fund Commissioners are authorised to contract loans by issuing state stock at a rate not exceeding six per centum per annum, and to an amount not exceeding eight millions of dollars, redeemable after 1870.

WORKS OF IMPROVEMENT PROVIDED FOR.

1. The Great Wabash river in co-operation with the state of Indiana, in that part over which both states have concurrent jurisdistion; appropriated $100,000.
2. Illinois rivers, $100,000.
3. Rock river, $100,000.
4. Kaskaskia river, $50,000.
5. Little Wabash river $50,000.
6. On the Great Western Mail Route leading from Vincennes to St. Louis. $250,000.
7. A railroad from the city of Cairo, at or near the junction of the Ohio and Mississippi rivers, via Vandalia Shelbyville, Decatur and Bloomington;—to cross the Illinois river, at the termination of the Illinois and Michigan canal, and from thence, via Savanna to Galena, appropriated $3,500,000.

This is called the "Central Rail road," by the people.

8. A southern cross railroad from Alton, via Edwardsville, Carlyle, Salem, Fairfield, Albion to mount Carmel; from whence it is expected a line will be extended through Indiana to New Albany, and become connected with the great railroad chartered and surveyed from the Ohio river to Charleston, South Carolina.

Also a railroad from Alton to Shawneetown, to diverge from the aforesaid southern cross railroad at Edwardsville, and pass through Lebanon, Nashville, Pinckneyville, Frankfort and Equality.

And further, a railroad from Belleville via Lebanon, and to intersect the road from Alton to Mount Carmel. This last will pass near Rock Spring. Appropriated $1,750,000.

9. A northern cross railroad from Quincy on the Mississippi river, via Columbus, Clayton, Mount Sterling, to cross the Illinois river at Meredosia, and to Jacksonville, Sprigfield, Decatur, Sydney, Danville, and thence to the state line in the direction of Lafayette, Indiana, and thus form a line of communication with the great works in Indiana, and to the eastern states. Appropriated $1,850,000.

10. A railroad from Alton via Upper Alton, Hillsboro, Shelbysville, charleston, Paris, and from thence to the state line in the direction of Terre Haute, Indiana, where it will be connected with railroad and canal communications through that state, both in an estern and southern direction. Appropriated, $1,250,000.

11. A railroad from Peoria, via Canton, Macomb and Carthage to Warsaw, on the Mississippi, at the foot of the Des Moines rapids. Appropriated $700,000.

12. A railroad from Bloomington, to Mackinau, and from thence two branches to the Illinois river;—one through Tremont to Pekin; the other to Peoria. Appropriated $350,000.

An appropriation of $200,000 was made to those counties through which no railroad or canal is made at the cost of the state, to be in a rateable proportion to the census of 1835, and to be applied in the improvement of roads, bridges and other public works by the counties.

INTERNAL IMPROVEMENT FUND.

The special fund for this purpose shall consist of all moneys raised from state bonds, or stock, or other loans, authorised by law;—all appropriations made from time to time out of the revenue of the state arising from land taxes; —all tolls and rents of water privileges and other tolls from the works when constructed;—all rents, profits and issues from lands to be purchased on the routes;—the proceeds of all donations of lands from the general government, or from individuals, companies, or corporations;—a portion of the proceeds of the surplus fund distributed by congress; together with the net proceeds of all bank and other stocks subscribed and owned by the state after liquidating the interest on loans contracted for the purchase of such bank or other stocks.

A subsequent enactment authorised the Fund Commissioners to subscribe two millions of dollars stock to the State Bank of Illinois, and one million four hundred thousand dollars to the Illinois bank at Shawneetown, by the creation of six per cent. stock. The net proceeds of this stock, after paying interest on the loans will equal six per centum per annum, or produce an annual revenue to the Internal Improvement fund of $180,000.

The interest of the state in all these works, all their proceeds, with the faith of the state, are irrevocably pledged for the payment of the interest and the redemption of the principal of all stock and loans for Internal Improvement.

The improvement of the great western mail route from Vincennes to St. Louis, and the special appropriation to to the counties, are to be provided for from the first loans made.

The improvement of the rivers is to be for steam, keel and flat boats; to be commenced at their mouths and continued up as far as the appropriations admit.

The rail roads are to be commenced at their intersection with navigable rivers, and commercial towns, and as soon as five miles of any one line is completed the commissioners are required to place thereon locomotives and facilities of transportation, to establish tolls, etc.

Congress has made an appropriation to improve the navigation of the Mississippi at the rapids—a work of immense inportance to the northern part of this state, and the Wisconsin Territory.

The improvement of the navigation of the Mississippi should be regarded and urged as strictly a national work. There are two rapids in the Mississippi river, which, in times of low water, impede the progress of steamboats. One is near the mouth of the Des Moines, and adjoining Hancock county, where the water descends over sand rocks 25 feet 5 inches in about 11 miles. The other commences at Rock Island and extends about fifteen miles. The descent of the water in that distance is 21 feet 10 inches. In both of these rapids there are ledges of rocks, with intervals of deep water, extending across the river.

The harbor at Chicago, nearly completed by the general government will be of immense benefit to that place and all the northern portion of the state. It will form one of the finest harbors in all the northern lake country.

The *National Road* is in progress through this state, and considerable inprovement has been made on that portion which lies between Vandalia and the boundary of Indiana. This road enters Illinois at the northeast corner of Clark county, and passes diagonally through Coles and Effingham counties in a southwesterly course to Vandalia, a distance of 90 miles. The road is established 80 feet wide, the central part, 30 feet wide, raised above standing water, and not to exceed three degrees from a level. The base of all the abutments of bridges must be equal in thickness to one third of the height of the abutment.

But little has been done on this road during the last two years. About $220,000 of appropriated funds now remain on hand, and arrangements are in progress to work out this fund during the present season.

From Vandalia, westward, the road is not yet located, but the legislature of Illinois with great unanimity have consented to its passage through the state, only on the contingency it shall pass Alton and cross the Mississippi, above the mouth of the Missouri.

Many companies have been incorporated for the construction of short canals, rail roads and turnpike roads, some of which will be noticed in connection with towns etc.

A railroad from Naples to Jacksonville, now undergoing construction;—another rail road from Jacksonville via Lynnville and Winchester to the Illinois river opposite Augusta. A third railway has been commenced from Chicago to the Des Plaines, twelve miles over level prairies and designed to extend across the state to Galena.

Another railroad is now under contract and working from the Mississippi, opposite St. Louis, across the American Bottom to the coal mines in the bluffs of St. Clair county. Governor John Reynolds, George E. Walker, Vital Jarrot, S. B. Chandler and Louis Boismenu own the land and have commenced this railroad, six miles long, which will be completed before the close of the present year. They own a strip of land along the bluffs for three miles in extent, filled with exhaustless beds of bituminous coal, from which it is expected that not less than one million of bushels of coal will be transported annually to the river.

No state in the union possesses such facilities for intercommunication by canals and railways, at so cheap a rate and which can be so equally distributed to its population, as Illinois.

EDUCATION.

The congress of the United States, in the act for admitting the state of Illinois into the union upon equal footing with the other western states, granted to it the section numbered *sixteen* in every township, or one thirty-sixth part of all the public lands within the state, for the use of schools. The avails of this section are understood to constitute a fund for the benefit of the families living within the surveyed township, and not the portion of a common fund to be applied by the state for the general purposes of education.

Three per cent of the net proceeds of all the public lands, lying within this state, which shall be sold after the 1st of January, 1819, is to be paid over by the general government, and constitute a common fund for education under the direction of the state authority. One sixth of this three per cent. fund, is to be exclusively bestowed upon a college, or university.

Two entire townships, or 46,080 acres selected from choice portions of the public lands, have likewise been given to education. Part of this land has been sold by state authority and the avails funded at six per cent. interest.

The amount of funds realised from these sources, and under charge of the state, (independent of the sixteenth sections,) is about $384,183, the interest of which is now distributed annually to such schools as make due returns to the proper authority.

By a recent act of the legislature, a moiety of the "*surplus fund*," received from the national treasury, is to be converted into bank stock, and the income to be distributed to common schools. The income of the three per centum from the sales of public lands, will continue as long as there are public lands to be sold.

The unsold lands in this state belonging to the general government, may be estimated at 18,000,000 of acres. Were this sold at the present minimum price, it would produce $22,500,000, of which three per cent. would be 675,000 dollars.

But it is highly probable that this immense domain will not all be sold at its present price; we will put the average value at 75 cents per acre, or $13,500,000, of which three per cent. belonging to this state, would give $405,000 for education purposes.

The amount of the sections numbered sixteen, and reserved for schools in the respective townships, was estimated by the commissioner of public lands, and reported to Congress in April, 1832, at 977,457 acres in Illinois.

This tract is not usually sold until the township in which it lies is somewhat populated, and hence commands a higher price than other lands. The section in the vicinity of Chicago was sold in November, 1833, (after reserving twelve acres,) for $38,705. Other tracts in settled portions of the state have been sold for from five to ten dollars per acre.

Estimating the whole at two dollars per acre, the value is $1,954,914.

Present fund at interest,	$ 384,183
Value of Seminary lands unsold,	20,000
Value of sections numbered sixteen,	1,954,914
Estimate of the three per cent. fund on all public land now unsold in the state, at 75 cents per acre,	405,000
	$2,764,097

To this add the moiety of the surplus fund to be invested in bank stock and the income to be distributed with the interest on the school fund, equal to 318,500 dollars; but as it is liable to be demanded by the general government, I have not considered it any portion of the permanent school fund.

The funds and claims of Illinois for education purposes may be estimatnd at *three millions of dollars.*

But it is sincerely and ardently hoped that the patriotism, foresight, intelligence, and liberality of congress, after reducing the price of the public lands to the actual settler and cultivator, will be manifested in applying all future proceeds to the object of common schools, by some equitable apportionment amongst the several states of the Union. Hitherto these lands have been pledged for the payment of the national debt. That being now accomplished, I cannot but hope this question will be settled to the entire satisfaction of all parties, by a consecration of the net proceeds to the noble, beneficent, and truly national purpose of educating every child in the Union. Such a disposition of the public domain would reflect more honor on this nation, and tend more to its aggrandisement, than a hundred wars or a thousand victories. It would provide for a triumphant conquest of human ignorance, and carry joy and gladness to millions of hearts.

Notwithstanding the liberal provision in funds and lands for education, little has yet been done by the legislature in providing a system for common schools. A law was framed in 1825, providing for school districts to become incorporated, by the action of the county commissioners' courts, upon a petition of a majority of the qualified voters of any settlement. The voters in each district, by a majority of votes, could levy a tax not exceeding one half per centum on property, and appoint trustees and other officers to manage the business.

This feature of the law was soon made unpopular, and a subsequent legislature repealed that portion that authorised the levying of a tax, and made other modifications, by which it remains on the statute book as a matter of very little value.

The preamble to this law establishes beyond controversy, the great principles for legislative authority and aid for common schools. It reads thus:—

"To enjoy our rights and liberties, we must understand them;—their security and protection ought to be the first object of a free people;—and it is a well established fact that no nation has ever continued long in the enjoyment of civil and political freedom, which was not both virtuous and enlightened;—and believing that the advancement of literature always has been, and ever will be the means of developing more fully the rights of man; that the mind of every citizen of every republic, is the common property of society, and constitutes the basis of its strength and happiness;—it is considered the peculiar duty of a free government, like ours, to encourage and extend the improvement and cultivation of the intellectual energies of the whole: Therefore,

"*Be it enacted, etc.*"

Provision now exists by law for the people to organise themselves into school districts, and to conduct the affairs of the school in a corporate capacity by trustees, and they can derive aid from public funds under control of the state.

Upon petition from the inhabitants of a township, the section numbered sixteen can be sold, and the proceeds funded, the interest of which may be applied annually to the teachers of such schools within the township as conform to the requisites of the law. To some extent the people have availed themselves of these provisions and receive the interest of the fund.

A material defect in all the laws that have been framed in this state, on this subject, has been in not requiring the necessary qualifications on the part of teachers, and a previous examination before a competent board or committee.

Without such a provision no school law will be of much real service. The people have suffered much already, and common school education has been greatly retarded by the imposition of unqualified and worthless persons under the name of school teachers; and were funds ever so liberally bestowed, they would prove of little real service, without the requisites of sobriety, morality, and sufficient ability to teach well on the part of those who get the pay.

A complete common school system must be organised, sooner or later, and will be sustained by the people. The lands, education funds, and wants of the country, call for it.

Many good primary schools now exist, and where three or four of the leading families unite and exert their influence in favor of the measure, it is not difficult to have a good school.

In each county a school commissioner is appointed, to superintend the sales of the sixteenth sections, loan the money, receive and apportion the interest received from this fund and from the state funds, receive schedule returns of the number of scholars that attend each school, and make report annually to the secretary of state.

The people in any settlement can organise themselves into a school district, employ a teacher, and obtain their proportion of the income from the school funds, *provided the teacher keeps a schedule of the number of scholars who attend, the number of days each one is present, and the number of days each scholar is absent, a copy of which must be certified by the trustees of the district, and returned to the school commissioners of the county semiannually.*

If the school is made up from parts of two or more townships, a separate schedule of the scholars from each township must be made out.

The term "township" in the school laws merely expresses the surveys of 36 sections, and not a civil organisation.

Several seminaries, and institutions for colleges, have been established and promise success.

Illinois College. This institution is located in the vicinity of Jacksonville, and one mile west of the town. Its situation is on a delightful eminence, fronting the east, and overlooking the town, and a vast extent of beautiful prairie country, now covered with well cultivated farms.

This institution owes its existence and prosperity, under God, to the pious enterprise of several young men, formerly members of Yale College, Connecticut. Most of its funds have been realised from the generous donations of the liberal and philanthropic abroad.

The buildings are as follows: a brick edifice, 104 feet in length, 40 feet in width, five stories high, including the basement; containing 32 apartments for the accommodation of officers and students. Each apartment consists of a sitting room, or study, 14 feet by 12, two bed rooms, each eight feet square, two dress closets, and one wood closet. The basement story embraces a boarding hall, kitchen, store rooms, etc. for the general accommodation.

To this main building are attached two wings, each 38 feet long, and 28 feet wide, three stories high, including the basement; for the accommodation of the families of the Faculty.

The chapel is a separate building, 65 feet long, and 36 feet wide, two stories high, including rooms for public worship, lectures, recitations, library, etc. and eight rooms for students.

There are also upon the premises a farm house, barn, workshops for students who wish to perform manual labor, and other out buildings.

The farm consists of 300 acres of land, all under fence. The improvements and stock on the farm are valued at several thousand dollars.

Students who choose are allowed to employ a portion of each day in manual labor, either upon the farm or in the workshop. Some individuals earned $150 each during the year.

The library consists of about 1,500 volumes. There is also a valuable chemical and philosophical apparatus.

The year is divided into two terms, of twenty weeks each. The first term commences eight weeks after the third Wednesday in September. The second term commences on the Wednesday previous to the 5th of May;

leaving eight weeks vacation in the fall and four in the spring.

There are 42 students connected with the college classes, and 22 students in the preparatory deparment. Of this number, several are beneficiaries, who are aided by education societies, with a view to the gospel ministry. A considerable number more are pious.

The trustees of the college are Rev. Edward Beecher, President, Hon. Samuel D. Lockwood, John P. Wilkinson, Esq., William C. Posey, Esq., Rev. Messrs. Theron Baldwin, John F. Brooks, Elisha Jenney, William Kirby, Asa Turner, John G. Bergen, and John Tillson, Esq., Rev. Gideon Blackburn, D. D, Gov. Joseph Duncan, Col. Thomas Mather, Winthorp S. Gilman, Esq., Frederick Collins, Esq., Nathaniel Coffin, Esq., Treasurer and Agent, Rev. J. M. Sturtevant, Secretary, Jeremiah Graves, Superintendant of the Farm.

Faculty. Rev. *Edward Beecher*, A. M. President, and Professor of Moral and Intellectual Philosophy and Political Economy.

Rev. J. M. Sturtevant, A. M. Professor of Mathematics and Natural Philosophy, and lecturer on Chemistry.

Truman M. Post, A. M. Professor of the Greek and Latin Languages.

Jonathan Baldwin Turner, A. M. Professor of Rhetoric and Belles Letters.

Reuben Gaylord, A. B. Instructor in the preparatory department.

Classes.—Senior, 3;—Junior, 11;—Sophomore, 12;—Freshman, 16. Total Collegiate department,   42
In the Preparatory department,   22
                                               64

The course of Instruction is intended to be equal to the first rate colleges in the eastern states.

Shurtleff College of Alton, Illinois, is pleasantly situated at Upper Alton. It originated in the establishment of a Seminary at Rock Spring, in 1827, and which was subsequently removed.

At a meeting held June 4th, 1832, seven gentlemen formed a written compact, and agreed to advance funds for the purchase of about 360 acres of land, and put up an academical building of brick, 2 stories with a stone basement, 40 feet long and 32 feet wide. A large stone building for a Refectory, and for Professors' and Students' rooms has since been erected. The Rev. Hubbel Loomis commenced a Preparatory school in 1833. In 1835 building lots were laid off within the corporate bounds of the town, a part of which was sold, and a valuable property still remains for future sale.

The same year funds to some extent were obtained in the eastern states, of which the liberal donation of *ten thousand dollars* was received from Benjamin Shurtleff M. D. of Boston, which gives name to the institution. Of this fund 5000 dollars is to be appropriated towards a College building, and 5000 dollars towards the endowment of a Professorship of Oratory, Rhetoric and Belles-lettres.

Regular College classes are not yet organised. The Preparatory department is in regular progress and contains about 60 students.

Rev. Washington Leverett, A. M. Professor of Mathematics, and Natural Philosophy.

Rev. Zenas B. Newman, A. M. Principal of the Preparatory Department. Measures are progressing to put up a large college building, and to complete the organisation of the College Faculty.

Alton Theological Seminary is an organisation distinct from Shurtleff College. Rev. Lewis Colby, A. M. is Theological Professor, with seven or eight students, licentiates of Baptist churches, under his charge.

Mc Kendreean College, under the supervision of the Methodist Episcopal Church, is located at Lebanon, St. Clair county. It has a commodious framed building, and about 50 Students in the Preparatory Department, under the charge of two competent instructors.

Mc Donough College, at Macomb, has just commenced operations. It is identified with the interests of the "old school" Presbyterians, as the Illinois college at Jacksonville is with the "New School" Presbyterians.

Canton College in Fulton county has recently been chartered as a college by the legislature, and is a respectable academical Institution, and has 70 or 80 students. Rev. G. B. Perry A. M. formerly pastor of the Spruce street Baptist Church Philadelphia, has recently been elected president of this Institution.

A Literary Institution, modeled somewhat after the plan of the *Oneida Institute* in the state of New York, is in progress at Galesboro, Knox county, under the supervision of the Rev. Mr. Gale and other gentlemen.

Belvidere College, in Winnebago county, has been recently chartered, and an effort is about being made to establish a respectable literary institution in this new and interesting portion of the state.

Several respectable academies and seminaries are also in operation, established chiefly by individual effort, where good schools are taught. Amongst these we notice the following, though some of equal importance may be overlooked.

The *Jacksonville Academy* conducted by Messrs. Charles E. Blood, and Charles B. Barton A. B. is established for the convenience of those whose studies are not sufficiently advanced to enter the Preparatory Department of Illinois College.

The *Jacksonville Female Academy* is a flourishing institution.

A respectable Academy is in operation at Springfield, another at Princeton, Putnam county, a third at Griggsville, and a fourth at Quincy.

The *Alton Female Seminary* is an institution projected for a full and useful course of instruction, on a large scale, towards the establishment of which Benjamin Godfrey, Esq., will contribute fifteen or twenty thousand dollars.

It is located at Monticello, a little more than four miles from Alton, on the borders of a delightful, elevated prairie, and is designed wholly as a boarding school. The business of instruction will be in the hands of competent ladies. The system of instruction will be extensive. The Rev. Theron Baldwin will exercise a general supervision over the institution, and lecture on scientific and religious subjects.

The project of establishing a Seminary, for the education of teachers at Waverley in the southeastern part of Morgan county, is entertained by several gentlemen.

A Seminary is about being established in a settlement of Reformed Presbyterians in the eastern part of Randolph county.

The "Reformers," or Campbellites, as some term them, have a charter and contemplate establishing a college at Hanover, in Tazewell county.

Thus a broad and deep foundation is about being laid in this state for the promotion of education.

Several lyceums and literary associations exist in this state, and there is in almost every county a decided expression of popular opinion in favor of education.

RELIGIOUS DENOMINATIONS.

The *Methodist Episcopal Church* is the most numerous. The Illinois Conference, which embraces this state and a portion of Wisconsin Territory, in 1835 had 61 circuit preachers, 308 local preachers, and 15,097 members of society. They sustain preaching in every county, and in a large number of the settlements.

The *Baptist Denomination* includes 22 Associations, 260 churches, 160 preachers and 7,350 communicants.

The *Presbyterians* have one Synod, 8 Presbyteries, and about 80 churches, 60 ministers, and 2,500 members.

There are 12 or 15 *Congregationalist* churches, united in an association, and several ministers.

The *Methodist Protestant Denomination* has one conference, 22 ministers and 344 members.

The *Reformers*, as they term themselves, or "Campbellites," as others call them, have several large, and a number of small societies, a number of preachers, and several hundred members, including the *Christian* body with which they are in union. They immerse all who profess to believe in Christ for the remission of sins, but differ widely from orthodox baptists on some points of doctrine.

The *Cumberland Presbyterians* have 2 or 3 Presbyteries, 12 or 15 preachers, and several hundred communicants.

There are two churches of *Reformed Presbyterians*, or *Covenanters*, 1 minister, and about 280 communicants, with a few families scattered in other parts of the state. There are also two or three societies of *Associate Reformed Presbyterians*, or *Seceders*.

In McLean county is a society of *United Brethren*, or, as some call them, Dutch Methodists.

The *Dunkards* have five or six societies and some preachers in this state.

There are several Lutheran congregations with preachers.

The *Protestant Episcopal Church* has an organised diocese, 8 or 10 congregations, and 7 or 8 ministers.

There are small societies of *Friends* or *Quakers* in Tazewell and Crawford counties; and a few *Mormons*, scattered through the state.

The *Roman Catholics* are not numerous. They have a dozen congregations, 8 or 10 priests, and a population between five and six thousand including old and young. A convent and boarding school for young ladies is in operation at Kaskaskia. The Roman Catholics are mostly about the old French villages, and the laborers along the line of canal.

There is considerable expression of good feeling amongst the different religious denominations, and the members frequently hear the preachers of each other, as there are but few congregations that are supplied every Sabbath. The qualifications of the clergymen are various. A number of them are men of talents, learning, influence, and unblemished piety. Others have had but few advantages in acquiring either literary or theological information, and yet are good speakers and useful men.

Some are very illiterate, and make utter confusion of the word of God. Such persons are usually proud, conceited, fanatical, and influenced by a spirit far removed from the meek, docile, benevolent, and charitable spirit of the gospel.

In general there are as many professors of religion, of some description, in proportion to the population, as in most of the states. The number will not vary far from 40,000, or one to ten.

PUBLIC LANDS.

In all the new states and territories, the lands which are owned by the general government, are surveyed and sold under one general system. In the surveys, "*meridian*" lines are first established, running north from the mouth of some noted river. These are intersected with "*base*" lines.

There are five principal meridians in the land surveys in the west.

The "*First Principal Meridian*" is a line due north from the mouth of the Miami.

The "*Second Principal Meridian*" is a line due north from the mouth of Little Blue river, in Indiana.

The "*Third Principal Meridian*" is a line due north from the mouth of the Ohio.

The *Fourth Principal Meridian*" is a line due north from the mouth of the Illinois.

The "*Fifth Principal Meridian*" is a line due north from the mouth of the Arkansas. Each of these meridians has its own base line.

The surveys connected with the third and fourth meridians, and a small portion of the second, embrace the state of Illinois.

The base line for both the second and third principal meridians commences at Diamond Island, in the Ohio, opposite Indiana, and runs due west till it strikes the Mississippi, a few miles below St. Louis.

All the *townships* in Illinois, south and east of the Illinois river, are numbered from this base line either north or south.

The third principal meridian terminates with the northern boundary of the state.

The fourth principal meridian commences on the right bank, and at the mouth of the Illinois river, but immediately crosses to the *east* shore, and passes up on that side, (and at one place nearly fourteen miles distant,) to a point in the channel of the river, seventy-two miles from its mouth. Here its base line commences and extends across the peninsula to the Mississippi, a short distance above Quincy. The fourth principal meridian is continued northward through the military tract, and across Rock river, to a curve in the Mississippi at the upper rapids, in township eighteen north, and about twelve or fifteen miles above Rock Island. It here crosses and passes up the *west* side of the Mississippi river fifty-three miles, and recrosses into Illinois, and passes through the town of Galena to the northern boundary of the state. It is thence continued to the Wisconsin river and made the principal meridian for the surveys of the territory, while the northern boundary line of the state is constituted its base line for that region.

Having formed a principal meridian with its corresponding base line, for a district of country, the next operation of the surveyor is to divide this into tracts of six miles square, called "*townships*."

In numbering the townships *east* or *west* from a principal meridian, they are called "*ranges*," meaning a range of townships; but in numbering *north* or *south* from a base line, they are called "*townships*." Thus a tract of land is said to be situated in township four north, in range three east, from the third principal meridian: or as the case may be.

Townships are subdivided into square miles, or tracts of 640 acres each, called "*sections*." If near timber, trees are marked and numbered with the section, township, and range, near each sectional corner. If in a large prairie, a mound is raised to designate the corner, and a billet of charred wood buried, if no rock is near. Sections are divided into halves by a line north and south, and into quarters by a transverse line. In sales, under certain conditions, quarters are sold in equal subdivisions of forty acres each, at one dollar and twenty-five cents per acre. Any person, whether a native born citizen, or a foreigner, may purchase forty acres of the richest soil, and receive an indisputable title, for fifty dollars.

Ranges are townships counted either east or west from meridians.

Townships are counted either north or south from their respective base lines.

Fractions are parts of quarter sections intersected by streams or confirmed claims.

The parts of townships, sections, quarters, etc. made at the lines of either townships or meridians are called *excesses* or *deficiencies*.

Sections, or miles square, are numbered, beginning in the northeast corner of the township, progressively west to the range line, and then progressively east to the range line, alternately, terminating at the southeast corner of the township, from one to thirty-six, as in the following diagram:

6	5	4	3	2	1
7	8	9	10	11	12
18	17	16*	15	14	13
19	20	21	22	23	24
30	29	28	27	26	25
31	32	33	34	35	36

* Appropriated for schools in the township.

I have been thus particular in this account of the surveys of public lands, to exhibit the simplicity of a system, that to strangers, unacquainted with the method of numbering the sections, and the various subdivisions, appears perplexing and confused.

A large tract of country in the north, and northeastern portion of this state is yet unsurveyed. This does not prevent the hardy pioneers of the west from taking possession, where the Indian title is extinct, as it is now to all lands within this state. They risk the chance of purchasing it when brought into market.

Land Offices and Districts. There are ten land offices in Illinois, in as many districts, open for the sale or entry of public lands.

The Land District of Shawneetown embraces that portion of the state, bounded north by the base line, east and south by the boundaries of the state, and west by the third principal meridian.

Office for the entry and sale of lands at Shawneetown.

The Land District of Kaskaskia is bounded north by the base line, and comprehends all that part of the state that lies between the third principal meridian and the Mississippi.

Land office at Kaskaskia.

The Land District of Edwardsville extends south to the base line, east to the third principal meridian, north to the line that separates the thirteenth and fourteenth townships north, and west to the Mississippi.

Land office at Edwardsville.

The Land District of Vandalia extends south to the base line, east to the line between ranges eight and nine, east of the third principal meridian, north to the south line of Springfield district, and west to the range line between ranges second and third west of the third principal meridian.

Land office at Vandalia.

The Land District of Palestine extends south to the northern boundary of the Shawneetown district, west to the eastern boundary of Vandalia district, north to the dividing line between townships sixteen and seventeen north; and east to the boundary of Indiana.

The Land District of Springfield extends south to Edwardsville district, east to the Palestine and Danville districts, and north and west to the Illinois river.

The Land District of Quincy embraces all the tract of country between the Illinois and Mississippi rivers to the line between townships 12 and 13 north and west of the third principal meridian.

The Land District of Danville includes that part of the state to its northern boundary, which lies north of Palestine, to the line between T. 30 and 31 N. of the 3d meridian and east of Springfield district.

Northwest District is in the northwestern portion of the state, and bounded south by the line between townships twelve and thirteen north, on the military tract, and east by the line between ranges three and four east of the third principal meridian, and north by the northern boundary of the state.

Land office at Galena.

Northeast District is in the northeast portion of the state, and bounded south by the line between townships thirty and thirty-one, on the third principal meridian, east by lake Michigan, and north by the boundary of the state.

Land office at Chicago.

The officers in each land district are a register and receiver, appointed by the president and senate, and paid by the general government.

The land, by proclamation of the president, is first offered for sale at auction, by half quarter sections. If no one bids for it at one dollar and twenty-five cents per acre or upwards, it is subject to private entry at any time after, upon payment at the time of entry. No credit is allowed.

In special cases congress has granted pre-emption rights, where settlements and improvements have been made on public lands previous to the public sale.

Pre-emption Rights confer the privilege only of purchasing the tract containing improvements at one dollar and twenty-five cents per acre, by the possessor, without the risk of a public sale.

All lands in this state, purchased of the general government, are exempted from taxation for five years after purchase.

All lands owned by private citizens ar corporate bodies, and not exempted as above, are divided by law into two classes for taxation, called "*first and second rates.*" First rate lands are taxed three dollars and twenty cents per quarter section of one hundred and sixty acres, per annum. Second rate lands are taxed two dollars and forty cents per quarter section, besides a county tax for roads. Resident and non resident landholders are taxed equally.

Residents owning lands in the different counties may list the same and pay taxes in the counties where they reside, or in the auditor's office, at their option.

Non residents must list their lands in the auditor's office.

Taxes of non residents are required to be paid into the state treasury, annually, on or before the first of August. If not paid at that time, a delinquent list of all lands, owned by non residents, on which taxes have not been paid, is sent to the clerk of the county commissioners' court of the county where the land lies, and a transcript of this list is to be published in some newspaper, printed within the state, at least sixty days previous to sale.

If the taxes are not paid to the clerk of the county by the first Monday in March, so much of the land, as is necessary to pay taxes and costs, is sold at the seat of justice of the county.

Lands sold for taxes may be redeemed within two years from the time of sale, by paying to the clerk of the county for the use of the purchaser, double the amount of taxes, interest, and costs for which the same may have been sold.

Lands belonging to minor heirs may be redeemed at any time before the expiration of one year from the time the youngest of said heirs shall become of lawful age.

Military Bounty Lands. The lands which constitute the Illinois military tract, given as a bounty to the soldiers in the last war with Great Britain, are included within the peninsula of the Illinois and Mississippi rivers, and extend on the fourth principal meridian, from the mouth of the Illinois, one hundred and sixty miles north. This tract embraces the counties of Calhoun, Pike, Adams, Schuyler, McDonough, Warren, Mercer, Knox, Henry, Fulton, Peoria, and a portion of Putnam.

For a particular description, reference may be had to each of these counties in part second.

In general terms however, this tract contains as much good land, both timber and prairie, as any portion of the state of equal extent. About three fifths of the quarter sections have been appropriated as military bounties. The remainder is to be disposed of in the same manner as other public lands. South of the base line, which passes across the tract through Schuyler and Adams counties, the public lands have been offered for sale. North of that line there is much excellent land yet for sale.

The disposition of so much of this fine country for military purposes has very much retarded its settlement. Most of the titles have long since departed from the soldiers for whose benefit the donations were made. Many thousand quarter sections have been sold by the state for taxes, and are past redemption. Much of it is in the hands of non residents, who hold it at prices too exorbitant to command sale. Some have doubted the legality of these sales at auction for taxes, but able lawyers, and those who have investigated the business, have expressed the opinion, that " tax titles," are valid. Within the last two years the military tract has received a great accession to its population. A large quantity of these military lands are now owned by a company, who have a land office, opened at Quincy, and offer tracts from three to ten dollars per acre.

The following particulars may be of use to non resident landholders:

1. If persons have held lands in the military tract, or

in the state, and have not atttended to paying taxes for more than two years, the land is sold and past redemption, unless there are minor heirs.

2. Every non resident landholder should employ an agent within the state to pay his taxes, and take the oversight of his property.

3. All deeds, conveyances, mortgages, or title papers whatsoever, must be recorded in the "*recorder's office,*" in the county where the land is situated. Deeds and title papers are not in force until *filed* in the recorder's office.

4. The words "*grant, bargain and sell,*" whatever may be the specific form of the instrument in other respects, convey a full and bona fide title, to warrant and defend, unless express provision is made to the contrary in the instrument.

[See revised laws of Illinois, of 1833, art. " recorder," page 510.]

HISTORY.

About 1670, the notion prevailed amongst the French that visited Canada, that a western passage to the Pacific ocean existed. They learned from the Indians that far in the west there was a great river; but of its course or termination they could learn nothing. They supposed that this river communicated with the western ocean.

To investigate this question, P. Marquette, a jesuit, and Joliet, were appointed by M. Talon, the intendant of New France. Marquette was well acquainted with the Canadas, and had great influence with the Indian tribes. They conducted an expedition through the lakes, up Green bay and Fox River, to the Portage, where it approaches the Wisconsin, to which they passed, and descended that river to the Mississippi, which they reached the 17th of June, 1673. These were the first Europeans that ever visited the " father of waters." They found a river much larger and deeper than it had been represented by the Indians. Their regular journal was lost on their return to

Canada, but from the account afterwards given by Joliet, they found the natives friendly, and that a tradition existed amongst them of the residence of a " Mon-e-to," or spirit, near the mouth of the Missouri, which they could not pass. They turned their course up the Illinois, and were highly delighted with the placid stream, and woodlands and prairies through which it flowed. They were hospitably received and kindly treated by the Illinois, a numerous nation of Indians who were destitute of the cruelty of savages.*

Marquette continued amongst these Indians with a view to Christianise them; but Joliet returned to Canada and reported the discoveries he had made.

Several years elapsed before any one attempted to follow up the discoveries of Marquette and Joliet. M. de La Salle, a native of Normandy, but who had resided many years in Canada, was the first to extend these early discoveries. 'He was a man of intelligence, talents, enterprise, and perseverance. After obtaining the sanction of the king of France, he set out on his projected expedition, in 1678, from Frontenac, with Chevalier Fonti, his lieutenant, and father Hennepin, a jesuit missionary, and thirty or forty men.

He spent about one year in exploring the country bordering on the lakes, and in selecting positions for forts and trading posts, to secure the Indian trade to the French. After he had built a fort at Niagara, and fitted out a small

* The word "Illim," from whence is derived the name "Oillinois," or "Illinois," as it was variously written by the French explorers, is said by Hennepin to signify " a full grown man." This nation, or confederacy, appears to have possessed originally, the Illinois country. The confederacy was formed of seven tribes:—the Illinois, Michigamies, Mascotans, Kaskaskias, Kahokias, Peorias, and Tau-mar-waus.

Their country was subjugated by the Iroquois or Mohawks about the close of the seventeenth century, who held dominion over the soil by right of conquest. In 1701 the Iroquois ceded all that part of Illinois that lies south and east of the Illinois river, to the British government.

vessel, he sailed through the lakes to Green bay, then called the "Bay of Puants." From thence he proceeded with his men in canoes towards the south end of lake Michigan, and arrived at the mouth of the "river of the Miamis" in November, 1679. This is thought to be Chicago. Here he built a fort, left eight or ten men, and passed with the rest of his company across the country to the waters of the Illinois river, and descended that river a considerable distance, when he was stopped for want of supplies. This was occasioned by the loss of a boat which had been sent from his post on Green bay. He was now compelled by necessity to build a fort, which, on account of the anxiety of mind he experienced, was called *Creve-cœur*, or broken heart.

The position of this fort cannot now be ascertained, but from some appearances, it is thought to have been near Spring bay, in the northeast part of Tazewell county.

At this period the Illinois were engaged in a war with the Iroquois, a numerous, warlike, and cruel nation, with whom La Salle had traded, while on the borders of Canada. The former, according to Indian notions of friendship, expected assistance from the French; but the interest and safety of La Salle depended upon terminating this warfare, and to this object he directed his strenuous efforts. The suspicious Illinois construed this into treachery, which was strengthened by the malicious and perfidious conduct of some of his own men, and pronounced upon him the sentence of death. Immediately he formed and executed the bold and hazardous project of going alone and unarmed to the camp of the Illinois, and vindicating his conduct. He declared his innocence of the charges, and demanded the author. He urged that the war should be terminated, and that the hostile nations should live in peace.

The coolness, bravery, and eloquence of La Salle filled the Indians with astonishment, and entirely changed their purposes. The calumet was smoked, presents mutually exchanged, and a treaty of amity concluded.

The original project of discovery was now pursued.

Father Hennepin started on the 28th of February, 1680, and having passed down the Illinois, ascended the Mississippi to the falls of St. Anthony. Here he was taken prisoner, robbed, and carried to the Indian villages, from which he made his escape, returned to Canada by the way of the Wisconsin, and from thence to France, where he published an account of his travels.

La Salle visited Canada to obtain supplies, returned to Creve-cœur, and shortly after descended the Illinois, and then the Mississippi, where he built one or two forts on its banks, and took possession of the country in the name of the king of France, and in honor of him called it *Louisiana*.

After descending the Mississippi to its mouth, he returned to the Illinois, and on his way back left some of his companions to occupy the country. This is supposed to have been the commencement of the villages of Kaskaskia and Cahokia, in 1683. La Salle went to France, fitted out an expedition to form a colony at the mouth of the Mississippi, sailed to the gulf of Mexico, but not being able to find the mouths of that river, he commenced an overland journey to his fort on the Illinois. On this journey he was basely assassinated by two of his own men.*

After the death of La Salle, no attempts to discover the mouth of the Mississippi, were made till about 1699; but the settlements in the Illinois country were gradually increased by emigrants from Canada.

In 1712, the king of France, by letters patent, gave the whole country of Louisiana to M. Crosat, with the commerce of the country, with the profits of all the mines, reserving for his own use one fifth of the gold and silver. After expending large sums in digging and exploring for

---

* La Salle appears to have discovered the Bay of St. Bernard, and formed a settlement on the western side of the Colorado, in 1685. This fact constitutes our claim to Texas. *See J. Q. Adams's Correspondence with Don Onis. Pub. Doc. first session 15th Congress*, 1818.

the precious medals without success, Crosat gave up his privilege to the king, in 1717. Soon after, the colony was granted to the Mississippi company, projected by Mr. Law, which took possession of Louisiana, and appointed M. Bienville governor. In 1719, La Harp commanded a Fort with French troops not far from the mouth of the Missouri river.

Shortly after, several forts were built within the present limits of Illinois, of which fort Chartres was the most considerable. By these means a chain of communication was formed from Canada to the mouth of the Mississippi.

The oldest record or document in the state is at Kaskaskia, dated 1725. It is a petition to Louis XV. king of France, asking a grant of common fields, commons, etc.; stating their great sufferings the preceding year, [1724] from the great flood which swept away all their improvements and obliged the people to flee to the bluffs opposite the village, and across the Kaskaskia river.

At the termination of hostilities between the French and English, in 1763, the Illinois country, with Canada, was ceded to the British government; and in 1765, Capt. Sterling, of the royal Highlanders, took possession of Illinois. He was succeeded by Major Farmer, who was relieved by Col. Reed, in 1766. The principal military post and seat of government during these changes, was at fort Chartres. The administration of Col. Reed was extremely unpopular with the inhabitants, and is said to have been a course of military oppression. In 1768 he was succeeded by Lieut. Col. Wilkins, who established a court of justice amongst the people, and appointed seven judges to settle all matters relating to debts and property.

They met for the first time at fort Chartres in December following, and continued to meet for business monthly. Still the people were dissatisfied, and demanded the right of trial by jury, which was denied them.

Affairs continued in this posture till the revolutionary war, when the Virginia militia, under command of Gen. George Rodgers Clarke, made an excursion through the

Indian country, subjugated fort Chartres, Kaskaskia, and other posts on the Mississippi, and then conducted a successful expedition against Port Vincent, now Vincennes. This was in 1778.

The same year the legislature of Virginia organised a county in this remote region, called "*Illinois*," and appointed a magistrate over it with extensive powers styled lieutenant governor. Timothy Demonbrun was appointed to this office.

This territory was afterwards ceded by Virginia to the United States, and formed a portion of the Northwestern Territory, by whose authority the county of Illinois was divided, and the names of St. Clair and Randolph given. In 1800, it was included within the limits of Indiana territory, and at that time the country that forms the present state of Illinois contained about 3,000 inhabitants.

Many of the officers and soldiers that accompanied General Clarke in his expedition became enamored with the country, returned with their families and formed the early American settlements. Other persons settled in Kaskaskia about the same time, to engage in the Indian trade.

In 1786, the Kickapoo, and other bands of Indians, commenced their predatory warfare, which greatly harassed the American settlers for the succeeding ten years.

After 1800, the population increased considerably from emigration. In 1809, a territorial government was formed, and the population the next year amounted to 12,282.

During the last war between Great Britain and the United States, Illinois, in common with other frontier districts, felt the calamities of warfare. The defence of the long line of frontier from the mouth of the Missouri, across the territory to Shawneetown, depended upon the energy and vigilance of the citizens, under the able and indefatigable governor, the late Ninian Edwards.

In 1812, the territory, which had been under the government of the governor and judges, entered upon the second grade of territorial government, with a legislature, and a delegate in congress.

In 1818, the constitution was framed and Illinois was received into the Union as the twenty-second state.

MISCELLANEOUS REMARKS.

1. This state presents many inducements to those who are emigrating to the west. It is now receiving large accessions from the north, the south, and from Europe. Many Germans have already entered it, and many more are shortly expected. An English colony was formed at Albion, in Edwards county, by Messrs. Birbeck and Flowers, in 1818.

Morgan county contains many English families, who came three or four years since. In general they have purchased lands, and are doing well.

Emigrants from New England, New York, Pennsylvania, and Ohio, pour into the middle and northern counties.

From the southern states there are hundreds visiting Illinois monthly, to find convenient residences, and a retreat from the inconveniences of slaveholding.

2. Farms, partially cultivated may be purchased, at a reasonable price, in almost every county. The prices vary from local situation, or factitious circnmstances. From three to ten dollars per acre, including improvements, is the common range of prices.

3. In no part of the United States can uncultivated land be made into farms with less labor than in Illinois. An emigrant may purchase a quarter section for $200, a proportionate supply of timbered and prairie land, and have a large farm under cultivation in a short time. His cattle, horses, and hogs will run upon the range around him, and find feed nine months in the year, and a small amount of labor will provide a supply of winter food. Hundreds of families, who have not the means to purchase, settle on public lands, make their farms and live unmolested. Any laboring man, with reasonable industry and economy, with a family, may arrrive here without any capital, and in

half a dozen years be the owner of a good farm, with stock in abundance. The prairies and woodland would furnish range until his farm was made.

Those who have one or two thousand dollars to commence with, have peculiar advantages.

4. Mechanics of every description, for the ordinary purposes of life, find abundant encouragement.

I could name common mechanics, whom I knew when apprentices, and who commenced business without a cent of capital, but who now own property valued from ten to twenty thousand dollars. They have gained it by steady, persevering industry. And yet, no one makes money rapidly, and grows rich suddenly. The great secret of the accumulation of property in any part of the " West," consists in the *gradual rise of property, by the advantageous application of manual labour.* As a general principle, with exceptions to particular places, this rise of property in Illinois, the last ten years, has equalled from twenty-five to thirty per cent. per annum. About some of our rising towns the rise has been 1000 per cent. in three years.

5. Good school teachers, who will follow the employment, are much needed. The usual method is to pay by the scholar per quarter. Prices for ordinary branches in the country settlements, including board $2 50, and $3 per scholar. Female teachers for schools, are inquired after.

6. The people of the West, and of Illinois, have much plain, blunt, but sincere hospitality. Emigrants who come amongst them with a disposition to be pleased with the people and country—to make no invidious comparisons—to assume no airs of distinction—but to become amalgamated with the people, where, of course every thing is different to what they have been accustomed, will be welcome.

PART SECOND.

GENERAL VIEW OF EACH COUNTY IN THE STATE OF ILLINOIS.

ARRANGED IN ALPHABETICAL ORDER.

ADAMS COUNTY.

Adams County was organised from Pike county, in 1825, and is thirty miles long, with an average width of twenty-four miles—containing about 810 square miles.

It is bounded north, by Hancock; east by Schuyler and a corner of Pike; south by Pike; and west, by the Mississippi river.

Its streams are Bear creek and branches, Cedar, Tyrer, Mill, Fall, and Pigeon creeks, on the western; and the north and west forks of M'Kees creek on its eastern border.

For quality of soil, well proportioned into timber and prairie, it is second to none in the state. Few tracts of country are equal, and none superior to the one on Bear creek.

Its productions are similar to other counties in the military district. The people in general are enterprising and industrious farmers. The population is about 8,500. Adams county is attached to the fifth judicial circuit, and sends one senator and two representatives to the legislature.

The seat of justice is *Quincy*.

ALEXANDER COUNTY.

Alexander County lies at the south end of the state, in the forks of the Ohio and Mississippi rivers, which wash its western, southern, and a portion of its eastern borders. More than sixty miles of its western side are along the curves and windings of the latter river. It has a fertile soil, covered with a heavy growth of timber, amongst which are oaks of various kinds, especially white oak, cypress, poplar, walnut, hickory, some cherry, elm, etc. and a tract of yellow pine in the northwestern part. A reef of rocks of limestone, intermixed with sand stone, forming the grand chain of the Ohio, six miles above America, is supposed to extend across this county, (below the surface of the earth,) to the Mississippi river. At least one third of the county is alluvion. On Cash river, and near the mouth of the Ohio, the land is inundated in times of high water. Along the Mississippi is an extensive tract of alluvial land, entirely above high water.

The streams in this county are Cash river and branches, Sexton's creek, and Clear creek. Cash river enters it at the northeastern part, passes in a circuitous course through it, and enters the Ohio six miles above its mouth, at *Trinity*.

Alexander county is about twenty-four miles long, and upon an average width of eighteen miles—containing about 375 square miles.

Alexander county is attached to the third judicial circuit, and sends one member to the house of representatives, and, with Union county, one member to the senate. Population about 2350. It was formed from Union county, in 1819.

The seat of justice is *Unity*.

BOND COUNTY.

Bond County was organised from Madison, in 1817. It

then embraced an extensive district of country, but has since been reduced to an area of twenty miles long, and eighteen miles wide, or 360 square miles. It has Montgomery on the north, Fayette east, Clinton south, and Madison on the west.

Shoal creek and its branches pass through the middle, and Hurricane fork waters the eastern portion of this county.

It is duly proportioned into timber and prairie. In some parts the latter is rather too level for convenience, but is good second rate land. The population generally are industrious, frugal, and intelligent farmers.

Bond county sends one member to the house of representatives, and with Montgomery one to the senate. It belongs to the second judicial circuit. Population about 3,980.

The seat of justice is *Greenville.*

BOONE COUNTY.

Boone County was formed from Winnebago and Mc Henry counties in February, 1837. It is bounded north by the Wisconsin territory; east by McHenry; south by Kane, and West by Winnebago county. It is about 24 miles long, and 21 miles wide; containing about 500 square miles.

It is watered on the western side by the northern and main branches of the Kishwaukee, and on its eastern side by branches of Fox river.

Its timber, scattered over the county, is found chiefly in groves and oak openings, with a large proportion of rich, undulating prairie. Its representative and its judicial connection is with Jo Daviess county. The seat of justice not yet located. Most of the land in this and the adjoining counties is unsurveyed and of course not in market, but is rapidly settling. I estimate its population at 600.

CALHOUN COUNTY.

Calhoun County was organised from Pike-county, in 1825. It is a long and narrow strip of country lying in the forks of the Illinois and Mississippi rivers. It is bounded on three sides by those rivers, and on the northern end, by Pike county, and is thirty-seven and a half miles long, and from three to ten miles in width from one river to the other—making about 260 square miles. The mouth of Bay creek is in the northern part of this county, which affords a harbor and navigation for steam boats seven miles. There are no other creeks worth naming. Several fine prairies lie at the foot of the bluffs on both sides of the county, amongst which are Illinois, Salt, Belleview. On the rivers considerable tracts are subject to inundation, and in the interior are bluffs, ravines and sink holes. Still there are considerable tracts of good land unoccupied.

The bottoms furnish excellent range for stock. Cattle, beef, pork, corn, honey, and beeswax are its exports.

Formerly honey from the trees was obtained in profuse quantities. It grows more scarce as the population increases. Calhoun belongs to the fifth judicial circuit, and is connected with Greene, in electing a representative, and senator. Population about 1200.

Surrounded by rivers and low bottoms, Calhoun county is less healthy than others on the military tract.

Coal, in large bodies, is found on the Mississippi in the south part of the county.

The seat of justice is *Guilford*.

CASS COUNTY.

Cass County was formed from the north part of the county of Morgan at the late session of the legislature, and decided by the votes of the people of Morgan county on the third Monday of April, 1837, as the law provided.

It is bounded north by Sangamon county and river, east

by the same county, south by Morgan, and west by the Illinois river which separates it from Schuyler county.

It is 27 miles long, and about 12 miles broad, containing about 256 square miles.

It is watered by various branches that fall into Sangamon river on the north, with the head branches of Indian and other small creeks that fall into the Illinois river, on the west and south. It is proportionably divided into timber and prairie, the surface undulating, and the soil geneally very rich.

The population is estimated at 6,500. Its representative and judicial connection is still with Morgan county.

The seat of justice is *Beardstown.*

CHAMPAIGN COUNTY.

Champaign County was organised from the attached part of Vermilion county, in February, 1833. It is bounded, on the north, by a strip of country not belonging to any county; on the east by Vermilion; on the south by Coles; and on the west by Macon and McLean counties. It is 36 miles long, and about 28 miles wide, and contains about 1008 square miles. The streams, are the Salt Fork of the Vermilion of the Wabash; the Vermilion of the Illinois, the Kaskaskia, and the North Fork of the Sangamon;—all of which take their rise in this county and run in opposite directions. Here are extensive prairies, indented with beautiful groves of fine timber, of which Big Grove, at the head of Salt Fork, is the largest. Around these groves the prairies are undulating, and very rich soil.

The settlements are not yet extensive. As an interior county, it will be further from market than those situated either on the Wabash or Illinois, but is well adapted to the growth of stock, and will be undoubtedly a healthy region.

Champaign county belongs to the fourth judicial circuit, and sends one representative and, with Vermilion county, one senator to the legislature. Population about 1250.

The seat of justice is *Urbanna.*

CLARK COUNTY.

Clark County was formed from Crawford county, in 1819; and is bounded on the north by Edgar; on the east by Indiana and the Wabash river; south by Crawford: and west by Coles.

It is twenty-four miles long, east and west; and twenty-one miles broad—containing about 500 square miles.

Its streams are, the North Fork of the Embarras, which crosses the northwestern part of the county; Mill creek, and Big creek, which cross its northeastern part.

Walnut, Union, Dolson, and Parker's prairies are found in this county.

At York, in the southeastern corner of the county, is a steam saw and flouring mill.

Its exports are corn, pork, and beef cattle. From 60,000 to 100,000 bushels of corn are sent out annually.

Clark county has 4,000 inhabitants, sends one member to the house of representatives, and, with Coles, one member to the senate. It belongs to the fourth judicial circuit.

The seat of justice is *Darwin*.

CLAY COUNTY.

Clay County was formed from portions of Wayne, Lawrence, Crawford, and Fayette, in 1824.

It is bounded on the north, by Effingham and Jasper; east, by Lawrence; south, by Wayne, and a corner of Edwards; west, by Marion, and a corner of Fayette.

Its medium length is thirty miles; width, twenty-one miles—containing about 620 square miles.

It is watered by the Little Wabash, and branches.

Probably two thirds of the surface is prairie of an inferior quality. The streams usually overflow their banks in freshets.

Clay county belongs to the fourth judicial circuit, and sends one member to the house of representatives, and also with Fayette and Effingham sends one member to the senate.

Population, at the last census, 1648; increase since, probably about twenty per cent.

Its seat of justice is *Maysville.*

CLINTON COUNTY.

Clinton County was formed from Washington and a portion of Bond, in December, 1824.

It is bounded north by Bond; east by Marion; south by Washington; and west by St. Clair, and a corner of Madison.

It is thirty miles long, and eighteen miles wide—containing about fourteen townships, or 504 square miles.

It is watered by the Kaskaskia river, which passes through it, and its tributaries—Crooked, Shoal, and Sugar creeks; and is about equally proportioned into timber and prairie.

Much of the land in this and the adjacent counties is not equal in quality to that further north. This is true especially of the prairies. The soil is thinner, the surface is less undulating, and farmers are subjected to greater inconvenience from wet seasons.

The timber, where it abounds, is generally of a good quality.

Clinton county belongs to the second judicial circuit, and sends one member to the house of representatives, and, with Marion, one to the senate.

Population about 3,000.

The seat of justice is *Carlyle.*

COLES COUNTY.

Coles County was organised, in 1830, from Clark and Edgar counties.

It lies in the eastern part of the state, and is bounded north by Champaign; east by Edgar and Clark; south by Jasper, and a corner of Effingham; and west by Shelby and Macon counties. It is forty-eight miles long, from north to south; and twenty-six miles wide on a medium; —containing about 1,248 square miles.

The Kaskaskia river passes through four townships in its northwestern part; the Embarras runs its whole length, with several branches; and the heads of the Little Wabash afford fine mill streams, and settlements, in its southwestern portion.

This county contains much excellent land, equal in quality to the country on the Illinois river.

The northern, and a tract through the middle portions of the county are prairies of considerable extent; but the other parts are duly proportioned into timber and prairie.

The timber is similar to the borders of the Kaskaskia; and much of the prairie land is moderately undulating, The southeastern part is rather wet or broken.

The streams are not large; they generally run over a bed of sand, and afford many good mill seats.

Most of the settlements are of recent formation, but its agricultural productions soon must exceed those of any other county near the Wabash, and will find their way to that river for market.

It belongs to the fourth judicial circuit, and sends two members to the house of representatives, and, with Clark, one to the senate.

The population is equal to 5800.

Pork, beef, cattle, and horses, will be the staple productions.

The seat of justice is *Charleston*.

COOK COUNTY.

Cook County was organised January 15th, 1831, and is bounded north by McHenry county, east by lake Michigan; south by Will county; and west by La Salle. It is about 42 miles long and 36 miles wide, but irregularly shaped on its eastern and southeastern sides. It has about 1330 square miles.

It is watered by the Des Plaines, the north and south branches of the Chicago, the Du Page, Hickory creek, and some smaller streams.

Its surface is tolerably level, of a rich soil, with large prairies, and the timber in groves. There is a fine body of timber on the north fork of the Chicago, and along the lake shore.

This county, and those adjacent, differ in several respects from the country below. The small streams run perennially, over rocky and gravelly beds through the prairies. The timber is not confined to the banks of the streams, but exists in groves and strips, often on the dividing ridges between the water courses. The summers are comparatively cooler, and the winters longer and more severe.

Cook county is rapidly settling, chiefly by emigrants from the northern states; and will be both a stock and grain growing region. Its market will be through the lakes to New York and Canada.

This county belongs to the seventh judicial circuit, and sends one senator and three representatives to the legislature.

The seat of justice is *Chicago.*

CRAWFORD COUNTY.

Crawford County was formed, in 1816, and lies north of Lawrence, east of Jasper, south of Clark, and west of the Wabash river, that separates it from Indiana.

It is twenty two miles long, and twenty miles broad,—containing 426 square miles.

Racoon, Hutson, Sugar, and La Motte creeks, are small streams, that rise in this county, and run east into the Wabash; its western border is watered by branches of the Embarras.

La Motte prairie is a level and rich tract, admirably adapted to the growth of corn. Its exports are similar to those of other counties along the Wabash, consisting chiefly of corn, beef, pork, and cattle.

Crawford county with Jasper sends one member to the house of representatives, and with Lawrence, one to the senate. It is attached to the fourth judicial circuit.

The seat of justice is *Palestine*.

EDGAR COUNTY.

Edgar County was formed from Clark, in 1823, and is bounded north by Vermilion; east, by the state of Indiana; south by Clark; and west by Coles county.

It is twenty-seven miles long, from north to south; and twenty-five miles wide, from east to west—containing eighteen townships, or about 648 square miles.

Edgar county is watered by Big Clear, and Brulette's creeks, which are small streams, and enter the Wabash. Little Embarras heads in the western and southwestern parts of this county, and runs southwest into Coles.

The south and east sides of this county are well timbered with all the varieties found on the eastern side of the state, including poplar.

The soil in general is rich, adapted to the various productions of this state. Pork and beef—especially the former—are its chief exports, which find a ready market at Terre Haute and Clinton, Indiana.

It belongs to the fourth judicial circuit, and sends two members to the house of representatives, and one to the senate.

The seat of justice is *Paris*.

EDWARDS COUNTY.

Edwards County was organised from Gallatin, in 1814. It lies on the Little Wabash river, and has Lawrence county on the north; Wabash county east; White county south; and Wayne county west.

It is twenty-two miles long, from north to south; and an average width of eleven miles—containing about 183 square miles, proportionably divided into timber and prairie. It is the smallest county in the state.

The prairies are small, high, undulating, and bounded by heavy timber. The English settlement formed by Messrs. Birbeck and Flowers is in this county.

Edwards county is watered by the Little Wabash river which runs along and near its western border; and the Bon Pas, which forms its eastern boundary, and their branches.

Its prairies are Boltenhouse, Burnt, Long, Bon Pas, Village, Bush and Mills, in all of which are flourishing settlements. A settlement of about 60 families is in the timbered country, in the south end of this county.

Edwards county is attached to the fourth judicial circuit; sends one member to the house of representatives, and, with Wabash and Wayne, one member to the senate. The seat of justice is *Albion*.

EFFINGHAM COUNTY.

Effingham County was laid off by the legislature from Fayette county, in 1831, but did not become organised by the election of officers and the possession of county privileges till the commencement of 1833.

It is bounded north, by Shelby, and a corner of Coles; east by Jasper; south by Clay, and a corner of Fayette; and west by Fayette. It is twenty-four miles long, and about twenty-one broad—containing 486 square miles. It is watered by the Little Wabash river and its branches, and contains good second rate land, tolerably level. The bottom lands on the Little Wabash are rich, and heavily timbered, but are inundated for a day when the river rises so as to overflow its banks.

Effingham county, in union with Fayette, sends two members to the house of representatives, and with Fayette and Clay, one to the senate. It belongs to the second judicial circuit.

The seat of justice is *Ewington.*

FAYETTE COUNTY.

Fayette County was formed from Bond, Edwards, Crawford, and Clark, in 1821, embracing a large extent of territory, extending northward to the Illinois river, which has since been formed into several counties. It is situated on the Kaskaskia river, and is bounded north by Shelby; east by Effingham; south by Marion, and a corner of Clinton; and west by Bond and Montgomery. It is about twenty-seven miles long, and twenty-four broad, with additional townships at the southeast and southern corners, and contains about 720 square miles. Vandalia the present seat of government for the state, is situated towards the southwestern part. Besides the Kaskaskia river, which passes through Fayette, it is watered by Hurricane fork, Higgin's, Ramsey's and Beck's creeks on the west, and by Big and Hickory creeks on the east. There is a heavy growth of timber in several parts of this county, especially along the Kaskaskia, and the Hurricane fork. Besides some prairies of convenient size, intersected with points of timber, about twelve miles in width of the eastern side of Fayette is in the Grand prairie.

The bottom lands of the Kaskaskia are low, subject to inundation, and contain many small lakes and ponds. The country around Vandalia is undulating and well timbered, and the soil is second rate.

The principal settlements in Fayette are Hurricane,

Seminary township, Buckmaster's, Hall's, Brown's, Wakefield's, Haley's and Big creek.

There are several grist mills propelled by water power in the county, and a valuable steam saw mill at Vandalia. Fayette belongs to the second judicial circuit; and with Effingham, sends two members to the house of representatives, and with Effingham and Clay, one to the senate The population is estimated at 4100.

The seat of justice is *Vandalia.*

FRANKLIN COUNTY.

Franklin County was formed out of Gallatin, White, and an attached part of Jackson county, in 1818, and is situated in the southern part of the state. It is bounded north by Jefferson county; east, by Hamilton and Gallatin; south, by Johnson and Union; and west, by Jackson and Perry counties. It is thirty-six miles long and twenty-four miles wide; making 864 square miles. Franklin county is watered by Big Muddy river and branches, and and the south fork of Saline creek. The prairies are generally small and fertile, but rather too level; the timber is good and in abundance; the soil rather sandy. Its products are similar to those of the counties adjoining, and it is capable of being made a rich agricultural county.

Franklin sends two members to the house of representatives, and with Jackson county, one member to the senate. It is attached to the third judicial circuit.

The county seat is *Frankfort.*

FULTON COUNTY.

Fulton County was formed from Pike county, in 1825, and is bounded north, by Knox, and a corner of Peoria; east by Peoria, and the Illinois river; south by the Illinois river, and Schuyler county; and west by Schuyler and McDonough and a corner of Warren counties.

The Illinois washes its southeastern side, and gives it an irregular shape. The Spoon river passes through it; and Otter creek waters the southwestern, and Copperas creek the northeastern portions.

It is from twenty-four to forty-two miles long, from north to south; and from twelve to thirty miles broad—containing 874 square miles.

Nearly one half of Fulton county is heavily timbered with the varieties that abound on the military tract; and much both of its prairie and timbered land, is of an excellent quality. It is in general well watered; the streams usually flow over a gravelly bottom, and furnish many good mill seats.

Its productions are and will continue to be similar to this region of country; and the Illinois and Spoon rivers will afford facilities to market. This whole region on the Illinois must shortly become a wealthy agricultural country.

Fulton county belongs to the fifth judicial circuit, and, with Knox and Henry, sends two members to the house of representatives, and one member to the senate. Population about 7000.

County seat *Lewiston.*

GALLATIN COUNTY.

Gallatin County joins the Wabash and the Ohio, in the southeastern corner of the state, and was organised in 1812. It is bounded north by White county; east by the states of Indiana and Kentucky; south by Pope county; and west by Pope, and Franklin counties.

It is from thirty to thirty-six miles long, and with a medium width of twenty-seven miles—containing about 760 square miles.

Its eastern boundary is washed by the Wabash and Ohio rivers, and the interior watered by the Saline creek and its tributaries.

Sand predominates in the soil of this part of the state.

The basis rock generally is sandstone, lying probably upon a stratum of clay slate.

This county is mostly covered with timber, amongst which are various kinds of oak, walnut, poplar, mulberry, hickory, beech, cypress, and the other kinds found in this part of the state.

The salines, in the vicinity of Equality, are sources of wealth; and furnish large quantities of salt for home consumption.

Other articles of export, are horses, beef, pork, cattle, lumber, some tobacco, etc. About one half of the salt manufactured at the salines is exchanged for corn, corn meal, flour, beef, pork, potatoes, and every species of produce raised in the country, to support the establishment.

This part of the state is well adapted to the growth of stock.

Gallatin county contains about 9,750 inhabitants. It is attached to the third judicial circuit, and sends three members to the house of representatives, and one member to the senate.

Shawneetown is an important commercial town on the Ohio.

The seat of justice is *Equality*.

GREENE COUNTY.

Greene County was formed from Madison, in January, 1821; and is bounded on the north by Morgan; east by Macoupin; south by Madison and the Mississippi river; and west by the Illinois river, which separates it from Calhoun and Pike counties.

Its medium length is thirty-eight miles; width, twenty-four miles; superficial contents 912 square miles. The Illinois and Mississippi washes its western and a portion of its southern borders; Apple and Macoupin creeks pass through it.

The banks of the Mississippi in the southern parts of this county are generally composed of perpendicular cliffs, varying in height from 80 to 200 feet, consisting of horizontal strata of lime and sandstone; frequently imbedded with coal. The latter does not show itself at the face of the cliffs, but is found in great abundance a short distance from it. These cliffs commence at Alton, and extend along the Mississippi and Illinois rivers to the northern part of the county; sometimes, however, receding several miles east, leaving a low and fertile alluvion which is usually timbered on the banks of the river, and a prairie surface towards the bluffs.

Greene county has much excellent land, both timber and prairie; the surface approaches nearer to a level than the counties further north, with proportionate quantities of timber and prairie, The population about 13,500.

Greene county is attached to the first judicial circuit, and sends three members to the house of representatives, and one to the senate, and unites with Calhoun in sending one additional representative and senator.

The seat of justice is *Carrollton*.

HAMILTON COUNTY.

Hamilton County was formed from White county, in 1821, and is bounded north by Wayne; east by White; south by Gallatin; and west by Franklin and Jefferson counties. It is twenty-four miles long, and eighteen broad—area 432 square miles.

This county is watered by branches of the Saline creek, and Little Wabash river, and contains a large proportion of timbered land. The soil generally is second and third rate, with a considerable tract of swamp in the northern part of the county.

Hamilton county belongs to the third judicial circuit; sends one member to the house of representatives, and, with Jefferson county, one to the senate.

The seat of justice is *Mc Leansboro'*.

HANCOCK COUNTY.

Hancock County was formed from Pike county, in 1825. It is thirty miles in length, and from twenty-four to thirty miles broad—containing about 775 square miles.

It lies north of Adams, west of McDonough, south of Warren, and is washed by the Mississippi on its western side.

Hancock prairie, from twelve to twenty miles in width, runs from south to north through this county. On the east, it is watered by the branches of Crooked creek; and on the southwest, by Bear; and on the northwest, by Camp creek. This county in the aggregate is deficient in timber. The banks of Bear creek furnish a supply for that portion of the county. A strip lines the bank of the Mississippi, in some places of considerable width and of excellent quality—in other places narrow and of inferior quality. A tolerably dense settlement extends along the line of this timber. Crooked creek furnishes a due proportion of timber and prairie, and a body of excellent land.

Hancock county belongs to the fifth judicial circuit, and sends one representative, and with McDonough one Senator to the legislature.

The county seat is *Carthage*.

HENRY COUNTY.

Henry Connty was formed in 1825, but not organised for judicial purposes till recently.

It is bounded north by Whiteside and Rock Island; east by Putnam; south by Knox, and west by Mercer and Rock Island counties. It is thirty miles long east and west, and about the same broad—area 840 square miles. It is watered by Edwards, and some of the head branches of Spoon river, Rock river, Green river and the Winnebago swamp and outlet.

About the Big Grove, Fraker's settlement, and on Edwards river is considerable good land, but in general Henry county is not equal to the counties contiguous. The Winnebago swamp spreads along its northern side; and there is considerable level, wet, swampy land between the waters that fall into the Mississippi and those that flow to the Illinois.

There is good land enough within its borders to make a respectable county. It belongs to the fifth judicial circuit, and with Knox and Warren, sends one member to each branch of the legislature. Its county seat not located.

IROQUOIS COUNTY.

This county was laid off by the legislature, in 1833. It is bounded on the north by Will county; east by the state of Indiana; south by Vermilion county; and west by an irregular strip of country, attached to Vermilion county.

It is about 42 miles long and thirty-four broad—containing about 1428 square miles.

Kankakee, Iroquois, Sugar, Spring and Beaver creeks are its water courses. A large proportion of this county is prairie; the timber is in groves, and strips along the streams.

Settlements have been formed to some extent on Iroquois and Sugar creeks. There are many sand ridges and plains in this region, but considerable portions of prairie are very rich. Iroquois is attached to the seventh judicial circuit, and sends one representative, and with La Salle, Kane and Boone, one senator to the legislature. Population about 1800. The seat of justice is not yet established.

JACKSON COUNTY.

Jackson County was formed from Randolph and Johnson, in 1816. It is situated on the Mississippi, and has Randolph county on the north, Franklin east, Union south, and the Mississippi river and a portion of Randolph west. It is twenty-four miles from north to south, and from eighteen to twenty-eight miles from east to west—its area is about 576 square miles. This county is watered by Muddy river and its tributaries.

On this stream, near Brownsville, is a saline where considerable quantities of salt are manufactured.

Jackson county is generally a timbered tract of country, except towards its northeastern part where are some fine prairies. The timber in this country and along the Muddy, is of the various kinds common to this portion of the state, as oaks of several species, hickory, elm, poplar, walnut, sugar maple, etc.

Its exports are salt, coal, pork, beef, horses, etc.

Jackson county belongs to the third judicial circuit, and sends one member to the house of representatives, and with Franklin, one member to the senate. Population about 3,150.

County seat *Brownsville.*

JASPER COUNTY.

Jasper County was formed out of Crawford, and small portions of Lawrence and Clay, in 1831.

It is bounded north by Coles; east by Crawford; south by Lawrence and Clay; and west by a corner of Clay, and Effingham. It is twenty-three miles long, and twenty-two wide—and contains about 508 square miles. The Embarras runs through it, and the Muddy Fork of the Little Wabash waters its western side. Much of the prairie and timbered land of this county is level, wet, and of an inferior quality. The settlements are small amounting to fifty or sixty families.

On the North Fork and the main Embarras are some good tracts of fertile soil.

The county seat is called *Newton*.

JEFFERSON COUNTY.

Jefferson County was organised from Edwards and White counties, in 1819. It is bounded on the north by Marion; east by Wayne and Hamilton; south by Franklin: and west by Perry and Washington. It is twenty-four miles long and the same in width—containing 576 square miles.

Jefferson county is watered by several branches of the Big Muddy, which head in this county, and a small branch of the little Wabash.

The soil is tolerable second rate land, about one-third prairie; the timbered land is covered with various kinds of oak, hickory, elm, sugar tree, etc.

Its productions find their market either at Shawneetown or St. Louis. Its prairies, all of which contain good settlements, are Casey's, Jordon's, Moore's, Walnut Hill, Arm of Grand, and Long prairie. Its streams are East, Middle, and West Forks of Big Muddy river, and Adams's branch of Skillet Fork.

Jefferson county is attached to the third judicial circuit, and sends one member to the house of representatives, and, with Hamilton county, one member to the senate.

The seat of justice is *Mount Vernon*.

JO DAVIESS COUNTY.

Jo Daviess County was formed in 1827, but has since been reduced to about the following extent. From east to west from 12 to 34 miles, and from north to south 37 miles, and extending by the curve of the Mississippi, in a triangular form nearly to a point at its northwestern corner;—containing about 724 square miles.

It is bounded by Wisconsin territory on the north, Stephenson on the east, Whiteside county south, and the Mississippi river west.

It is watered by Fever river, Apple, Rush, and Plum creeks, and some smaller streams.

This county is rich, both for agricultural and mining purposes. Lead and copper are in abundance here. Like all the northern part of Illinois, timber is scarce. The surface is undulating—in some places hilly—well watered, both with springs and mill streams.

The timber is in groves, and upon the margins of the streams.

The county was named in honor of the late general Joseph H. Daviess, of Kentucky, who gallantly fell, in the disastrous battle of Tippecanoe, in 1811. It was bad taste, however, in the legislature, to affix the appellation of *Jo* to a name that has received marked respect in the western states.

The chief export of this region is lead; but it is a fine country for both grain and stock.

Jo Daviess county is attached to the sixth judicial circuit, and, with Mercer and Rock Island, Stephenson, Winnebago, Ogle and Boone, sends two representatives and one senator to the legislature.

The seat of justice is *Galena*.

JOHNSON COUNTY.

Johnson County was organised from Randolph in 1812, and is situated in the southern part of the state. It is bounded north by Franklin; east by Pope; south by the Ohio river; and west by Union and Alexander counties.

It is from twenty-five to thirty miles long; breadth, eighteen; its area, about 486 square miles.

The interior of the county is watered by Cash river and

Big Bay creek. Between these streams and ten or twelve miles from the Ohio river, which washes its southern boundary, is a line of ponds, interspersed with ridges and islands of rich land; and at high water, a large current passes out of Big Bay into Cash river.

On the south side of these ponds is very rich land with a string of settlements; but an unhealthy region. Between this tract and the Ohio river, is a tract of barrens and timber, with a tolerably good soil, but not much population. A line of settlements contiguous to the Ohio river extends through the county.

Johnson county contains considerable quantities of good land, tolerably level, well timbered, and inclining to a sandy soil. The principal timber in this region, is cypress, sugar maple, oaks of various species, hickory, sweet gum, with some poplar, elm, walnut, and cedar.

Johnson county sends one member to the house of representatives; and with Pope, one to the senate. It belongs to third judicial circuit.

The seat of justice is *Vienna*.

KANE COUNTY.

Kane County was formed from the attached portion of La Salle, January, 1836. It is bounded north by Boone and McHenry, east by Cook, south by La Salle, and west by Ogle county.

It is thirty-six miles square, and contains 1296 square miles.

It is watered by Fox river in its southeastern parts, and Indian creek, Somonauk, Rock and Blackberry, Wabonsic, Morgan and Mill creeks that enter Fort river, and on its western and northwestern portion, several small streams, and the south and main branches of the Kishwaukee or Scyamore, that enters Rock river. These are all excellent mill streams, and already saw and flouring mills are built or in progress.

The timber is in groves, of which Au Sable, Big-woods,

Little-woods and various others are thickly settled around. There is white, black, red, yellow and bur oaks, sugar maple, linden or basswood, black and white walnut, hickory, ash of various species, white poplar, ironwood, elm, some cherry, and occasional clumps of cedar along the cliffs that overhang Fox river, and other streams.

Population from twelve to fifteen hundred and rapidly increasing.

Kane county belongs to the seventh judicial circuit and is represented in connection with La Salle, and Iroquois.

The seat of justice is not permanently located.

KNOX COUNTY.

Knox County is bounded north by Henry; east by Peoria, and a corner of Putnam; south by Fulton; and west by Warren, and a corner of Mercer.

It is thirty miles long, and from twenty-four to thirty miles broad—containing 792 square miles.

It is watered by Henderson and Spoon rivers, and their tributaries.

The prairies in this county are large and generally of the best quality; and there are several large and excellent tracts of timber on the water courses. The soil in general is of the first quality.

Knox county was laid off by the legislature in a general distribution of counties on the military tract, in January, 1825, though not organised for judicial purposes till about five years after.

It belongs to the fifth judicial circuit, and with Warren and Henry sends one member to each branch of the legislature.

Population about 2000.

Seat of justice, *Knoxville.*

LA SALLE COUNTY.

La Salle County was formed in 1831. It is bounded north by Kane, east by Will, south by Livingston and M'Lean, and west by Putnam. It is 48 miles long from east to west, and 36 miles wide, with an addition of four townships projecting south from its southwest corner—containing about 1864 square miles.

Besides the Illinois river, which passes through it, Fox river, Big and Little Vermilion, Crow creek, Au Sable, Indian creek, Mason, Tomahawk, and several smaller streams water this county. In general, the streams in this part of the state run over a rocky or gravelly bed, and have but few alluvial bottoms near them.

Like the adjacent counties, La Salle is deficient in timber; but contains abundance of rich, undulating, dry prairie, fine mill streams, extensive coal beds, and must eventually become a rich county. Its situation will enable the population to send off their produce either by the Illinois river to a southern market, or by the lakes to the north.

La Salle county belongs to the seventh judicial circuit and with Kane sends one representative, and, with the addition of Iroquois, one senator to the legislature.

The seat of justice is *Ottawa*.

LAWRENCE COUNTY.

Lawrence County was formed in 1821, from a part of Edwards and Crawford, and is situated on the eastern side of the state, opposite Vincennes.

It is bounded north by Crawford, and a corner of Jasper; east by the Wabash river; south by Wabash and Edwards counties; and west by Clay.

It is twenty miles across, north and south, and a medium length of twenty-eight miles—containing about 560 square miles.

It is watered by the Embarras river, and Racoon creek, which pass through it, and Fox river on its western border. The banks of these streams are low and subject to inundation.

In the low prairies, near the Wabash, are swamps and sloughs, known by the name of "purgatory," which, in a wet season, are miry, and extremely unpleasant to the traveler. Over some of these, bridges and levees are now constructed. In a dry season, the water evaporates, and the ground becomes firm.

Lawrence county contains about an equal proportion of timber and prairie, some of which is inferior land, and other portions of an excellent quality.

Its exports are corn, beef, pork, cattle, etc., much of which is sent down the Big Wabash in flat boats to New Orleans.

This county belongs to the fourth judicial circuit, and sends two members to the house of representatives, and, with Crawford and Jasper one to the senate.

The county seat is *Lawrenceville*.

LIVINGSTON COUNTY.

Livingston County was formed from La Salle, McLean, and an attached portion of Vermilion county, in February, 1837. It is 36 miles long, and about 30 miles wide; containing about 1040 square miles.

It is bounded north by La Salle, east by a strip of country attached to Vermilion, south by the same tract, and McLean, and west by McLean and La Salle counties.

It contains some rich tracts of timbered land, and a large quantity of fine rich undulating prairie. It is watered by the Mackinau and its branches, and by the Muddy Fork, Otter Fork, and other small streams.

Limestone and coal are its principal minerals. Livingston county belongs to the first judicial circuit, while one portion is represented in the legislature by the representation of La Salle, and the other by that of McLean.

Its seat of justice is not yet established.

MACON COUNTY.

Macon County was formed from the attached part of Shelby, in 1829, and is bounded north by McLean; east by Champaign and Coles; south by Shelby; and west by Sangamon.

It is thirty-nine miles long, and thirty-six broad—containing 1,404 square miles.

The southeastern portion is watered by the Kaskaskia and its tributaries; the middle and northern portions by the North Fork of the Sangamon; and the northwestern part by Salt creek.

There is much first rate land in Macon county. Some of the prairies are large, and, in the interior, level and wet; but generally dry, rich, and undulating near the timber.

Macon county is attached to the first judicial circuit and sends one representative, and with McLean county, one senator. The population is estimated at 3,600.

The county seat is *Decatur*.

MADISON COUNTY.

Madison County was organised from St. Clair county, in 1812, and then embraced a large portion of the state. It is now bounded north by Greene, Macoupin, and a corner of Montgomery counties; east, by Bond, and a corner of Clinton; south by St. Clair; and west by the Mississippi.

It is 24 miles from north to south; and from 28 to 36 miles from east to west—and contains about 750 square miles.

It is watered by Silver and Cahokia creeks, and Wood river, and their branches.

A portion of this county lies in the American bottom, but much of it is high, undulating, and proportionably divided into timber and prairie.

Settlements were formed in this county about thirty-five years since. Coal, and building stone, are abundant.

Around Alton, and along Wood river, and Cahokia creek, is one of the finest bodies of timber in this part of the state.

The prairies are very advantageously situated for settlements, and will soon be covered with well cultivated farms. .Wheat, corn, beef, pork, horses, cattle, and almost every production of Illinois, are raised in this county, and find a ready market.

Madison county belongs to the second judicial circuit, and sends one senator and two representatives to the legislature, and unites with St. Clair and Monroe in another senator.

The seat of justice is *Edwardsville.*

MACOUPIN COUNTY.

Macoupin County was organised from the attached portion of Greene county, in 1829. It is bounded north by Sangamon and Morgan; east by Montgomery; south by Madison; and west by Greene. It is thirty-six miles long, from north to south; and twenty-four miles broad—containing 864 square miles.

The Macoupin creek and its branches water the middle and western parts, the Cahokia creek the southeastern, and the heads of Wood river and Piasau, the southwestern parts of the county.

Some of the prairies on the eastern side are large, level, and wet; but a large portion of the county is excellent soil, and well proportioned into timber and prairie, and rapidly settling. About one-third of the county is timbered land. It is an excellent agricultural county, and will soon produce large quantities of pork, beef, wheat, etc., which will naturally reach the market at Alton.

Macoupin county sends one member to the house of representatives, and one to the senate. The county seat is *Carlinville.*

MARION COUNTY.

Marion County lies in the interior of the state, and is bounded north by Fayette; east by Clay, and a corner of Wayne; south by Jefferson; and West by Clinton, and a corner of Fayette.

It was formed from Jefferson and Fayette counties, in 1823, is twenty-four miles in extent, and contains 576 square miles.

Marion county embraces the southern part of the Grand prairie, and is watered by Crooked creek, and the East Fork of the Kaskaskia, on its western, and Skillet Fork on its eastern side.

It has considerable land of second quality; about one third timber, and the rest prairie. Considerable post oak timber is found in this county.

Marion county is attached to the third judicial circuit, sends one member to the house of representatives, and, with Clinton, one member to the senate.

The county seat is *Salem.*
Population, 3,000.

MCDONOUGH COUNTY.

McDonough County was formed from Pike county, in 1825, but not organised till 1829. It is situated in the centre of the military tract; is bounded north by Warren; east by Fulton; south by Schuyler; and west by Hancock.

It is twenty-four miles square, with an area of sixteen townships, 576 square miles, and 368,640 acres.

Crooked creek and its branches water most of this tract. The eastern side of McDonough county for eight or ten miles in width is prairie; the remainder is suitably proportioned into timber and prairie of the richest quality. A tract of country, fifteen or twenty miles square, taken from the eastern side of Hancock and the western half of

McDonough, is not excelled for agricultural purposes by any portion of the great valley.

Most of the streams have good mill seats for a portion of the year.

McDonough county is attached to the fifth judicial circuit, sends one representative, and, with Hancock, one senator to the legislature.

The seat of justice is *Macomb*.

MCHENRY COUNTY.

McHenry County was formed from Cook county, January, 1836, and is bounded north by Wisconsin Territory; east by lake Michigan; south by Cook; and west by Boone county.

It is about forty miles long and twenty-four miles wide, containing about 960 square miles. This includes only its land area. Its legal boundary extends east to the middle of Lake Michigan.

It is watered by the north branch of the Chicago, Des Plaines, Fox river and branches, together with Cache Mère, Crystal and other small lakes. Some of these lakes have limpid water, gravelly beds, with ridges of gravel and sand around them.

East side of Fox river, the soil approaches to a clay, while on the western side it is a rich, sandy loam. Timber abounds along the lake shore, and near the streams, with many beautiful groves and oak openings in the interior. It is similar in quality to Kane and Ogle counties. Limestone is plenty.

McHenry belongs to the seventh judicial circuit, and is connected with Cook and Will counties in its representation.

The seat of justice is not yet located.

MCLEAN COUNTY.

McLean County has Livingston and La Salle on the north; an irregular strip of country, and a corner of Champaign county, east; Macon, south; Sangamon touches it on the southwest; and Tazewell lies west.

It is from twenty-eight to forty-eight miles long, and forty-two to twelve broad, having 1,675 square miles.

One third of the eastern, and a portion of the northern side of this county is one vast prairie, and yet it has large tracts of the finest timbered land in the state. The timber is beautifully arranged in groves of various shapes and sizes, from those of fifteen or eighteen square miles, down to those of a few acres.

McLean county is watered by the Kickapoo, Sugar creek, and Salt creek, all which take their rise in the prairies of this county. The heads of the Vermilion river of the Illinois are found in the northeastern corner and those of Sangamon are on the eastern skirts. These streams furnish good mill seats when the water is not too low.

The country is elevated, moderately undulating, and of a rich soil. Where timber exists it is usually of excellent quality. Here are to be found oak of various species, walnut, hickory, ash, sugar maple, elm, hackberry, linden, cherry, and many other kinds. Papaw is frequently amongst the smaller growth.

Of the minerals, limestone is found on the branches of the Vermilion. Granite, in detached masses, or *boulders*, called by the settlers "lost rocks," and used for mill stones, are plentifully scattered over the country. Coal is found in several settlements.

McLean county sends two representatives, and, with Macon, one senator to the legislature.

The seat of justice is *Bloomington*.

MERCER COUNTY.

Mercer County lies north of Warren; west of Henry; and south of Rock Island counties, and has the Mississippi on its western side.

It is about thirty-two miles long and eighteen miles wide, containing about 550 square miles.

It is watered by Edwards and Pope rivers, and the northern branches of Henderson river, along which are excellent tracts of timber, as there is on the borders of the Mississippi. Its middle and eastern parts have extensive tracts of prairie.

It is said that the seasons are more uniform, the winters more severe, and the summers more pleasant than in the counties further south; but the frosts of spring do not injure the labours of the husbandman.

The soil is rich, undulating and excellent for farming.

Mercer is attached to the sixth judicial circuit, and unites with Rock Island and Jo Daviess counties, in sending two representatives and one senator to the legislature.

The seat of justice is *New Boston.*

MONROE COUNTY.

Monroe County was formed out of Randolph and St. Clair counties, in 1816. It is bounded north by St. Clair; east by St. Clair and Randolph; south by Randolph; and west by the Mississippi. Its shape is quite irregular; its average length is twenty miles; average width eighteen miles, containing about 360 square miles.

It is watered by Horse, Prairie de Long, and Eagle creeks. The American bottom, which is alluvion, runs through the county adjacent to the Mississippi, and is divided into timber and prairie. On the bluffs, the country is hilly and broken, with sink holes. Around Waterloo, and New Design, and on the eastern border of the county, is considerable good land, and a mixture of timber and prairie.

Monroe county is attached to the second judicial circuit, and sends one member to the house of representatives, and one to the senate.

The seat of justice is *Waterloo*.

MONTGOMERY COUNTY.

Montgomery County was formed from Bond, in 1821. It is bounded north by Sangamon; east by Shelby and Fayette; south by Bond; and west by Madison and Macoupin counties.

It is thirty-four miles long, with an average width of twenty-seven miles, and has about 960 square miles.

It is watered by Shoal creek and its branches, some of the heads of the Macoupin, a branch of the South Fork of the Sangamon, and the Hurricane Fork, and is proportionably divided into timber and prairie. The surface is generally high and undulating.

Montgomery county belongs to the second judicial circuit, and sends one member to the house of representatives, and, in connection with Bond one to the senate.

The seat of justice is *Hillsboro'*.

MORGAN COUNTY.

Morgan County, one of the most flourishing counties in the state, lying on the east side of the Illinois river, was formed from the attached part of Greene, in January, 1823.

It is bounded north by Cass; east by Sangamon; south by Macoupin and Greene; and west by the Illinois river, which separates it from Pike and Schuyler. It is thirty-four miles long; medium width, twenty-seven; area 918 square miles.

The Illinois river washes its western border; Indian,

Mauvaiseterre, Apple, Sandy, and several smaller creeks rise within its borders, and pass through it, furnishing many good mill seats.

Morgan county is destined to become one of the richest agricultural counties in the state. In 1821, the tract of country embraced within the limits of this county, contained only twenty families. In 1825, its population was 4,052; in 1830, it was 13,281; and now, is estimated at 20,000, without Cass county.

It is well proportioned into timber and prairie, well watered, and contains many extensive and well cultivated farms. In this county are more than thirty mills for sawing and grinding, propelled by animal or water power. Seven large steam mills are in operation, and two more have been commenced, and will be finished the present year.

Improved farms, in the populous parts of the county, sell for from ten to twenty dollars per acre; several towns and villages have been commenced besides Jacksonville, which are in a thriving condition.

Emigration, attended with industry and enterprise, in a few fleeting years, has changed a region that we have seen in all the wildness of uncultivated nature, into smiling villages and luxuriant fields, and rendered it the happy abode of intelligence and virtue.

Morgan county belongs to the first judicial circuit, sends six members to the house of representatives, and three to the senate.

The seat of justice is *Jacksonville.*

OGLE COUNTY.

Ogle County was formed from Jo Daviess, and a part of the attached portion of La Salle, January, 1836. It is from 36 to 42 miles long, and 36 miles wide;—containing about 1440 square miles.

Rock river passes diagonally through its northwestern portion. Winnebago Swamp and Inlet, and several other swamps are in its southern part. Pine, Leaf, and Kite rivers, and several smaller streams, all of which empty themselves into Rock river, furnish good mill seats. The timber is chiefly in groves, many of which are peculiarly beautiful, and of various shapes and sizes. Much of the surface is undulating, the soil calcareous, deep and rich, and the country is rapidly settling. The present population may be estimated at 1200.

Ogle county belongs to the sixth judicial circuit;—its representative connection is with Jo Daviess and several other counties. Its courts are held temporarily at Oregon city, but its seat of justice is not permanently established.

PEORIA COUNTY.

Peoria County lies on the west side of the Illinois river, about two hundred miles by water, and a hundred and fifty by land, above the junction of the Mississippi. This county contains considerable tracts of excellent land.

Its principal settlements are Peoria, Kickapoo creek, La Salle prairie, Senatchwine, Prince's and Harkness' settlements.

It is watered by the Kickapoo, the heads of Spoon river, Copperas creek and the Senatchwine. On the Kickapoo, and on the shore of Peoria lake, for several miles, the timber is good but the prairie predominates.

Peoria county was formed from Pike county, in 1825, and is bounded north by Putnam; east by Tazewell; south by Fulton; and west by Knox. It is about twenty-seven miles long, and has an average width of twenty-four miles—containing about 648 square miles.

One of the principal roads to Galena passes through this county.

The surface of the land is moderately rolling; on the Kickapoo it degenerates into bluffs and ravines. In the western and northwestern portion there is a scarcity of timber. Between Peoria and La Salle prairie is heavy timber, from two to five miles in width, and in places beyond the bluffs. In the bottom land adjoining the lake, are spots that overflow; but, in general, it is fit for cultivation. The bottom timber consists of oaks of various species, white and black walnut, ash, hackberry, locust and some hickory, buckeye, coffee nut, and grape vines.

Peoria County belongs to the sixth judicial circuit, and sends one representative, and with Putnam, one senator to the legislature.

The seat of justice is *Peoria*.

PERRY COUNTY.

Perry County was organised from Randolph and Jackson counties, in 1827, and is bounded north by Washington; east by Jefferson and Franklin; south by Jackson; and west by Randolph. It is twenty-five miles long, from east to west, and eighteen miles wide—containing 447 square miles.

The Big Beaucoup and its tributaries run through the middle of this county, from north to south, and the Little Muddy touches its eastern border.

About one third of Perry county is prairie, tolerably level, good soil, and susceptible of immediate cultivation.

Its productions are corn, beef cattle, pork, tobacco, and some cotton. This little county has sent to market many fat steers and fat hogs per annum.

Perry sends one member to the house of representatives, and with Washington, one member to the senate. It belongs to the third judicial circuit.

Pinckneyville is the seat of justice.

PIKE COUNTY.

Pike County is the oldest county on the military tract, and was erected from Madison and other counties, in

1821. It then embraced the whole country north and west of the Illinois river; but by the subsequent formation of new counties, it is now reduced to ordinary size. containing about twenty-two townships, or 800 square miles.

It is bounded north, by Adams; east, by Schuyler, and the Illinois river; south, by that river and Calhoun; and west by the Mississippi.

Besides the Mississippi and Illinois rivers, which wash two sides, it has the Snycartee slough running the whole length of its western border, which affords steamboat navigation to Atlas at a full stage of water. Pike county is watered by the Pigeon, Hadley, Keys, Black, Dutch, Church, Six Mile, and Bay creeks, which fall into the Mississippi; and Big and Little Blue, and the North and West forks of McKee's creeks, which enter the Illinois. Good mill seats are furnished by these streams.

The land is various. The section of country, or rather island between the Snycartee slough and the Mississippi, is a sandy soil, but mostly inundated land at the spring floods. It furnishes a great summer and winter range for stocks, affording considerable open prairies; with skirts of heavy bottom timber near the streams. Along the bluffs, and for two or three miles back, the land is chiefly timbered but cut up with ravines, and quite rolling. In the interior, and towards Schuyler county, excellent prairie and timbered uplands are found especially about the Blue rivers and McKee's creek. This must eventually become a rich and populous county.

In Pleasant Vale, on Key's creek, is a salt spring, twenty feet in diameter, which boils from the earth, and throws off a stream of some size forming a salt pond in its vicinity. Salt has been made here though not in great quantities.

Pike county is connected with Adams and Hancock, and sends two representatives and one senator to the legislature, and belongs to the fifth judicial circuit.

The seat of justice is *Pittsfield*.

POPE COUNTY.

Pope County was formed from Gallatin and Johnson counties, and is situated in the southern part or the state, and is bounded north by Gallatin, east and south by the Ohio river; and west by Johnson county.

It was organised as a county, in 1816, by the territorial government; and, after having been subsequently reduced, is now thirty-six miles long, with a medium width of about sixteen miles, and an area of 576 square miles.

The Ohio makes a bend so as to wash its eastern and southern sides, and project into the interior. Big Bay creek rises towards its northwestern corner, and, after entering Johnson county, turns again into Pope, and runs a southeastern course to the Ohio. Lusk's creek, and some smaller streams, give it the character of a well watered county. It is generally well timbered with the varieties that abound on that side of the state; the surface is tolerably level; the soil of a good quality, but rather sandy.

Corn, beef, pork, oats, potatoes, horses, etc., are articles of exportation in considerable quantities.

Pope county sends one member to the house of representatives, and with Johnson, one to the senate. It belongs to the third judicial circuit.

The seat of justice is *Golconda*.

PUTNAM COUNTY.

Putnam County was formed from Pike county in 1825, but not organised for judicial purposes till 1831, when the boundaries were altered.

It is now situated on both sides of the Illinois river. and is bounded north by Ogle, and Whiteside counties; east by La Salle; south by Tazewell and Peoria; and west by Henry and a portion of Knox counties.

It is thirty-six miles long, and thirty six miles broad, besides a fractional portion in its south eastern part—and contains about 1,340 square miles.

The Illinois river enters this county on its eastern border, makes a large bend and passes out at its southern side. The Bureau, Crow, and some smaller streams enter the Illinois within this county, and Spoon river waters its western border.

Some of the finest lands in the state are in this county; beautiful groves of timber, and rich, undulating, and dry prairies.

There are a number of large settlements of industrious and thrifty farmers, amongst which are Bureau Grove, Ox Bow Prairie, Knox's settlement, Spoon river settlement, and Strawn's settlement. Population about 4,800.

There are many fine springs in the county, and excellent mill seats on the streams.

Besides oaks of several species, there are most of the varieties of timber common to the state, as black and white walnut, sugar maple, blue, white, and hoop ash, elm, cherry, aspen, iron wood, buckeye, linden, locust, mulberry, etc.

Lime stone, sand stone, free stone and bituminous coal, are its principal mineral productions, and in sufficient quantities.

Produce will be sent down the Illinois river in steam boats from Hennepin.

A few tracts of prairie in this country are level and wet, and there are some small ponds and swamps in the northern part.

In this county are three Presbyterian, two Baptist, one Congregational, and three or four Methodist societies, a county Bible society that has twice supplied all the destitute with Bibles, a temperance society, a county Sunday School Union, ten Sunday schools, a county lyceum, and several other philanthropic societies.

Putnam county belongs to the sixth judicial circuit, and sends one representative, and with Peoria one senator to the legislature.

The seat of justice is *Hennepin*.

RANDOLPH COUNTY.

Randolph County was formed before the organisation of the territory of Illinois, and is the oldest county, except St. Clair, in the state.

It is bounded north by Monroe, St Clair, and Washington counties; east by Perry; south by the Mississippi river and a corner of Jackson county; and west by the Mississippi.

Its medium length and breadth is about twenty-four miles, though from curvatures of the Mississippi, it contains but about 540 square miles.

It is watered by the Kaskaskia river, and St. Mary, Horse, and some smaller creeks. The soil is of various kinds; from first rate to indifferent, and has a diversity of surface, from the low alluvion, and the undulating prairie, to the rugged bluffs and abrupt precipices.

Randolph county belongs to the second judicial circuit, sends two members to the house of representatives, and one to the senate.

County seat, *Kaskaskia*.

ROCK ISLAND.

Rock Island is a small irregularly shaped county, formed from portions of Mercer and Jo Daviess counties, in 1831, but subsequently organised by the judge of the fifth judicial circuit. The boundaries of this county, as defined by law, begin " at the middle of the main channel of the Mississippi, where the north line of township fifteen north intersects the same; thence east, to the fourth principal meridian; thence north, with said meridian, to the middle of the main channel of Rock river; thence up said channel to the confluence of the *Marais d'Ogee* slough or creek; thence along said slough to the middle of the Mississippi river, and down that channel to the place of beginning." It contains about 400 square miles.

Rock river, and some minor streams, water this county. Rock Island, in the Mississippi, is included in this county. The soil along the Mississippi for twenty-five miles is alluvion, sandy, and rich, including the site of the old Sauk village. There is much good land in the interior of the county, between the rivers.

This county elects a senator and representative in conjunction with Jo Daviess and Mercer.

The county seat is *Stephenson*.

SANGAMON COUNTY.

Sangamon County is one of the largest and most flourishing, counties in the state. It is bounded on the north by Tazewell; east, by Macon; south by Montgomery and Macoupin; and west by Cass and Morgan counties. The northwestern corner runs down between the Sangamon river, which separates it from Cass county, and Tazewell county, to the Illinois river.

It is forty-eight miles long, besides the corner mentioned; and forty-five miles wide—containing, in the whole, an area of about 1,270 square miles.

Sangamon county is watered by the Sangamon river and its numerous branches. Those which take their rise within the limits of the county are Clary's, Rock, Richland, Prairie, Spring, Lick, Sugar, Horse, and Brush creeks, on the south side, proceeding upward in the arrangement; and Crane, Indian, Cantrill's, Fancy, Wolf, and Clear creeks, which enter from the opposite side. Those branches which rise without the county, and yet run a considerable distance within it, are Salt creek and branches, North Fork, and South Fork. These streams not only furnish this county with an abundance of excellent water and a number of good mill seats, but are lined with extensive tracts of first rate timbered land.

Here are oaks of various species, walnut, sugar maple, elm, linden, hickory, ash, hackberry, honey locust, mulberry, sycamore, cotton wood, sassafras, etc., together with the various shrubs, common to the country.

The size of the prairies in Sangamon county is seized
upon as an objection, by persons who are not accustomed
to a prairie country. But were the timber a little more
equally distributed with prairie surface, its supply would
be abundant. The prairies vary in width from one to eight
or ten miles, and somewhat indefinite in length, being con-
nceted at the heads of the streams.

Much of the soil in this county is of the richest quality, being a calcareous loam, from one to three feet deep,
intermixed with fine sand. The point of land that lies
between the Sangamon and the Illinois rivers, which is
chiefly prairie, is divided betwixt inundated land, dry
prairie, and sand ridges. A stranger to observations upon
the surface of Illinois, upon first sight, would pronounce
most parts of Sangamon county a level or plane. It is
not so. With the exception of the creek bottoms and the
interior of large prairies, it has an undulating surface,
quite sufficient to render it one of the finest agricultural
districts in the United States. These remarks are not
meant exclusively for Sangamon. They apply with equal
propriety to many other counties on both sides of the Illinois river. What has been heretofore known to persons
abroad as the Sangamon country, may now be included
in a large district, containing a number of large and populous counties.

This county contains a larger quantity of rich land than
any other in the state, and therefore can maintain a larger
agricultural population, which is the great basis of national wealth. A distinguished writer, speaking of the
state of Illinois, and particularly of this portion of it, remarks in a letter to a friend from Springfield, Illinois,—of
March 2d:

"Our 'far west' is improving rapidly, astonishingly.
It is five years since I visited it, and the changes within
that period are like the work of enchantment. Flourishing
towns have grown up, farms have been opened, comfortable dwellings, fine barns and all appurtenances, in a
country in which the hardy pioneer had at that time
sprinkled a few log cabins. The conception of Coleridge

may be realised sooner than he anticipated. The possible destiny of the U. States as a nation of a hundred millions of freemen—stretching from the Atlantic to the Pacific, living under the laws of Alfred, and speaking the language of Shakspeare and Milton, is an august conception—why should we not wish to see it realized? On the subject of internal improvements the young giant of the west is making Herculean efforts—a bill passed the legislature last winter appropriating eight millions of dollars for railroads, canals, &c., works which, when completed, will cost twenty millions. A bill also passed transferring the seat of government from Vandalia, in Fayette county, to this place, Springfield, which is in the fertile district of Sangamon county, and as near as may be to the geographical centre of the state, and soon will be the centre of population.

"The state of Illinois has probably the finest body of fertile land of any state in the Union, and the opportunities for speculation are numerous—property will continue to advance—admirable farms and town lots may be purchased with a certainty of realising large profits. The country here is beautiful—equal in native attractions though not in classic recollections to the scenes I visited and admired in Italy. The vale of Arno is not more beautiful than the *valley of Sangamon*, with its lonely groves and murmuring brooks and flowing meads.—

'Oh Italy, sweet clime of song, where oft
The bard hath sung thy beauties, matchless deemed,
Thou hast a rival in this western land.'"

The first settlement on the waters of the Sangamon, made by white people for a permanent abode, was in 1819; the county was organised in 1821, and then embraced a tract of country 125 miles long, and seventy-five broad.

The public lands were first offered for sale in November, 1823, by which time, however, farms of considerable size, even to 100 acres of cultivated land, had been made.

At the present time, the borders of the prairies are covered with hundreds of smiling farms, and the interior animated with thousands of domestic animals. The rough and unseemly cabin is giving place to comfortable framed or brick tenements, and plenty every where smiles upon the labors of the husbandman.

This county is in the geographical centre of the state, and will eventually be in the centre of population.

Its river market and deposit is Beardstown; but much of its imports will be received and its exports sent off by its own river, which has already been navigated by steam to the vicinity of Springfield, and when some of its obstructions are removed, will afford convenient navigation for steamboats of the smaller class. Its exports now are beef cattle, pork, wheat, flour, corn meal, butter, cheese, etc. and soon will include almost every article of a rich, agricultural country.

Sangamon county belongs to the first judicial circuit, sends seven members to the house of representatives, and two members to the senate.

Its population, at the last census, was 17,573, its number now would exceed 20,000.

Villages and towns are springing up, some of which may become places of note, as Athens, New Salem, Richland, Salisbury, Greenfield, Rochester, etc.

The seat of justice is *Springfield*.

SCHUYLER COUNTY.

Schuyler County was formed from Pike county, in 1825, and lies on the Illinois river, opposite Morgan county. It is bounded north by McDonough, and a corner of Fulton; east by Fulton, and the Illinois river; south by the Illinois river, and Pike; and west by Adams and a corner of Hancock.

The southeastern side is washed by the Illinois, the interior is watered by Crooked and Crane creeks, the south western by McKee's creek, and the northeastern part by Sugar creek.

Schuyler county is of an irregular shape, thirty miles

long, and from eighteen to thirty broad—containing about 864 square miles.

Along the Illinois river is considerable land inundated at high floods, generally heavily timbered, as is more than one half of the county. The middle and northern portions are divided into timber and prairie of an excellent quality. Along Crooked creek is an extensive body of fine timber. Sugar creek also furnishes another body of timber eight or ten miles wide.

Schuyler county is attached to the fifth judicial circuit, and sends two members to the house of representatives, and one member to the senate.

Rushville is the county seat.

SHELBY COUNTY.

Shelby County was formed from Fayette, in 1827, and is bounded on the north by Macon; east by Coles; south by Effingham and Fayette: and west by Montgomery, and a corner of Sangamon.

It is thirty-six miles long and thirty broad—area, 1,080 square miles.

It is watered by the Kaskaskia and tributaries.

Shelby county contains a large amount of excellent land, both timber and prairie, and is one of the best inland agricultural counties in the state.

Shelby sends one member to the house of representatives, and one to the senate. It belongs to the second judicial circuit. The population is about 5,500.

The seat of justice is *Shelbyville*.

ST. CLAIR COUNTY.

St. Clair County is the oldest county in the state, and was formed by the legislature of the Northwestern Territory in 1794 or '95, and then included all the settlements on the eastern side of the Mississippi. It now lies on

that river opposite St. Louis, and is bounded north by
Madison county; east by Clinton and Washington; and
south by Randolph and Monroe counties—containing
1,030 square miles.

The land is various, much of which is good first and
second rate soil, and is proportionably divided into timber, prairie, and barrens. The prairies are distinguished
as Looking Glass, Twelve Mile, Ogle's, Ridge, Bottom,
and Du Pont prairies.

The streams are Cahokia, Prairie du Pont, Ogle's creek,
Silver creek, Richland creek, Prairie de Long, and the
Kaskaskia river.

Its timber comprises the varieties found on the western
side of the state.

The exports are beef, pork, flour, and all the varieties
in the St. Louis market.

Extensive coal banks exist in this county, along the
bluffs, from which St. Louis is partially supplied with
fuel. The quantity hauled there in wagons, in 1836,
amounted to about 300,000 bushels. A railroad is now
making from these mines to the river, opposite St. Louis,
by a private company.

There are five steam mills in this county, besides a
number propelled by water and animal power. Belleville
and Lebanon are its principal towns. Cahokia and Illinois are small villages. The people of this county are a
mixture of Americans, French, and Germans, about 10,000
in number.

St. Clair county belongs to the second judicial circuit,
and sends one senator and two representatives to the legislature, and, with Madison and Monroe, an additional
senator.

The seat of justice is *Belleville.*

STEPHENSON COUNTY.

Stephenson County was formed from Jo Daviess and
Winnebago counties, in February, 1837, and is bounded

north by Wisconsin Territory, east by Winnebago county, south by Ogle and Jo Daviess, and west by Jo Daviess county.

It is 27 miles long, and 21 miles wide, containing about 560 square miles.

It is watered by the Peekatonokee and its tributaries on the north, and the heads of Plum river and smaller streams in the southwestern part.

The timber is mostly in groves; the prairies generally undulating and rich, with tracts of hilly barrens and oak openings. The population is not large, but rapidly settling, as are all the northern counties.

For judicial and representative purposes it is attached to Jo Daviess county.

TAZEWELL COUNTY.

Tazewell County was formed from Peoria county, in 1827. It is bounded north by Putnam; east by McLean; south by Sangamon; and has the Illinois river along its northwestern border, which gives it a triangular form.

Its extreme length is forty-eight miles, and its extreme width forty-two miles—containing about 1,130 square miles.

It is watered by the Illinois river, which extends the whole length of its northwestern side, Mackinaw, and its branches, Ten Mile, Farm, and Blue creeks, all which enter the Illinois, with some of the head branches of the Sangamon.

A strip of this county, consisting mostly of sandy prairies, puts down the Illinois river, and between that and Sangamon county. On the bluffs of the Mackinau and the other streams, the land is broken, and the timber chiefly oak; in other portions of the county it has an undulating appearance and has much good land.

Below Pekin, and towards Havanna, are swamps, ponds, and sand ridges. The south eastern portion of the county is watered by Sugar creek and its branches.

This will soon be a rich agricultural county. Pleasant Grove and the adjacent country is delightful.

Tazewell county belongs to the first judicial circuit, and sends one senator and two representatives to the legislature.

The county seat is *Tremont.*

UNION COUNTY.

Union County was formed from Johnson county, in 1818, and is bounded north by Jackson; east by Franklin; south by Alexander; and west by the Mississippi river.

It is twenty-four miles long, and from twenty to twenty-six miles broad, containing above 396 square miles, and is watered by Clear creek, some of the south branches of Big Muddy, and the heads of Cash river. A large bend of the Big Muddy projects a few miles into the county towards its northwestern portion, and some sloughs and ponds are found on the Mississippi bottom. Much of this county is high, rolling, timbered land. Here are found oaks of various kinds, hickory, white and black walnut, poplar, some beech, and other species of timber common to the country. There is considerable German population in this county.

Union county belongs to the third judicial circuit, and sends one member to the house of representatives, and, with Alexander, one to the senate.

The exports from this county are corn, beef, pork, horses, etc. Large quantities of produce from this county go down the river to New Orleans in flat boats.

The county seat is *Jonesboro'.*

VERMILION COUNTY.

Vermilion County was formed from Edgar, in 1826, and lies north of Edgar and Coles; east of Champaign; south of Iroquois, and west of the state of Indiana.

It is forty-two miles long, and about twenty-four miles wide, containing about 1,000 square miles.

Vermilion county is watered by the Big and Little Vermilion rivers, and tributaries, and contains large bodies of excellent land. In the eastern part of the county the timber predominates, amongst which is the poplar and beech. Along the streams are oaks of various species, hickory, walnut, linden, hackberry, ash, elm, and various other kinds common to Illinois. The soil of the prairies is a calcareous loam, from one to three feet deep. Their surface is generally dry and undulating.

The exports are pork, beef, corn, salt, etc., which find a convenient market at the towns on the Wabash, and down that river to New Orleans. In due time much of the produce of the Vermilion country will pass by the way of Chicago and the lakes; and up the Wabash, and through a canal to Lake Erie. It would be no difficulty matter to open a water communication between the Wabash and Illinois rivers, and thus furnish an outlet for the productions of this part of the state in every direction. Population about 9,500.

It is attached to the fourth judicial circuit, and sends three members to the house of representatives, and, with Champaign, one to the senate.

The seat of justice is *Danville*.

WABASH COUNTY.

Wabash County was formed from Edwards county, in 1824, and is bounded north by Lawrence; east by the Wabash river; south it terminates in a point between the Bon Pas which divides it from Edwards county, and Wabash river; and west by Edwards county.

It is eighteen miles long, and from ten to fifteen miles broad, with the eastern side irregularly curvated by the Wabash river. It has about 180 square miles.

Wabash county is watered by the Wabash river on its

eastern, and Bon Pas creek on its western border, and Crawfish, Jordan, and Coffee creeks, from its interior.

It contains considerable good land, both timber and prairie, and a full proportion of industrious and thriving farmers. This county sends one member to the house of representatives, and, with Edwards and Wayne, one to the senate. It belongs to the fourth judicial circuit.

The seat of justice is *Mount Carmel.*

WARREN COUNTY.

Warren County was formed from Pike county, in 1825, but not organised till 1830. It contains extensive tracts of first rate land, and several fine settlements. It lies on the Mississippi, north of Hancock and McDonough, west of Knox, and south of Mercer.

Its prominent stream is Henderson river and branches; Ellison, Honey, and Camp creeks are in Warren. The land on these streams is generally a little undulating, rich, and where timber exists, it is excellent. A number of good mill seats exist.

Much of the bottom in this county that lies on the river is low, subject to inundation, and has a series of sand ridges back of it, with bold and pointed bluffs further in the rear.

North of Henderson river is an extensive prairie, which divides it from Pope and Edwards rivers.

Warren county is about thirty miles in extent, and contains about 900 square miles. It belongs to the fifth judicial circuit, and, with Knox and Henry counties, sends one member to each branch of the legislature.

The seat of justice is *Monmouth.*

WASHINGTON COUNTY.

Washington County was formed from St. Clair, in January, 1818, and is bounded north by Clinton; east by

Jefferson; south by Perry, and a corner of Randolph, and west by St. Clair. It is thirty miles long and from fifteen to twenty miles broad, containing about 656 square miles.

The Kaskaskia river runs along the northwestern side for eighteen miles, Elkhorn creek waters its western, Beaucoup and Little Muddy its southeastern, and Crooked creek, and some smaller streams, its northern portions. Considerable prairie, especially the southern points of the Grand prairie, is found in this county, some of which is rather level and wet, and of an inferior quality. A large body of timber lines the banks of the Kaskaskia river.

The produce of this county is pork, beef cattle, and other articles common to the adjacent parts. The timber is oak of various kinds, hickory, elm, ash, and the timber common to the Kaskaskia river.

Washington county is attached to the second judicial circuit, and sends two members to the house of representatives, and unites also with Perry in sending one to the senate.

The county seat is *Nashville*.

WAYNE COUNTY.

Wayne County was formed from Edwards, in 1819, and is situated in the southeastern part of the state, and is bounded on the north by Clay; east by Edwards; south by Hamilton, and a corner of White; and west by Jefferson and Marion.

It is thirty miles long, twenty-four miles wide, and contains 720 square miles.

The Little Wabash passes through its eastern part, and Elm river and Skillet fork water the northern portions of the county. It is proportionably interspersed with prairie and woodland, generally of a second quality. The productions of this county for exportation are beef, pork, cattle, and some peltry, which are sent down the Little Wabash in flat boats to New Orleans, or find a market over land to Shawneetown.

Wayne county belongs to the fourth judicial circuit, and sends one member to the house of representatives, and, with Edwards and Wabash, one member to the senate.

County seat *Fairfield.*

WHITE COUNTY.

White County was organised from Gallatin county, in 1815. It is situated in the south eastern side of the state. Its form is nearly square, about twenty-two miles in extent,—containing an area of nearly 480 square miles.

It is bounded north by Wabash, Edwards, and Wayne counties; east by the Big Wabash river, south by Gallatin, and west by Hamilton counties.

The eastern side of this county is washed by the Big Wabash, along which is a low bottom, subject to inundation; the interior is watered by the Little Wabash and its tributaries,. The banks of these streams are heavily timbered, among which are oaks of several species, hickory, walnut, hackberry, elm, ash, and poplar. Between the streams are fine prairies most of which are cultivated; the principal of which are the Big, Burnt, and Seven Mile.

The exports of White county are pork, beef, and beef cattle, corn, flour, venison hams, horses, and some tobacco. Horses and cattle are sent in droves to the south, and produce descends the river to New Orleans from this and the adjacent counties, in large quantities.

There are three water mills in this county for flouring and sawing, which do good business.

White county is attached to the fourth judicial circuit, has a population of between six and seven thousand inhabitants, and sends two members to the house of representatives, and one to the senate.

The seat of justice is *Carmi.*

WHITESIDE COUNTY.

Whiteside County was formed from Jo Daviess in January, 1836, and is bounded north by that county; east by Ogle; south by Henry and Putnam, and west by Rock Island county, and the Mississippi river.

It is from 27 to 36 miles long, and about 24 miles wide —containing about 770 square miles.

It is watered by Rock river, which passes diagonally through it, Little Rock, Marais d' Ogee lake and Swamp that divide it from Rock Island county, Cat-tail swamp, and several small streams.

It has some tracts of heavy timber along Rock river and Little Rock, besides groves, copses, and brushy swamps. Some of its prairie land is flat, while other portions are beautifully undulating and rich. Its population is yet small, and in its judicial and representative connections, it is attached to Jo Daviess county.

WILL COUNTY.

Will County was formed from portions of Cook and Iroquois counties in January, 1836, rather irregularly shaped on its northern side, and is bounded north by Cook; east by the state of Indiana; south by Iroquois, and west by La Salle.

It is from 30 to 24 miles from north to south, and from 12 to 38 miles from west to east; and contains about 1228 square miles.

Its timber is in detached portions in groves and along the water courses of the streams;—in some parts are large bodies; in other parts are extensive prairies. Much of Will county is excellent, first rate land.

It is watered by the Kankakee and branches, the Des Plaines, Du Page, Hickory, Forked, Rock, Soldier, Hawkins and Dennis creeks, and some of the tributaries of the Calumet. The Illinois and Michigan Canal will pass along the Valley of the Des Plaines.

Will county belongs to the seventh judicial circuit and is united with Cook county in its representation to the legislature.

The seat of justice is *Juliet.*

WINNEBAGO COUNTY.

Winnebago County was formed from Jo Daviess and the attached portion of La Salle county in January, 1836, from which parts of Stephenson and Boone counties have since been detached. It is bounded north by Wisconsin territory, east by Boone, south by Ogle, and west by Stephenson.

It is 24 miles long and 21 miles broad, having about 504 square miles. Rock river passes through it from north to south; the Peekatonokee comes in on its western border and enters Rock river in township 46 north; Kishwaukee waters its southeastern part and enters Rock river in township 43 north, besides some smaller streams. There is much excellent land in Winnebago county;—the timber is in groves and detached portions, and the prairies undulating and abundantly rich. Rock river furnishes immense water power, especially at Rockford, and all the streams abound in good mill seats. The Polish emigrants receive their lands, granted by Congress, in this county.

Winnebago county belongs to the sixth judicial circuit and is attached to Jo Daviess county in its representation.

The county seat is not yet permanently located.

NEW COUNTIES.

Besides several new counties formed at the last session of the legislature, and which are placed in alphabetical order, provision was made by law for the formation of the following counties on condition that a majority of the voters in the counties from which they were detached, at an election provided to be held subsequently, should decide in favour of such organisation.

Coffee County to be formed chiefly from Putnam with two townships from Knox, and one from Henry county, and will be bounded on the north by Putnam and Henry; east by Putnam; south by Peoria, and west by Knox and Henry; being 18 miles square, and containing 324 square miles.

It is watered by Spoon river and its branches, and contains excellent land—valuable timber on the large streams and in groves, and rich, undulating prairies. Much of the county will admit of a dense population.

De Kalb County, to be formed from the western part of Kane county, will be bounded north by Boone; east by Kane; south by La Salle, and west by Ogle county. It will be 36 miles long, and 18 broad, containing 648 square miles. It is watered by the south branches of the Kishwaukee, Wabonsic, Morgan and Blackberry creeks, and some smaller streams.

The timber resembles that of the adjacent counties, and is in groves, and scattered portions of oak openings. The surface generally is undulating, and the soil rich.

Michigan County, to be formed from the western part of Cook county, will be bounded north by McHenry; east by Cook; south by Will, and west by Kane county. It will be 30 miles long, and 24 miles broad, with an additional township at its southeastern corner. Fox river and its branches will water its western and northwestern portions, the heads of the Du Page its southwestern, Des Plaines will run through its southeastern corner, and Salt creek and Flag creek its eastern side.

The southern portion of this county is a superior region with some large groves of timber and rich, undulating prairie. Along Fox river are cedar cliffs, and in the northeastern and middle portions are extensive prairies.

PART THIRD;

CONTAINING A PARTICULAR DESCRIPTION

OF EACH TOWN, SETTLEMENT, STREAM, PRAIRIE,

BOTTOM, BLUFF, &c.

ALPHABETICALLY ARRANGED.

Apakeesheek Grove, in La Salle county, lies three miles north of Holderman's grove.

Adams's Fork, a branch of the Skillet fork of the Little Wabash. It rises in the prairies of Marion county, passes southeast, across the corner of Jefferson, and enters the Skillet fork in Wayne. The land is well timbered and of a good quality.

Alabama Settlement, in the northeastern part of Union county, of about thirty families. The timber, chiefly white oak, with a thin soil.

ALBION, the seat of justice for Edwards county, situated in section two, of township two south, in range ten, east of the third principal meridian. It was laid out by Messrs. Birbeck and Flowers, in 1819, and settled principally by English emigrants. The situation is high and healthy. It contains three stores, three houses of entertainment, an ox flouring mill, a cotton gin, and thirty or forty families. The court house is of brick, forty-four feet square, two stories, and finished. Albion is forty miles southwest of Vincennes.

Allen's Prairie and Settlement, in Greene county, twelve miles northeasterly from Carrollton. The land is good, the prairie large, with good timber on the water courses.

Allison's Prairie, (sometimes improperly spelt *Ellison*) in Lawrence county, five miles northeast from Lawrenceville. It is ten miles long, and five broad. The eastern part towards the Wabash, contains some wet land and purgatory swamps, but the principal part is a dry, sandy, and very rich soil, covered with well cultivated farms. Few tracts in Illinois are better adapted to corn than this. The population equals 200 families. This prairie was settled in 1816 and '17, by emigrants from Ohio and Kentucky, and mostly of the religious sect known in the west by the name of *Christians*, and the settlement is sometimes called by that name. In a few years death had thinned their numbers. The purgatory swamps, as they are called, around the prairie, had a deleterious influence, and retarded the progress of population. In later years but little sickness has existed, and this settlement furnishes one of many evidences that upon the subjugation of the luxuriant vegetation with which our rich prairies are clothed, and the cultivation of the soil, sickly places will be changed to healthy ones.

Alton, an incorporated town on the bank of the Mississippi, is thought by many to possess advantages for commerce equal to any in the state. It is situated on fractional sections thirteen and fourteen, in township five north, in range ten west of the third principal meridian.

It is two and a half miles above the mouth of the Missouri, and at the place where the curve of the Mississippi penetrates the furthest into Illinois, eighteen miles below the mouth of the Illinois river, and at the point where the commerce and business of the wide spread regions of the northeast, north, and northwest must arrive.

The legislature of Illinois have memorialised congress repeatedly to have the great national road, now constructing through Ohio, Indiana, and Illinois, cross the Mississippi at this place, and sanguine hopes are entertained that the rights of Illinois in this particular will be duly regarded.

Lower Alton has the best landing for steamboats on the east bank of the Mississippi, having a rock of level surface, of suitable height, forming a natural wharf. The state penitentiary has been established here, and many are sanguine that it will be the future seat of government.

One of the finest bodies of timber in the state surrounds it for several miles in extent, from which vast quantities of lumber may be produced. Bituminous coal exists in great abundance but a short distance from the town. Inexhaustible beds of limestone for building purposes, and easily quarried, are within its precincts. A species of free stone, easily dressed and used for monuments and architectural purposes, and that peculiar species of lime, used for water cement, are found in great abundance in the vicinity.

The corporate bounds extend two miles along the river, and half a mile back. The town plat is laid out by the proprietors upon a liberal scale.

There are five squares reserved for public purposes, a large reservation is made on the river for a public landing and promenade. Market street is 150 feet wide, other streets are one hundred, eighty, and sixty feet, according to the situation and public accommodation.

Alton, contained at the commencement of 1837, 20 wholesale and 32 retail stores and groceries, 8 attorneys, 7 physicians, 7 clergymen devoted to their calling, (besides several preachers of the gospel, who follow secular business during the week,) 4 hotels, 2 of which have large accommodations, a large steam flouring mill, four large slaughtering and packing houses for putting up pork, which do a large business, and mechanics' shops of various descriptions.

There are three printing offices which issue weekly papers, the Spectator, Telegraph and Observer; besides the Illinois Temperance Herald issued monthly. There is a large temperance society, that holds monthly meetings; a lyceum that holds weekly meetings, and two schools.

The public buildings are four houses for public worship, and two others expected to be erected soon. The Baptist church has a large stone edifice, with a handsome spire, bell, clock and organ. The basement furnishes three store rooms in front for rent, and a Sunday school room, and a committee room in the rear. The Presbyterian church has a moderate sized stone edifice with a cupola and bell, and a basement Sunday school room. The Methodist Episcopal church has a neat framed edifice with a stone basement and a cupola. The Methodist Protestant church has a small stone building. The Protestant Episcopal church, the Unitarian church, and the German Evangelical church, each meet in private rooms prepared for the purpose.

Among the public institutions are a bank, (a branch of the state bank of Illinois,) an insurance office, a Masonic lodge of independent odd fellows, a lyceum and a mechanics' association.

Depositories of the Illinois Bible, Sunday school, Tract, and Temperance societies are kept in this town for the supply of the state, and a spacious edifice, four stories high, with a front of hewn stone, is about to be erected by the citizens, by subscription, for which purpose two liberal and wealthy gentlemen have given a lot of the value of more than 5000 dollars. A large proportion of the funds for the erection of the building has been secured.

In no western town of the size, population, and business, has an equal amount been given by its citizens for religious and benevolent purposes within the last two years.

The state penitentiary is located in Alton. It has the warden's house, guard house, twenty-four cells, and the exterior wall around the yard erected.

The rapidity with which Alton has grown up from a business state to its present prosperous condition has been hardly equalled in the enterprising West. Mercantile business was commenced here in 1831. Its facilities are now great. Real estate has risen here more than 1000 per cent. within two years.

The prices of lots depend upon their location. The best stands for business near the river sell from 300 to 400 dollars per foot front. Lots more retired, for private residences, from 100 to 50 and 25 dollars per foot. Stores rent from 1500 to 400, and dwelling houses from 600 to 200 dollars. Some of the large wholesale stores do business from 250,000 to half a million of dollars annually.

Seven or eight steamboats are owned here in whole or in part, and arrivals and departures occur every day and at all times in the day during the season. Alton now commands a large proportion of the trade of the Upper Mississippi and Illinois rivers, and of the interior country for one hundred miles. Besides the public railroads that concentrate here, noticed under the head of "Internal Improvement," a survey has been made and the stock taken for one from Alton to Springfield, 72 miles, which will open an important line of communication with the interior, and eventually become connected with the great line to the Atlantic cities.

The natural surface of much of the town site of Alton is broken by bluffs and ravines, but the enterprise of its citizens and the corporation is fast removing these inconveniences by grading down its hills and filling up its ravines. A contract of 60,000 dollars has recently been entered upon to construct a culvert over the little Piasau creek that passes through the centre of the town, over which will soon be built one of the most capacious and pleasant streets. Since its settlement the citizens of Alton have enjoyed as good health, as those in any river town in the West. Its population is about 2500.

We close this article with the following extract from Beck's Gazetteer of Illinois and Missouri, written in 1821.

"Alton, although yet small, possesses natural advantages rarely equalled. Situated as it is, at the junction of three large and navigable rivers; possessing a fine, commodious harbor, and landing for boats at all seasons of the year; surrounded by a fertile country, rapidly settling, it bids fair to become a populous, wealthy, and commercial town."

Aikin's Grove, in Ogle county, lies five miles southeast of Oregon city, and east of Rock river, on the road from Dixonville to Princeton and Peoria. Here are three or four small groves, and thirty families.

America, the former county seat of Alexander county, situated on the west bank of the Ohio, on the first high land, and twelve miles above its mouth. The landing at this place is much injured by a sand bar.

Appanooce, a town site and post office on the Mississippi, in Hancock county, ten miles above Commerce, and eighteen miles northwest from Carthage.

Apple Creek post office. (*See Waverley.*)

Apple Creek Prairie, in Greene county, lies north of Apple creek, to the left of the road from Carrollton to Jacksonville. It is ten miles long, and from two to four miles wide, of good quality, and spread over with large farms, and populous settlements.

Apple River, in Jo Daviess county, rises near the boundary line, where its branches interlock with the waters of the Pee-ka-ton-o-kee, runs a southwestern course about forty-five miles, and enters the Mississippi twenty miles below Galena. It is a rocky and rapid stream, with good mill seats, and fifty yards wide at its mouth. The bottoms are excellent land. The uplands hilly and broken. Large bodies of timber are on its banks. Towards its heads is a fine undulating country.

Apple Creek rises near the borders of Sangamon county, runs a southwestern course through the southeastern part of Morgan into Greene county, and enters the Illinois river in section thirty-six, fractional township eleven north, fourteen west. It has several tributaries, which are noticed under their respective names, and which water a valuable tract of country, with a large population.

Arm of the Grand Prairie, in Jefferson county, lies eight miles northwest from Mount Vernon. The soil is tolerably good, and the settlement contains about fifty families.

Armstrong Post Office is in Wabash county, seven miles above Mount Carmel.

Arrowsmith's Settlement is towards the east side of Mercer county.

Ashmore's Settlement, in Coles county, fifteen miles north of Charleston, and on the east side of the Embarras. Timber and prairie good.

Ashton, a post office and town site in Adams county, nine miles south of Quincy.

Athens, a village in Sangamon county, on the east side, and four miles from the Sangamon river, and fifteen miles north from Springfield. It has several stores, one steam mill for sawing and flouring, and about seventy-five families. It has timber of the Sangamon on the west, and the prairies east, with a large settlement around.

Athens, a town site on the left bank of the Kaskaskia river, in St. Clair county, known as *Hill's Ferry*.

Atherton's Settlement, in Alexander county, two miles east from Unity, containing about one-hundred families. The upland tolerably good.

Atlas, a small town in Pike county, situated on the northwest quarter of section twenty-seven, township six south, range five west. It is on a handsome tract of ground, under the bluffs, half a mile from Snycartee Slough, which is navigable for steamboats to this place, in high water.

Aubuchon, a passage from the Mississippi to the Kaskaskia river, about four miles above the town of Kaskaskia.

Augusta, a town site and post office in Hancock county, on southwest section twenty-three, township three north, range five west, sixteen miles southwest from Carthage.

It has several families, and a respectable school.

Augusta, a town site on the west bank of the Illinois river, in Pike county, ten miles east of Pittsfield, and twenty-two miles from Jacksonville. It is opposite the termination of the Jacksonville, Lynnville and Winchester railroad, which is now under contract. Another company has been chartered to extend this line from Augusta, by Pittsfield and Atlas to Louisiana, Mo., from whence another line of railroad has been projected and a charter granted by the legislature of Missouri, across to Columbia and the Missouri river.

Auburn, a town site, in Sangamon county, on the north side of Sugar creek, on the stage road, and contemplated railroad route from Alton to Springfield. It has two stores, one grocery, one tavern, and ten or twelve families, surrounded with a beautiful prairie.

Au Sable, [Fr. *sandy—gravelly*,] a small stream in the eastern part of La Salle county. It rises near the west fork of Du Page, runs south mostly through prairie, and enters the Illinois three miles below the junction of the Des Plaines, and Kankakee.

Au Sable Grove is in the northeastern part of La Salle county, at the heads of the Au Sable creek. Here is a fine body of timber surrounded with an extensive and rich prairie.

Aviston, a town site and post office, in Clinton county, on the Vincennes and St. Louis stage road, with a dozen houses.

Bachelder's Grove, in Cook county, eighteen miles southwest of Chicago, contains about two sections of timber, and a large settlement.

Budgley's Settlement, in St. Clair county, five miles northwesterly from Belleville, one of the oldest American settlements in the county.

Bailey's Point, a branch of the Vermilion, and a settlement in La Salle county, fourteen miles southwest from Ottawa. Here is a small tract of excellent timber, surrounded with the choicest prairie. The settlement contains about twenty families.

Baker's Grove, in Ogle county, lies bordering on Rock river, between Grand Detour and Oregon city. It is eight miles long and three miles wide; timber good and land excellent.

Bankstone's Fork, in Gallatin county, rises in the interior, runs a southeastern course, and enters the South Fork of Saline creek, fourteen miles above Equality.

It has a fine country on its borders, and a large settlement.

Banning's Settlement, in Shelby county, near the Kaskaskia river, twelve miles south of Shelbyville. The land is good, and plenty of timber and prairie.

The bottom on the opposite side of the river is overflowed in high water.

Barney's Prairie, in Wabash county, seven miles north of Mount Carmel, is a good tract of land well cultivated.

Barbee's Settlement, seven miles northwest of Palestine, in Crawford county, with timber and prairie.

Bartlett's Settlement, in the southwestern part of McDonough county, on Crooked creek, fifteen miles from Macomb. The land is good, and the settlement extensive.

Bath, a post office and settlement on the south side of Cass county, on the road from Jacksonville to Beardstown.

Batcheldorsville post office is on the east side of Coles county, seven miles from Charleston.

Bay Creek rises in the prairies towards the eastern part of Pike county, and running westward enters Calhoun county, and forms a kind of bay at its mouth, which is navigable for some miles.

The land on its borders is generally good, except about the bluffs, where it is broken.

Beardstown, the seat of justice for Cass county, is situated on the Illinois river, twenty-five miles northeast from Jacksonville, on fractional township eighteen north, and twelve west. It is on elevated ground, sandy soil, and entirely above the highest floods. It has thirteen stores, four of which do commission and forwarding business, three groceries, two druggists, four physicians, one large hotel, and several boarding houses, two bakeries, two shoemakers, three tailors, two blacksmiths, two cabinet makers, one silversmith, one watchmaker, four carpenters and housejoiners, three cooper shops, one painter and glazier, two tinners, two brick and one stone masons, one carriage maker, two steam flouring mills, with six pairs of stones, one steam sawmill, one steam distillery, and a large brewery, one lawyer, one minister of the gospel, and about 1,000 inhabitants. There is a Methodist and an Episcopalian congregation, but no house of worship.

Canal project. A company has been chartered and surveys made preparatory to the construction of a canal from this place to Sangamon river, at Huron, and from thence to improve the river by slack water navigation to the head And it has been ascertained that a water communication may be opened at moderate expense across the state to the Vermilion of the Wabash. The construction of that portion of the canal from Beardstown to the Sangamon river can be easily effected.

Bear Creek, a small branch of the Macoupin, twelve miles west from Carlinville.

Bear Creek heads in String prairie, and enters Apple creek, in Greene county. A considerable settlement is on its borders.

Bear Creek, a small stream and branch of the middle fork of Shoal creek, and a settlement in Montgomery county. The land is rather level, and inclined to be wet, but fertile.

Bear Creek, a small stream in the southeastern part of Sangamon county, with a considerable settlement. It enters the South Fork of Sangamon from the south side.

Bear Creek, a small stream that rises in the north part of Gallatin county, runs south, and enters the North Fork of Saline creek, ten miles above Equality. Here is much good land, and a large settlement.

Bear Creek, is a fine stream in Adams county, with two principal forks. South Fork rises in one north, six west. North Fork rises in five north, seven west, in Hancock county, and interlocks with the western branch of Crooked creek. They unite in section thirteen, two north, eight west. After passing through the bluffs into the Mississippi bottom, this stream divides into two prongs; one runs a northwest course and enters the Mississippi—the other prong bears a little south of west, receiving several small streams, and enters Boston Bay, one mile above Quincy.

This stream is about forty yards wide at its separation, and has a number of mill seats. Few bodies of land in the state equal that which lines its banks.

Large settlements extend along its timber.

Bear Prairie is a small tract in Wayne county, five miles east of Fairfield, with twenty families.

Beaucoup is a large settlement on Beaucoup creek, in Washington county, south of New Nashville. The land is a mixture of timber and prairie, and good second rate soil.

Beaucoup Settlement is in Jackson county, twelve miles northeast from Brownsville, between the Big Beaucoup creek and Big Muddy river. The land is rich, heavily timbered, with a considerable settlement.

Beaver Creek, called also Stinking creek, rises in Bond county, runs south into Clinton county, crosses the Vincennes and St. Louis road, four miles west of Carlyle, and empties into Shoal creek, in the northeastern part of township one north, four west. It is about twenty-five miles in length, is a sluggish, muddy stream, and waters a fine tract of country.

The settlement extends its whole length.

Beaver Creek rises in Boone county, runs southwest and enters Kishwaukee, twelve miles above its mouth. It is sparsely timbered with walnut, linden, oaks of various species, and oak openings. Soil, sand and clay; prairies, rolling; fine springs.

Beaver Creek, a branch of Iroquois river in Iroquois county.

Beck's Creek heads in the western part of Shelby county, runs southeast, and enters the Kaskaskia in the northern part of Fayette, eighteen miles above Vandalia. It is a mill stream, has much good land on its banks, and rolling prairie adjoining.

The timber is oak of various kinds, walnut, locust, coffee nut, cherry, elm, etc.

Begg's Settlement, in the southeast part of Union county, on the waters of Cash river. It is a fine, undulating, timbered region, and contains about 120 families.

Bellefountaine, a large spring and settlement in Monroe county, near Waterloo. In the vicinity of this place, several attacks were made by the Indians, forty years since; some of the inhabitants were killed and others taken prisoners.

Belleville, the seat of justice for St. Clair county, is situated on sections twenty-two, twenty-three, twenty-seven, and twenty-eight, of township one north, in range eight west of the third principal meridian. It is a neat flourishing village, on high ground, six miles from the American bottom, and thirteen miles east southeast from St. Louis. The public buildings are a handsome court house of brick, finished in a superior style, a brick jail, a clerk's office, a public hall belonging to a library company, and a framed Methodist house of worship. It has two select schools; one for boarders half a mile distant.

There are two large merchant steam flouring mills, with six pairs of stones, a brewery, a steam distillery, a wool carding machine, eight carpenters, one cabinet maker, five blacksmith's shops, one tinner's shop, two silversmiths, three wagon makers, one turner and wheelwright, two shoemakers' shops, one millwright, two coopers, two saddlers, two tailors, one bakery, one high school, one common school, a Presbyterian, Baptist and a Methodist congregation, and about 700 inhabitants, of which about 100 are Germans, twenty French, and the residue Americans. There are three lawyers, four physicians, and four resident ministers of the gospel.

It is surrounded with a rich and extensive agricultural settlement, and a fine body of timber. Belleville contains a printing office, which issues the *" St. Clair Gazette,"* and is a place of considerable business.

Belleview Prairie, is a rich, dry, prairie, at the foot of the bluffs, in Calhoun county. It is six miles long, and three fourths of a mile wide, with a gradual descent from the bluffs. Belleview post office, is in this settlement, which contains about forty families.

Belvidere, a village of a dozen families, two stores, a post office, saw and grist mill, and rapidly increasing, in the western part of Boone county on the stage road from Chicago to Galena. It is situated on Squaw prairie, and has a delightful appearance. Near the town site is a mound, fifty rods long and about thirty rods wide, elevated seventy feet above the bottom lands of Rock river. On the top of this mound is the cemetery of an Indian called *Big Thunder*. He died about the period of the Sauk war in 1831 or '32, and was placed in a sitting posture on a flag mat, wrapped in blankets, his scalping knife by his side to cut the plugs of tobacco that are offered him. Over the body is constructed a covering of wood and earth, with an opening in front, where Big Thunder may be seen sitting with his tobacco lying before him. The Indians still visit the place to replenish his stores of tobacco, whiskey, &c.

The citizens of this region are about to erect a College edifice on this spot, in a vault under which the bones of Big Thunder will repose unmolested. A charter was granted for the purpose at the recent session of the legislature. The Rev. S. S. Whitman, formerly Professor in the Hamilton Literary and Theological Institution, New York, is engaged in the enterprise.

Beman's Mill and settlement on Apple creek, in Greene county, seven miles northwest from Carrollton.

Bennington, a post office in the western part of Fulton county.

Berlin, a town site and post office, in Sangamon county, on the west side of Island Grove, seventeen miles west from Springfield, on the main road to Jacksonville.

Bernadotte, a town on Spoon river, in Fulton county, on section nineteen, five north, two west, 12 miles southwest from Lewistown. It has one sawmill, one flouring mill with three runs of stones, three stores, two groceries, one tavern, and a common school.

Spoon river can easily be made navigable to this place.

Berry's Settlement is in the forks of Crooked creek, in Clinton county, eight miles southeasterly from Carlyle.

Bethel, a populous settlement in St. Clair county, ten miles north of Belleville. Here is a Baptist meeting house and congregation, and a moral, religious society of industrious farmers.

Bethany, a post office and settlement, in Sangamon county, twenty-one miles southeast from Springfield, on the road to Shelbyville.

Big Barren Grove is in the western part of Putnam and eastern part of Henry county, 25 miles long, and from 2 to 3 miles wide; and forms the dividing ridge between the waters of Spoon river and the Winnebago Swamp. The timber is scattering, resembling barrens, with various kinds of oaks, hickory, &c. The west end is called Black Oak Ridge where a colony from Wethersfield, Con., is settled.

Big Bay Creek, a small stream that rises in the north eastern part of Johnson county. It takes a southeastern direction, receiving Cedar creek in that county, and Little Bay creek in Pope county, and enters the Ohio about six miles below Golconda. Its bottoms are wide, and the bluffs rather broken; and towards the Ohio the bottom land produces large quantities of cypress with other growth.

Big Bottom is a settlement in the northwest corner of Alexander county, on Clear creek. The soil is first rate alluvion.

Big Beaucoup Creek, one of the four heads of Big Muddy river. It rises in the southeastern part of Washington county, township three south, in range two west, runs a south course through Perry county and enters the Big Muddy in section thirty-five, eight south, two west, eight miles above Brownsville. It has much good land on its borders, some excellent prairies, and fine timber, consisting of oak, hickory, ash, poplar, elm, walnut, etc. The bottom land is rather wet. Big Beaucoup is navigable for flat boats.

Big Creek, in Pope county, rises in the northern part of the county, runs south, and enters the Ohio, fifteen miles above Golconda.

Big Creek, in Crawford county, a small stream that enters the Embarras in the southwestern part of the county.

Big Creek is a small stream that rises on the Grand Prairie, in Edgar county, runs a southeast direction, passes through a corner of Clark, and enters the Wabash near the point at which the dividing line of the two states leaves that river. The land through which it passes is good, well timbered, and densely settled with a farming population.

Big Creek, in Effingham county, a branch of the Little Wabash, running a southeast course through Brockett's settlement to that river.

Big Creek, in Macon county, a branch of the North Fork of Sangamon. It is formed from Long creek, and Findley's fork.

Big Creek, a stream in Fayette county, which rises in the Grand prairie, northeast from Vandalia, crosses the national road twelve miles east of that place, runs southwest, and enters the Kaskaskia in the lower part of the county.

Big Creek, in the western part of Crawford county, runs south and enters the Embarras.

Big Creek, in Fulton county, a small stream that rises near Canton, runs southwest, and enters Spoon river one mile above the road from Rushville to Lewistown. A considerable settlement and good land towards its head.

Big Grove, in Champaign county, is on a branch of the Salt Fork of the Vermilion river, and is about the centre of the county. It is a body of heavy timbered, rich land, twelve miles long, and of an average of three miles in width. The country around is most delightful, the prairie is elevated, dry, and of a very rich soil, the water is good, and the country very healthy. The population at Big Grove must now exceed 200 families.

Big Grove, in Kane county, is on the South Fork of the Kishwaukee. The surface around undulating, and the soil a black sandy loam.

Stratified limestone, flint, pebbles and coal abound in this region.

Big Grove, in La Salle county, twenty miles northeast from Ottawa, is about three miles in diameter. The land in the timber is wet, but the surrounding prairie is dry, undulating and rich.

Big Grove, a timbered tract, or rather several groves, connected, for twelve miles in length, in the southwestern part of McLean county, on the third principal meridian, and township twenty-one north. It is a fine tract of country, rich in soil and well timbered, on the Kickapoo creek. Bloomington, the county seat, is eighteen miles from the heart of the settlement, which contains from one hundred and fifty to two hundred families.

Big Grove, a beautiful, high, undulating, and rich tract of timber, near some of the heads of Spoon river, in Henry county. It is twelve or fifteen miles long, and about three miles wide, surrounded with extensive and rather level prairies.

Big Mound Prairie, in Wayne county, is five miles west from Fairfield, three miles in extent, undulating surface, thin soil, and has about fifty families.

A large mound gives the name to this prairie.

Big Muddy river, (called by the French who discovered it, *Riviere au Vase*, or *Vaseux*) a considerable stream in the southwestern part of the state.

It has four principal heads, which, rising in Washington, Jefferson, and Hamilton counties, and uniting in Jackson county, form the main stream.

They are the Beaucoup, Little Muddy, and Middle Fork. The general course of the stream is southwest, and it is navigable some distance above Brownsville. Below Brownsville it turns south to the county line, makes a short bend, and enters the Mississippi near the northeastern corner of township eleven south, in range four west of the third principal meridian.

Its bluffs generally are abrupt, the land along its borders and branches is undulating, and for most of its length well timbered. Valuable salines exist on its banks, and are worked about Brownsville, where there is an inexhaustible bed of bituminous coal. Native copper has been found on its banks in detached masses. It runs through a fine agricultural and grazing country.

Big Neck is a settlement in one south, six west, at the head of the South Fork of Bear creek, in Adams county: a tract of good land.

Big Prairie, in White county, between the Little and Big Wabash, about three miles in diameter, and nearly all in a state of cultivation. The soil is sandy, but of great fertility.

Big Rock Creek, is a branch of Fox river in Kane county.

Big Woods, a large tract of timbered land, lying on the east side of Fox river, in Kane county, and provided the surveys were run it would lie mostly in townships 38 and 39 N., range 8 east. It is about 10 miles in length and from 4 to 5 miles in width. The timber consists chiefly of white, black, yellow, and bur oaks, sugar maple, linden, black and white walnut or butternut, hickory, ash of various species, poplar, ironwood, elm, cherry, etc. The soil is generally a dark sandy loam; sometimes approaches to clay, generally a little undulating, but in some places quite level and a little wet. The Big Woods are thickly settled on all sides, as is the prairie country adjoining.

Bethel a post office and town site with a dozen families in Morgan county, 12 miles west of Jacksonville.

Bethesda, a post office in Coles county, 8 miles west of Charleston.

Birch Creek, is a small stream that rises in Morgan county, and enters Apple creek in Greene county. The settlement contains about twenty-five families.

Blackberry Creek, in Kane county, rises in the central part of the county, runs south and enters Fox river near the south line of the county. Groves of timber, barrens, and rich undulating prairie along its course.

Black Creek is an insignificant stream, in Pike county, that enters the Snycartee.

Black Partridge Creek, a post office, and a small stream in the upper part of Tazewell county, that enters the Illinois river.

Bloomfield, a town and post office in Edgar county, 10 miles north of Paris, with three stores, two groceries, one tavern, one physician, various mechanics, and about 20 families.

Blooming Grove, a tract of timbered land and a large settlement, in McLean county, adjoining Bloomington. It is about six miles long from northwest to southeast, and varying in width from one to four miles, containing about twelve square miles of beautiful timber, with a large settlement of industrious farmers around it. Nearly all the land is already occupied with settlers, a majority of whom are from Ohio. Both timbered land and prairie are first rate.

Bloomingdale is the locality of a colony in Tazewell county.

Bloomington, is the seat of justice for McLean county and is beautifully situated on the margin of a fine prairie and north side of Blooming-Grove, on section four, township twenty north, range two east. It has eight or ten stores, three groceries, two taverns, two lawyers, three physicians, a handsome academy building, various mechanics, two steam mills for sawing, a Presbyterian and a Methodist meeting house, and ministers, and about 700 population. The surrounding country is most delightful.

Block House, a name given to an American settlement formed about forty years since, in the American bottom, in the southwestern part of St. Clair county. At the foot of the bluffs, near this, is a spring that regularly ebbs and flows, once in twenty-four hours.

Blue Creek, in the upper part of Tazewell county, rises in the prairie, runs west, and enters the Illinois below Spring bay.

Bluffdale, a settlement in Greene county, ten miles west of Carrollton, and under the bluffs that overhang the Illinois bottom. The land is rich, dry, and beautifully situated for six miles in extent, under overhanging bluffs and precipices from which springs of "crystal waters" gush forth. The settlement is generally arranged along the bluffs from Apple creek to the Macoupin, from three to four miles from the Illinois river, and consists of fifty or sixty families. The settlement of Bluffdale has two stores, one grocery, one tavern, one minister of the gospel, and a Baptist congregation, one post office, one school, and various mechanics.

Blue Point, a point of timber projecting into the prairie, in Effingham county, five miles north west of Ewington.

Blue River. There are two small streams of this name in Pike county distinguished as *Big* and *Little Blue.* They rise in the middle of the county, run a southeast course and enter the Illinois, in three south, two west, about six miles apart. The land through which they pass is fertile.

Bolive, a town site in the forks of Sangamon river, ten miles southeast from Springfield, surrounded with a large and flourishing settlement.

Boltinghouse Prairie, lies south of Albion, in Edwards county. It is about four miles long and three broad, dry, undulating surface, and good soil.

Bon Pas (-*Bumpau*,) a small village near the creek of the same name in the northeast part of White county.

Bon Pas, a creek that divides Wabash and Edwards counties. It rises near the Vincennes road, fifteen miles west of Lawrenceville, and taking a southeasterly course, enters the Wabash river in section fourteen, township three south, range fourteen west of the second principal meridian, at the corner of Wabash and White counties. Its banks are low and swampy.

Bon Pas Prairie, four miles northeast from Albion, in Edwards county, and about two miles in diameter. It contains good land, and a settlement.

Bon Pas Settlement, near the southeast corner of Edwards county, between the Bon Pas creek and Little Wabash river. It is a timbered tract, good land, and contains about sixty families.

Boston Bay is an arm of the Mississippi, above Quincy in Adams county, which, at a tolerable stage of water, furnishes a fine harbor for boats.

Boston, a town site in Canaan settlement, Shelby county

twelve miles north of Shelbyville, township thirteen north, four east, on the west fork of the Kaskaskia.

Bostwick's Settlement, is three miles northeast from Hillsboro' in Montgomery county, a dry, rolling, fertile, prairie.

Bottom Settlement, commences in the northwestern part of Union county, and extends down the Mississippi. This bottom is timbered, and is from three to four miles wide but part of it is wet and inundated.

The settlement lies chiefly along the bank of the river.

Bottom Settlement, in Alexander county; lies along the Mississippi, on rich alluvial land, heavily timbered, and contains sixty or seventy families.

Bradley's Settlement is at the head of Kincaid creek, in the north part of Jackson county. It is a timbered region, tolerable land, and has twenty-five or thirty families.

Brattleville, a post office, in Carter's settlement, in McDonough county, twelve miles south of Macomb, and on the mail road to Rushville.

Bridge's Settlement, in Johnson county, ten miles west from Vienna, contains some tolerably good land. Population about sixty families.

Brighton, a town site and post office in Brown's prairie, the southwest corner of Macoupin county, 12 miles north of Alton. It has two stores, a castor oil factory and a dozen families.

Broad Run, a small stream in Coles county. It rises in the Grand prairie, and runs southwest into the Kaskaskia. Settlement small.

Brocket's Settlement on the west side of the Little Wabash, eight miles southwesterly from Ewington, in Effingham county. The surface is tolerably level and the settlement contains forty or fifty families.

Brooklyn, a town site laid off on the bank of the Mississippi river, in St. Clair county, opposite North St. Louis.

Brown's Point, a settlement at the head of timber in

a large prairie in Morgan county, ten miles south of Jacksonville.

Brown's Prairie, in the corner of Macoupin and Greene counties and extending into Madison county, between Wood river and the Piasau. It is rich, dry soil, and is about twelve miles north from Alton.

BROWNSVILLE, the seat of of justice for Jackson county, is situated on the north side of Big Muddy river, on section two, nine south, and three west of the third principal meridian. It is twelve miles by land, and twenty-five by water from the Mississippi, and is surrounded by hills.

The Big Muddy Salines and coal banks are near this place. The population is about twenty families.

Brulette's Creek rises in the north part of Edgar county, and runs eastward across a portion of Indiana into the Wabash. The timber on its banks is chiefly oak. The settlement is in the forks, and along the north fork of the creek. The land is good. Prairie predominates over the timbered land. The post office is called *Bloomfield*.

Brush Creek rises in the east part of Shelby county, runs a southwest course, and empties into the Kaskaskia river, in the south part of the county. The timber is indifferent, and the prairies are level and wet.

Brush Creek rises in the prairies in the south part of Sangamon county; runs north and enters Horse creek, a little above its junction with the Sangamon.

Brush Hill post office is in Cook county, in the northeast corner of township thirty-eight north, range eleven east, and sixteen miles west of Chicago.

Brush Prairie Creek, a trifling stream in Franklin county, rises in a prairie of the same name, runs west, and enters the middle fork of Muddy river. Good timbered land.

Brushy Fork, a small branch of the Embarras on the east side, and in the northern part of Lawrence county. It runs a south course, and enters the main stream six miles above Lawrenceville.

The settlement is new, containing twenty-five or thirty families, and a portion of the country barrens.

Brushy Fork, a small stream that rises in the prairie, near the borders of Edgar county, and taking a southwest course, enters the Embarras in Coles county, fourteen miles above Charleston. On the east side the land is rolling and fertile, and there is a settlement of fifteen or twenty families; on the west side the land is level and rather wet.

Brushy Prairie, on the east side of the Little Wabash, in Wayne county, eleven miles east of Fairfield, and contains about fifty families.

Buck-heart Prairie, in Fulton county, is northeast from Lewistown, and joins Canton prairie. It is six or eight miles in extent, and has a considerable settlement.

Buck-heart Creek rises near the South Fork of the Sangamon river, runs northwest, and enters the North Fork. It has a considerable settlement.

Buck-heart Grove, at the head of Buck-heart creek, in Sangamon county, fifteen or twenty miles southeast from Springfield. It is a fine tract of timber, about 1000 acres, surrounded with high prairie and settlement.

Buck Prairie lies in Edwards county, six miles northeast from Albion, and is about two miles and a half across.

Buck-horn Prairie is in Morgan county, six or eight miles south of Jacksonville. The soil is rich, but its surface is rather level and wet.

Buckle's Grove, at the head of the north branch of Salt creek, in McLean county, contains about twelve sections of timbered land, surrounded with rich prairie. It is in twenty-two north, four east, and is about six or eight miles east from Bloomington.

Timber principally oak, with some sugar maple, and the land around it rather level.

Buffaloe Grove, in Jo Daviess county, twelve miles north of Dixon's ferry, and on the road to Galena. It contains four or five sections of timber, surrounded with the richest prairie, a post office called Buffaloe Grove, and a town site called St. Marion.

Buffaloe-heart Grove lies in Sangamon county, fourteen

miles northeast from Springfield and six miles southeasterly from Elk-heart grove, which it resembles. It is about three miles long, and one mile and a half wide, containing about four sections of timber and twenty-five or thirty families. The rushes, which cover the prairies around, furnish winter food for cattle.

Buffaloe Rock, a singular promontory on the north side of the Illinois river, in La Salle county, six miles below Ottawa. It rises fifty or sixty feet nearly perpendicular on three sides, and contains on its surface about six hundred acres of timber and prairie.

Bullard's Prairie, sometimes called Gardner's prairie, in the western part of Lawrence county, sixteen miles from Lawrenceville. It is eight or ten miles long, and two miles wide, second rate soil, and has considerable settlements on its borders.

Bullbona Grove in sixteen north, eight east, in Putnam county. Prairie rich and undulating.

Buncombe Settlement, in Johnson county, eight miles northwest from Vienna, contains forty families; soil rather broken, thin and rocky.

Bunker Hill, an elevated town site in the south part of Macoupin county, section fourteen, seven north, eight west, in a large undulating prairie.

Bureau Creek rises in the northern part of Putnam county, runs southwest, receives Little Bureau, turns thence southeast, and enters the Illinois river nearly opposite Hennepin. It is a fine mill stream, with a bold current, rock, gravel, and sand in its bottom, and receives a number of branches. About the bluffs of the Illinois the surface of the land is broken, but in general it is excellent the whole length of the stream. Between its branches are fine prairies, undulating, rich, and dry, and along its borders is much excellent timber.

Burnside's Settlement, in Clinton county, five miles north of Carlyle, called by some the Irish settlement.

Burnt Prairie, in the northwestern part of White, and extending into Wayne county, is about two miles in dianieter, contains some good land and a dense settlement. Here is a post office and town site.

Burnt Prairie, in Edwards county, four miles northwest from Albion. It is about six miles long and two miles wide, interspersed with small groves and points of timber. The soil is good, and the population dense. Here is a windmill erected by a Mr. Clark, an English gentleman, which does good business as a grist mill.

Byron, a town site in Champaign county in Big Grove, three and half miles northwest from Urbanna, with three or four families.

Cache Merè, a small lake in McHenry county.

Cadwell's Branch, a small branch of the Mauvaiseterre, which it enters from the south, ten miles below Jacksonville. It is a mill stream and rocky.

Cahokia, and old French village, and one of the earliest in Illinois, situated in the American bottom, in St. Clair county, five miles south of Wiggin's Ferry, and ten miles north of west from Belleville.

The Cahokias, (or according to the orthography of the early French explorers, the *Caoquias*,) one of the tribes of the great nation of Illini, had made this a resting place for a long time previous to the discovery of the Mississippi, probably on account of the game which abounded in the vicinity. It is probable that the first settlement was made here by the French, shortly after La Salle descended the Mississippi, in 1683.

Charlevoix, who visited the place in 1721, expresses his astonishment that his countrymen had pitched upon so inconvenient a situation, being "half a league" from the river. He says, however, the people told him that the Mississippi once washed the foot of the village, but that in three years it had receded half a league, and that the people were talking of removing to a more eligible situation.

In 1766, it contained forty families; and at the commencement of the revolutionary war they had increased to fifty. This is about their present number. It was once the seat of a considerable fur trade.

Both the Spanish and French governments, in forming settlements on the Mississippi, had special regard to convenience of social intercourse, and protection from the Indians. All their settlements were required to be in the form of villages or towns, and lots of a convenient size for a door yard, garden and stable yard were provided for each family. To each village were granted two tracts of land at convenient distances, for "*common fields*" and "*commons.*"

A *common field* is a tract of land of several hundred acres, enclosed in common by the villagers, each person furnishing his proportion of labor, and each family possessing individual interest in a portion of the field, marked off, and bounded from the rest. Ordinances were made to regulate the repairs of fences, the time of excluding cattle in the spring, and the time of gathering the crop and opening the field for the range of cattle in the fall. Each plat of ground in the common field was owned in fee simple by the person to whom granted, subject to sale and conveyance, the same as any landed property.

A *common* is a tract of land granted to the town for wood and pasturage, in which each owner of a village lot has a *common*, but not an individual right. In some cases this tract embraced several thousand acres. The "common" attached to Cahokia, extends up the prairie opposite St. Louis.

Cahokia creek rises in Macoupin county, runs in a southwesterly direction through Madison into St. Clair county, and empties into the Mississippi two miles below the ferry at St. Louis. Through the American bottom the course of this stream is very sluggish, and meanders greatly. A mill dam backs up the water fifteen miles. Near its borders are several lakes and ponds rendering this portion of the American bottom unhealthy.

Formerly this creek passed Cahokia village, and entered the Mississippi further down, but a mischievous Frenchman, from some pique against the village, cut a channel from the creek to the river, and formed its present outlet. Along its borders are sixty or seventy mounds of various shapes and sizes.

Cairo is located near the mouth of the Ohio and extends across the point of land from river to river. The termination of the great central railroad is to be at or near the site of Cairo.

Calamic, a stream at the south end of lake Michigan. It rises in Indiana, runs westward into Illinois, turns north and enters the lake. Much of the country near the lake is low and swampy. Further up are rapids and falls in the stream.

Caledonia, a town laid off on the bluffs of the Ohio in Alexander county, three miles above America. A wharf is here constructing to secure a good landing for boats which is wanted at America.

It has two or three stores, a dozen families, and is thought to be an important site for business.

Calumet, a large stream that rises in Indiana, winds into Illinois, turns again and enters the lake Michigan, near the boundary line. Much of the country near the lake is low and swampy. Further up are rapids, and good water power.

Calumet, a town site with 8 or 10 houses and a post office near the mouth of the Calumet.

Camden, a town site at the mouth of the Illinois river in the southwest part of Green county.

Cameron's Settlement, in Fulton county, eight miles northwest from Lewistown, is in a tract of good land, a mixture of timber and prairie, with a considerable population.

Campbell's Island, in the Mississippi, ten miles above Rock Island, in the upper rapids of the Mississippi.

Camp Creek, a small stream in Randolph county, that enters the Kaskaskia river on the west side, in five south, eight west.

Camp Creek is an insignificant stream that rises in the prairies which divide Hancock from Warren county, and runs west into the Mississippi.

Camp Creek in Mercer county, rises in the interior of Henry county, runs west and enters Edwards river in township fifteen north, range one west; high, rolling prairie, and Richland grove.

Camp Fork, a branch of Crooked creek in McDonough county, rises in Hickory grove, on the north side of seven north, two west, runs south, and unites with Drowning fork. The land on these creeks is of the first quality.

Canaan is a rich settlement in Shelby county, twelve miles north of Shelbyville: a very superior tract.

Canaan, a post office, in Rock Island county, 20 miles north of Stephenson.

Canteen Creek rises in ridge prairie, in the south part of Madison county, runs a western course, and enters the Cahokia creek in the American bottom. Little Canteen creek rises in St. Clair county, and enters the main creek about the bluffs.

Canteen Settlement, in Madison county, about six miles south of Edwardsville.

Canton, a pleasant town in Fulton county, on the borders of a large prairie, fifteen miles north of Lewistown on section twenty-seven, seven north, four east.

It is a respectable town, has eight or ten stores, a large academy and a charter for a college, and a population of five or six hundred. The country around is high, undulating, fertile and healthy, with a due mixture of timber and prairie.

Canton Prairie, in Fulton county, commences near Spoon river and runs northward, dividing the waters that fall into Spoon river on the left, from those that enter the Illinois on the right, till it becomes lost in the interminable prairies on Rock river. At Canton it is from two to three miles in width, dry, undulating, and inexhaustibly rich. Further north it becomes inferior.

Cantrill's Creek rises on the eastern side of Sangamon county, runs west, and enters Sangamon river about fifteen miles above Salt Fork. The land on this creek is rather level, the soil rich, and about equally divided into timber and prairie.

Cape au Gris. A small French settlement of this name, (which means *Cape of Grit or Grindstone,* from the rocks near,) was formed on the Mississippi, above the mouth of the Illinois, at the most southern bend of the river in Calhoun county, about forty years since. In 1811, it consisted of about twenty families, who had a village on the bank of the river, and cultivated a common field of about five hundred acres in the prairie, one mile from the river. They were driven off by the Indians during the last war with Great Britain. The American population began to enter this county, in 1818.

CARLINVILLE, the seat of justice of Macoupin county, is situated on the north side of the Lake Fork of the Macoupin, in a beautiful prairie.

It is on section twenty-eight, ten north, seven west of the third principal meridian.

Carlinville has several stores, one grocery, two lawyers, two physicians, and about 80 families, and is improving rapidly. The state roads from Vandalia to Carrollton, and from Springfield to Alton, intersect at this place.

It is fifty-five miles northwest from Vandalia, forty-five miles southeast from Jacksonville, forty-five miles southwest from Springfield, thirty-five east of Carrollton, thirty-five miles north from Edwardsville, and thirty-five northeast from Alton. The country around Carlinville is proportionably divided into timber and prairie.

A theological Seminary, under patronage of the Presbyterian Synod of Illinois is about to be established at this place, and the railroad from Alton to Springfield will pass through it.

CARLYLE, the seat of justice for Clinton county, is situated on the west side of the Kaskaskia river, 215 miles by water above its mouth, and on the Vincennes and St. Louis road.

It was laid out as a town site, in 1818, on section eighteen, two north, two west, on elevated ground, on the border of a large prairie. The intersection of several public roads from different parts of the state, gives it an appearance of life and business, rarely to be seen in a place so remote from commercial advantages.

Carlyle contains five stores, three taverns, a grist and saw mill by water power, and forty families. The court house is of wood.

CARMI, the seat of justice of White county, situated on the west bank of the Little Wabash, and nearly in the centre of the county. It is surrounded by lands of a good quality, and an extensive settlement, and is in latitude thirty-eight degrees five minutes north, eighty miles southeast of Vandalia. It is now in an improving condition, has four stores, a saw and flouring mill, and a neat brick court house, forty feet square, with a cupola, the whole painted and neatly finished.

Carmi has many good framed houses, and about fifty families, 2 lawyers, and 3 physicians.

Carolus, a post office in Vermilion county, about twenty miles from Danville, west of south, and on the mail route from Vincennes to Chicago.

CARROLLTON, the seat of justice for Greene county, is a flourishing and pleasant village, situated on the borders of String prairie, nearly equidistant from Macoupin and Apple creeks, and on the dividing line of sections twenty-two and twenty-three, ten north, and twelve west.

It has 17 stores, 6 groceries, 2 taverns, 7 lawyers, 6 physicians, 4 ministers of the gospel, 2 male and 2 female schools, 2 steam flouring mills, 2 steam saw mills, one tannery, and about 1000 inhabitants.

The court house is neatly built of brick; forty-four by forty-six feet, two stories, with a handsome spire.

Around Carrollton is a beautiful country, tolerably level, rich soil, suitably proportioned into timber and prairie, and densely populated with industrious and thriving farmers.

Here are Presbyterian, Baptist, Methodist and Reformer societies.

Houses of worship for the Baptists, Reformers, and Methodists are erected, and the Presbyterians are preparing to build.

Improved farms around Carrollton sell for ten, fifteen, and twenty dollars per acre. The houses mostly are framed, or of brick, built in a plain but convenient style.

Carter's Settlement, near the south part of McDonough county, twelve miles from Macomb, on the road to Rushville. The land is gently undulating, soil rich, timber and prairie proportioned, and an extensive settlement.

It is in the south part of four north, two west, between the heads of Sugar creek and Grindstone fork. This is the oldest settlement in the county.

CARTHAGE, the seat of justice for Hancock county, is situated in the prairie, one mile from timber between the head waters of Bear and Long creeks, and nine miles from the Mississippi, on the northwest quarter of section nineteen, township five north, in range six west. The town was laid off by commissioners in March, 1833, and about one hundred lots sold the following June; averaging about thirty dollars each. It now contains three stores, one grocery, three carpenters, one blacksmith, two cabinet makers, one wheelwright, one tavern, one brick maker, one physician; but no lawyer.

The adjoining prairie is dry, and beautifully undulating. The timber adjacent is excellent. Good water in all this region is obtained by digging wells from fifteen to twenty-five feet deep. Coal is near and in abundance. Since the sale of lots, property has risen in value about fifty per cent.

Cass Post Office is in Cook county, 22 miles from Chicago, on the road to Ottawa.

Casey's Grove is fifteen miles northeast from Jacksonville, on the road to Beardstown. It is a small grove of from five to six hundred acres on Clay creek.

Casey's Prairie, in Jefferson county, adjoining Mount Vernon, is five miles long and two miles broad; surface tolerably level, soil second rate, and the population consists of about 130 families.

Cash river, a stream in the southern part of the state, which is formed from several branches, and a series of ponds that exist in Union and Johnson counties. These unite in Alexander county, through which the main stream follows a devious course, at one time approaching within a mile and a half of the Mississippi, and again approaching near the Ohio, till it empties its waters into the latter river, at Trinity, six miles above its mouth.

One of its principal branches rises in Union county, and forms the " Scatters of Cash," which see.

Another source of its waters is in Johnson county, in a series of ponds which are connected with the waters of Big Bay creek, in Pope county. The outlet of these ponds is known by the name of *Pond Slough.*

The alluvions of Cash river, where not inundated, are wide, of a rich soil, and heavily timbered.

Cato, a post office on the west side of Clay county, and on the Vincennes and St. Louis stage roads.

Cat Tail Swamp, is in Whiteside county, and connects the waters of the Mississippi and Rock river. It is navigable for small craft at some seasons.

Cave-in-Rock. This natural curiosity, well known to all the navigators of the Ohio river, is situated on the bank of the Ohio, where the dividing line between Pope and Gallatin counties strikes the river. Such caves and piles of rock, as are described in the following sketch, are called by the Indians *Mon-e-to*—a name spelled *Man-i-teau*, by the French, and sometimes *Mon-it-to* by other authors. It signifies "*the residence of a spirit*," either good or bad.

There are several Mon-e-toes in Illinois, Missouri, and other western states. One is at the precipices of the Mississippi adjoining Lower Alton. Two more that give names to streams in Boone and Coles counties, Missouri. The Indians relate some wild and extravagant legends of the freaks of these imaginary beings at their " residences," and they usually propitiate the favour of the Mon-e-to, by liberal offerings, and the firing of guns, as they pass his habitation.

The one at the head of this article, known to Americans by the name *Cave-in-rock*, was long the rendezvous of a class of beings, far more formidable and dangerous to the whites, than the Indian Mon-e-toes.

In 1797, it was the place of resort and security to Mason and his gang of robbers; who plundered and murdered the crews of boats, while descending the Ohio. It still answers as a temporary residence for those who need shelter while on the river. The rock is limestone abounding with shells.

The following description of this cave is given by Thaddeus M. Harris, an English tourist, made in the spring of 1803, a writer who has done justice to the West in his descriptions generally.

"For about three or four miles before you come to this place, you are presented with a scene truly romantic. On the Illinois side of the river, you see large ponderous rocks piled one upon another, of different colours, shapes and sizes. Some appear to have gone through the hands of the most skilful artist; some represent the ruins of ancient edifices; others thrown promiscuously in and out of the river, as if nature intended to show us with what ease she could handle those mountains of solid rock. In some places, you see purling streams winding their course down their rugged front; while in others, the rocks project so far, that they seem almost disposed to leave their doubtful situations. After a short relief from this scene, you come to a second, which is something similar to the first; and here, with strict scrutiny, you can discover the cave.

"Before its mouth stands a delightful grove of cypress trees, arranged immediately on the bank of the river. They have a fine appearance, and add much to the cheerfulness of the place.

"The mouth of the cave is but a few feet above the ordinary level of the river, and is formed by a semicircular arch of about eighty feet at its base, and twenty-five feet in height, the top projecting considerably over, forming a regular concave. From the entrance to the extremity, which is about 180 feet, it has a regular and gradual ascent. On either side is a solid bench of rock; the arch coming to a point about the middle of the cave, where you discover an opening sufficiently large to receive the body of a man, through which comes a small stream of fine water, made use of by those who visit this place. From this hole, a second cave is discovered whose dimensions, form, etc., are not known. The rock is of limestone. The sides of the cave are covered with inscriptions, names of persons, dates, etc."*

The trees have been cut down and the entrance into the cave exposed to view.

Cedar Creek post office is in Warren county, section thirty-five, township twelve north, range three west, and about seven miles northwest from Monmouth.

Cedar Creek, in Adams county, which rises in one south, eight west, runs west, and enters Boston bay.

A saw and grist mill has been erected on this stream and the land contiguous is good.

Cedar Creek, in Johnson county, rises in the northeastern part, runs south, and enters Big bay creek. It has large, abrupt bluffs, covered with cedar, and a settlement near it.

Cedar Creek, a branch of Big Muddy river in Jackson county, rises in Union county, and runs first north, and then a western course, and enters Muddy river twelve miles above its mouth. This creek has high bluffs towards its mouth, which abound with cedar.

The country is broken, timbered, well watered with springs, and contains about one hundred families. The main settlement is six miles from Brownsville.

Cedar Fork, a branch of Crooked creek, in the northwest corner of Schuyler county, runs through a dry and rather hilly tract of country.

Cedar Fork of Henderson river rises in the great prairie between Henderson and Spoon rivers and taking a northwestern course, enters the main Henderson. The land along its borders is first rate, and begins to receive cultivation from an industrious settlement.

Centerville, called also " Virginia Centerville," a settle-

---

* Harris's Tour, etc., Boston, 1805.

ment at the intersection of the base line of the fourth principal meridian, with the boundary line betwixt Adams and Schuyler counties. Excellent prairie and timbered land, undulating, healthy, and watered by the head branches of McKee's and crooked creeks.

A post office is here called *Daviston*, within Schuyler county, twenty-five miles from Rushville.

Centerville, a post office in Wabash county, situated five miles northwest from Mount Carmel.

CHARLESTON, the seat of justice for Coles county, is situated on the border of the Grand prairie, two and a half miles from, and on the west side of, the Embarras river, on section eleven, township twelve north, nine east. The surface around is tolerably level, the soil fertile, and the settlements already considerable, will soon be extensive. It has three stores, three groceries, and about twenty-five families. It was laid out in 1831, and the first sale of lots took place in that year.

Charter's Grove, a small tract of timber on the waters of Kishwaukee in Kane county.

Chatham, a post office in Sangamon county, north of Sangamon river, and on the road from Springfield to Havanna.

Cheyney's Grove, a settlement near the head waters of the Sangamon, on the east of McLean county, twenty-three north, six east. This timber is an island in the great prairie, of three or four square miles, twenty-five miles east of Bloomington, and on the road to Danville. The population is 24 families.

Cherry Grove, a settlement in St. Clair county, eight miles northeasterly from Belleville, with a dense population of Germans.

Cherry Grove, a post office, in Jo Daviess county.

Chester, a town on the bank of the Mississippi river, in Randolph county, and about two miles below the mouth of the Kaskaskia river. It is situated on an elevated strip of bottom land at the foot of the bluffs and is a commercial depot for the country back.

Exports by steamboats for 1836, $150,000; imports,

130,000. It has five stores, three groceries, one tavern, one physician, two ministers of the gospel, four warehouses, one steam saw and grist mill, one castor oil factory, and 280 inhabitants.

CHICAGO, the seat of justice for Cook county, is situated on a river or bay of the same name, at the junction of North and South branches, and from thence to lake Michigan. The town is beautifully situated on level ground, but sufficiently elevated above the highest floods, and on both sides of the river.

Its growth, even for western cities, has been of unparalleled rapidity. In 1832 it contained five small stores, and 250 inhabitants. In 1831, there were four arrivals from the lower lakes, two brigs and two schooners, which was sufficient for all the trade of the northeastern part of Illinois, and the northwestern part of Indiana. In 1835 there were about 267 arrivals of brigs, ships and schooners, and 9 of steamboats, and brought 5015 tons of merchandise and 9400 barrels of salt. The value of merchandise imported equal to two and a half millions of dollars, besides a vast number of emigrant families, with their furniture, provisions, &c. Owing to the vast influx of emigration, the exports have been but small. There are about 60 stores, 30 groceries, 10 public houses, 23 physicians, 41 lawyers, five ministers and about 5000 inhabitants.

The Presbyterians, Methodists, Baptists, Episcopalians, and Roman Catholics, each have houses of worship. The harbor constructed by the United States government is now nearly completed and will afford one of the safest and best on the northern lakes.

Chicago is now an incorporated city, under the usual municipal regulations. It has one or more insurance companies, fire companies, water works for the supply of the city from the lake, several good schools and a respectable academy, three printing offices that publish weekly papers and mechanics of every description.

The natural position of the place, the enterprise and capital that will concentrate here, with favorable prospects for health, must soon make this place the emporium of trade and business for all the northern country.

Back of the town, towards the Des Plaines, is a fertile prairie, and for the first three or four miles, elevated and dry.

Along the north branch of the Chicago, and the lake shore, are extensive bodies of fine timber. Large quantities of white pine exist in the regions towards Green bay, and about Grand river in Michigan, from which lumber in any quantities is obtained and conveyed by shipping to Chicago. Yellow poplar boards and plank are brought across the lake from the St. Joseph's river.

The mail in post coaches from Detroit, arrives here tri-weekly, and departs for Galena, for Springfield, Alton, and St. Louis, and for Danville and Vincennes.

The United States owns a strip of elevated ground between the town and lake, about half a mile in width, on which Fort Dearborn and the light house are situated, but which is now claimed, as a pre-emption right, and is now in a course of judicial investigation.

Chicago, the stream or bay, on which the town of Chicago is situated. It is made by *North* and *South* branches, which form a junction in the upper part of the town, about three fourths of a mile from the lake. The Chicago resembles a vast canal, from fifty to seventy-five yards wide and from fifteen to twenty-five feet deep. Northerly and easterly storms throw the cool waters of the lake into this channel, and raise it about three feet.

North Branch, which is the largest, rises a short distance above the boundary line, and near the lake, and runs parallel with the lake shore a southerly course, and is navigable for small boats. Its banks are well timbered, and the land fertile.

In spring floods, its waters, in one or two places, flow across the prairie and commingle with those of Des Plaines.

South Branch rises in an opposite direction, in the prairies towards the Saganaskee swamp, runs a northern direction about twenty miles, and forms a junction with the *North* branch, in the town of Chicago. The timber is rather scarce on South branch.

Chillicothe, a town site and 20 or 30 families, in Peoria county at the upper end of Peoria lake.

Chippewa, a town site in Madison county, directly opposite the mouth of the Missouri. A steam mill and several buildings are going up.

Choteau's Island, is in the Mississippi river, in the southwestern part of Madison county. It is four miles long, and a mile and a half wide, and has several families and farms on it. In extreme high floods the water of the river nearly covers it.

Christian Settlement, see *Allison's Prairie.*

Christy's Prairie, sometimes called *Lewis's Prairie,* is in Lawrence county ten miles west of Lawrenceville, moderately rolling, and good second rate land. Population 150 families.

Clary's Grove is a beautiful tract of timber and flourishing settlement, in Sangamon county, eighteen miles northwest from Springfield, and surrounded with excellent prairie. The timber is three or four miles in diameter, consisting of oaks, sugar maple, walnut, hickory, linden, elm, locust, and various other species. Clary's creek issues from this grove, runs northwesterly, and enters the Sangamon river near the corner of Morgan county.

Little Grove is a smaller tract contiguous to Clary's Grove; timber and prairie of the same quality.

Clayton is a town site on the east side of Adams county, on section thirty-five, township one north, range five west.

Clay Creek rises in the prairies in the northeastern part of Morgan county, passes through two lakes in the bottom, and enters the Illinois river below Beardstown.

Clay Lick, a branch of Cedar creek, in Union county. The land is hilly, and heavily timbered.

Clay Prairie, in Clark county, lies west from Union Prairie, and eight miles southwest from Darwin. It contains a large settlement.

Clear Creek, a small stream that rises in the prairies near Paris, Edgar county, and leaving the county at its

16

southeast corner, passes across a strip of Indiana, and enters the Wabash. It is a mill stream, and the land on each side is good.

Clear Creek, a small stream in Putnam county, ten miles south of Hennepin. Along its banks are fine timber, and the adjoining prairies are excellent.

Clear Creek, a stream that rises in Union county, runs south and enters the Mississippi in the northwestern part of Alexander county. One branch rises in the northern part of Union, the other in the neighbourhood of Jonesboro'.

Clear Creek, in Sangamon county, rises in the prairies between Salt creek and the North Fork, runs a southwestern course, and enters the Sangamon river near the junction of the North and South Forks. This is a good mill stream; the country on its borders rather level, timber good, considerable prairie, and a population of 200 or 300 families.

Clear Creek, a small stream in Morgan county, that passes through the narrows and enters the Illinois river below Beardstown.

Clear Creek, post office, is at Mechanicsburg, 14 miles east of Springfield, and on the road to Decatur.

Clear Lake, an expansion of water in the American bottom, St. Clair county, about ten miles westerly from Belleville.

Clendening's Settlement, in Greene county, six miles southwest of Carrollton.

Clifton, a post office on Sugar creek, Clinton county.

Clifton, on the bank of the Mississippi, four miles above Alton. Here is a landing, a steam saw mill, an excellent free stone quarry, and a quarry of water cement lime stone, and a town site.

Clinton, a town site, post offices and half a dozen families, in the northern part of Macon county, 24 miles from Decatur.

Clinton Hill is three miles north of Belleville, in St. Clair county, and the residence of John Messenger, Esq. It is an elevated timbered tract, containing some excellent springs, and a valuable stone quarry. The Richland Baptist church have their house of worship here.

Clio, a post office in the northwest corner of Pike county, 22 miles northwest from Pittsfield.

Coal Banks, in the bluffs of St. Clair county, east side of the American bottom, and seven miles from St. Louis ferry.

Several beds have been opened along the bluffs, within three miles. The coal is bituminous, burns well, and appears to be inexhaustible. About 300,000 bushels are now taken to St. Louis annually, and the demand for it is rapidly increasing.

Coal Creek, in Schuyler county, heads near Crane creek, runs east, and enters the Illinois, four miles above Beardstown.

Coal Creek, in the northwest part of Putnam county, 3 miles west of French grove, and runs into swamps. Here is coal in abundance and a beautiful grove of timber.

Cochran's Grove, a post office and settlement in Shelby county, ten miles east of Shelbyville.

Coffee Creek, an inconsiderable stream in Wabash county, that enters the Wabash river, six miles below Mount Carmel. A settlement of the same name is along its course. It is a timbered country, undulating, and broken.

Cold Prairie is in the American bottom, in St Clair county, on the road from St. Louis to Belleville.

Cold Spring Settlement and post office is in Shelby county, on the road from Vandalia to Shelbyville, twelve miles south of the latter place. The land is second rate, and proportioned into timber and prairie. This was formerly called *Wakefield's Settlement*.

Collinsville, a village, post office, and settlement, in the south part of Madison county.

Here is a store, a large mill for sawing and grinding, and several mechanics. A meeting house and Presbyterian church of fifty members, a large Sabbath school, and a body of sober, moral and industrious citizens, render this an interesting settlement.

Columbus, a town near the centre of Adams county, of 40 or 50 families.

Columbo Creek rises in Perry county, runs a southeast course, and enters Big Beaucoup, in Jackson county.

Columbus, a town site in Randolph county, near the Flat prairie, eighteen miles east of Kaskaskia, on section one, five south, six west. Here is an academy, a congregation of Reformed Presbyterians, and an industrious and large settlement.

The post office is called " *Shannon's Store.*"

Commerce, a town, landing and post office on the Mississippi, in Hancock county, 16 miles northwest of Carthage, and at the head of the Lower rapids, in seven north, one west. It has two stores, one grocery, and 12 or 15 families.

Compton's Prairie, in Wabash county, twelve miles west of Mount Carmel. This is a small, rich, level prairie, inclined to be wet, and has twenty-five or thirty families.

Concord, a post office and settlement, sometimes called "Slocumb's," in White county, between the Little and Big Wabash, below Big prairie.

Concord, a town site on the Iroquois river, opposite Iroquois town. It has a steam saw and grist mill, and two or three families.

Coon Creek, a branch of the North Fork of the Kishwaukee in Kane county. It rises in township forty north, range four east, and runs west.

Coonsville, a small creek and settlement, on the south side of Apple creek, in Greene county, and six miles northwest from Carrollton.

Coop's Creek, a branch of the Macoupin, in Macoupin county. It rises in the prairies towards the head of Cahokia creek, runs a northwesterly course, and enters the main stream below the forks. Timber and prairie, undulating and rich.

Copperas Creek, in Fulton county, towards the eastern part. It rises near Canton, runs a southeastern course, and enters the Illinois river in six north, five east. Much of it is a timbered tract; some good prairie, and a large settlement.

Cottonberger's Settlement, on Salt creek, in the northwest part of Macon county, eighteen miles north from Decatur.

Cotton Hill Prairie is in Sangamon county, between South Fork and Horse creek, twelve miles south of Springfield.

Court Creek runs through Knox county, from northwest to southeast, and enters Spoon river.

Covington was formerly the seat of justice of Washington county, but after its division in forming Clinton, this place was left in the northwest corner of the county, and now contains half a dozen families. It is situated on the left bank of the Kaskaskia river, in section thirty-three, township one north, three west. Should the contemplated improvements of the Kaskaskia river be carried forward so as to be navigated by steam, Covington may become a place of some importance.

It is fourteen miles from Nashville.

Cownover's Branch, in Morgan county, rises at the head of Jersey prairie, and enters Indian creek near Smart's mill.

Cox's Grove, a small body of timber on the line of Cass and Sangamon counties.

Cox's Prairie, northeast of Brownsville, in Jackson county, near Big Beaucoup, contains about four sections of good rolling land.

Crab Orchard, a small creek that rises in the south part of Franklin county, passes into Jackson, and enters the Big Muddy, fifteen miles above Brownsville. The country adjoining is level and good, and the settlement has forty or fifty families.

Crawfish Creek, a small stream in Wabash county, that enters the Wabash river six miles above Mount Carmel. The adjacent country is sterile and broken.

Crawford's Creek is an insignificant stream in Adams county, containing excellent land and timber. It enters the south prong of Bear creek.

Crane Creek, a small stream in Schuyler county, which rises near Rushville, runs south through a timbered region, and enters the Illinois a few yards above the mouth of Crooked creek.

Crane Creek, a trifling stream that enters the Sangamon river from the north side, below Miller's ferry.

Crane Creek, in Whiteside county, rises near the south fork of Plum creek, runs west, then south, and enters Rock river fifteen or twenty miles below Dixon's ferry, near the foot of the second rapids. Its length is about twenty-five miles. The timber near it is in groves, and the country generally the finest for farming purposes. It is a good mill stream.

Crooked Creek, on the military tract, from its size, length, and number of its branches, should be called a river; but it is not our province to make or alter names. The term "creek" is applied to this stream on the maps, and in the vocabulary of the country. It rises in numerous branches in McDonough and Hancock counties, and near the borders of Warren, runs a southern course through McDonough and Schuyler counties, and enters the Illinois in section thirteen, one south, one west, six miles below Beardstown. It can easily be made navigable some distance. No better land can be found in Illinois than the country in general watered by this stream; and the many small tributaries emptying into it from the east and west not only afford many mill seats, but apportion the timber and prairie so nearly equal as to render almost every tract capable of immediate settlement. It is to be regretted that much of the land in this section of the country is owned by non residents, and that it is held at prices much too high to suit the circumstances of settlers, or the relative value of land in this state.

The country generally on Crooked creek is gently undulating, dry soil, inexhaustibly rich, and where timber exists it is of excellent quality. Here are found oaks of different species, walnut, sugar maple, linden, hackberry, hickory, cherry, honey locust, mulberry, elm, ash, and various other growth common to the state. The soil is an argillaceous mould, from one to four feet deep. Near the mouth of Crooked creek is an extensive bottom on the Illinois, inundated in high water, but affording an extensive range for stock during the greatest part of the year.

Bituminous coal is found in great abundance along this stream and its tributaries, with several quarries of free stone.

Crooked Creek, in Marion county, rises in the Grand prairie near Salem, runs a southwesterly course, and enters the Kaskaskia river above Covington.

Crooked Creek, an insignificant stream and branch of the Little Wabash, in White county, eight miles above Carmi.

It is a timbered region, and the settlement is large.

Crow Creek rises in the north part of McLean county, passes through the southwestern part of La Salle, and enters the Illinois river in Putnam county below Hennepin.

There is a fine skirt of timber and much good prairie along its borders.

Crow Creek, a small stream in Putnam county that enters the Illinois river from the west side. It rises in Crow grove, (Boyd's) and runs an east course.

Crow Grove, or Boyd's settlement, forty miles above Peoria, on the stage road to Galena. It is a beautiful tract of country, in fourteen north, eight east from the fourth principal meridian, and thirteen miles west of Hennepin.

Crow Meadow post office is in Putnam county, on the road from Peoria to Ottawa.

Crow Prairie lies near the Illinois river, in Putnam county, on the east side, twelve miles below Hennepin. It is six miles long and three miles wide, good soil, and timber around it.

Crow Prairie is in Putnam county, on the west side of the Illinois river. It is twelve miles long, four miles wide, and dry, rich, farming land.

Cumberland, a post office on the National Road, 6 miles east of Vandalia.

Curran, a post office in Gallatin county, 13 miles northwest from Equality.

Cutler's Settlement, in Coles county, eight miles northeast from Charleston, on the east side of the Embarras. The soil, both of the timbered land and prairie, is good, and the settlement contains from forty to fifty families.

Cypress, a sluggish creek in Gallatin county, between Equality and Shawneetown, which runs into the Saline creek.

The land in the vicinity is generally good and heavily timbered.

Crystal Lake, a beautiful sheet of water in McHenry county, with gravelly banks and a delightful prospect.

Dad Joe's Grove, so called from Joseph Smith, but more commonly known to the people, by the euphonious name of "*Old Dad*." It is in Putnam county, section four, eighteen north, nine east.

DANVILLE, the seat of justice for Vermilion county, is situated on the Vermilion river of the Wabash, on section eight, in township nineteen north, and in range eleven west from the second principal meridian.

It is on a dry, sandy, and elevated surface, surrounded with heavy timber on the east, north, and west, but open to the prairie on the south.

It has fourteen stores, three groceries, three taverns, five lawyers, six physicians, various mechanics, a public land office for this district, and a printing office from which issues weekly the "*Danville Enquirer*, and 700 inhabitants.

The Methodists, Baptists, and Presbyterians each have congregations. There are about 120 families. The country around is populous, and rich land.

DARWIN, the seat of justice of Clark county. It is situated on the Wabash, in section twenty-seven, ten north, eleven west from the second principal meridian, adjoining Walnut prairie, and contains about twenty families.

Daviston Post Office is at the place where the base line of the fourth principal meridian crosses the dividing line of Adams and Schuyler counties, twenty-five miles south of west from Rushville on the road to Quincy.

Dawson's Grove, called sometimes "*Old Town Timber*,"

in McLean county, twelve miles east from Bloomington, and at the heads of Kickapoo and Salt creek, in twenty-three north, and three and four east. The road from Pekin to Danville passes through this grove. It is long, and intersected with some barrens. Timber principally oak with some sugar maple. The prairie around it is very rich.

Dead Man's Grove, in Coles county, six miles west of Charleston. It is almost circular, about two miles in diameter, and contains three or four sections of indifferent timber, surrounded with a rich and undulating prairie, and is monopolised by two or three families. It receives its name from the circumstance of a man perishing here with cold several years since. The old Kickapoo towns were adjoining this grove.

Deaton's Mill, one of the first settlements in Morgan county, on the Mauvaiseterre, three miles northwest from Jacksonville. Here is a steam mill and a large and flourishing settlement.

Deausix, a trifling stream, and branch of the Kaskaskia river, in the southeastern part of St. Clair county.

Decker's Prairie, a small tract of second rate, undulating land, in Wabash county, twelve miles northeast from Mount Carmel, with about twenty-five families.

DECATUR, the seat of justice for Macon county, is situated on the west side of the North Fork of Sangamon river, and on the borders of an extensive prairie. It is on the northeast quarter of section fifteen, in sixteen north, two east from the third principal meridian. It is dry, elevated, and bids fair for health. The country around is elevated, rich, and has a fine settlement.

Decatur has three stores, several mechanics and about thirty families.

Delhi, a post office and town site in the south part of Greene county, 22 miles from Carrollton. It was formerly called "*Lurton's.*"

Des Plaines River [*Riviere des Plaines*, Fr.] rises in the Wisconsin territory, a few miles above the boundary line of Illinois, and about six miles from lake Michigan. It runs a south course, generally over a bed of limestone rock, and forms one of the prominent branches of the Illinois river, by its junction with the Kankakee.

Groves of timber are found on its banks, and interspersed through the vast prairie region. The country along its borders is rapidly populating, notwithstanding the apparent deficiency of timber.

In many places along the Des Plaines rock may be easily obtained both for fencing and building. The country is well watered, the streams perennial, and the soil rich, and covered with luxuriant herbage. It is frequently written and pronounced *Aux Plaines* or *O'Plane*.

Devil's Anvil is a singular rock, of considerable elevation, and the top jutting over its base, near the road from Equality to Golconda. The surrounding country is very hilly, with rocky precipices, and exhibits all the desolation and wildness of a mountainous region.

Devil's Oven is a singular promontory of sand rock that projects into the Mississippi, in Jackson county, one mile above the *Grand Tower*. It has a cave resembling the mouth of a mammoth oven, to be seen from the river.

Diamond Grove, a most beautiful tract of timber in Morgan county, two miles southwest from Jacksonville. It is elevated above the surrounding prairie, and contains 700 or 800 acres, and surrounded with beautiful farms.

Diamond Grove Prairie, in Morgan county, south and adjacent to Jacksonville. It is four miles in extent, rich soil, undulating, dry surface, and mostly covered over with fine farms.

Dickerson's Lake is in the Illinois bottom, in Morgan county, near the bluffs.

Dillard's is a large settlement in Gallatin county, eight miles northwest of Shawneetown. The land generally is good.

Dillon's Post Office is in the town of Liberty, Tazewell county. Here is a large settlement called Dillon's.

Dixon's Ferry, and post office in Ogle county, on Rock river, on the stage road from Peoria to Galena.

The country around is excellent, but there is a deficiency of timber for dense settlements. Formerly called *O'Gee's Ferry*.

Dixonville, a town site at Dixon's Ferry, on the south side of Rock river, in Ogle county. It contains 2 stores, 2 taverns, 1 grocery, a steam saw mill, 10 or 12 families, and is a pleasant site. Here the stage roads from Chicago by Napiersville:—from Ottawa by Troy grove;—and from Peoria by Windsor and Princeton all concentrate, and pass into Galena. Rock river here is 206 yards wide and is crossed by a rope ferry boat.

Dolson's Prairie is on the west side of Clark county, six miles wide, and twice as long, level, considerably wet and a rather thin and clay soil.

Donohue's Settlement is in the northeast corner of Jefferson county, on Adams's creek, ten miles from Mount Vernon. It is mostly a timbered tract, and has twenty or thirty families.

Downing's Settlement, in Bond county, nine miles south of Greenville. It is on the waters of Beaver creek, and is well furnished with timber and prairie.

Douglass, a post office on the east side of Macoupin county fifteen miles northeast from Carlinville.

Dresden, a town site near the junction of the Des Plaines and Kankakee, and on the line of the canal. It has one store and two or three families.

Drewry's Creek, a branch of Crab Orchard. It rises in Union County, runs a devious course northeasterly into Jackson county, and has a settlement of fifteen or twenty families. The land timbered, and second rate soil.

Driftwood, a post office in Iroquois county, on the road from Danville to Chicago.

Drowning Fork, in McDonough county. It rises in the prairies six north, one west, runs a southwestern course, and uniting with other branches, forms Crooked creek. It has a large body of excellent timber, surrounded with extensive prairies.

Dry Fork, a small stream in Macoupin county. It rises towards Cahokia creek, runs a northwesterly course, and enters the Macoupin above the forks.

Dry Fork, a branch of Shoal creek, in the northwest part of Bond county.

Dry Grove is a timbered tract in McLean county, in twenty-four north, one east, six miles north of west from Bloomington, and lies at the head of Sugar creek. It is about ten miles long, from east to west, high, dry, and undulating, and contains a settlement of about fifty families.

Dry Point, a small branch of Lake Fork of the Macoupin. The head of the timber is well known on the old road from Edwardsville to Springfield, and is nine north, six west, nine miles southeast from Carlinville.

Duck Grove, a small body of timber north of Holderman's Grove in La Salle county.

Dudley's Settlement, in Coles county, seven or eight miles east from Charleston.

Including *Richwood's*, a fine body of timber south, it is an excellent tract of country, and contains more than 120 families.

Duncanton, a post office in Mantua settlement, in the southwestern part of White county, on the mail road from McLeansboro' to Shawneetown.

Dunwoody's Mill is on Indian creek, Morgan county, eight miles north of Jacksonville,

Du Page, [*Riviere du Page*, Fr.] a beautiful stream in Cook county. It rises in two forks, which unite in the settlement of Fountaindale. One fork rises near the Des Plaines, and runs a western course, and forms a junction with the other fork, which rises towards Fox river. After the junction it runs a southwestern course through groves and prairies, and enters the Des Plaines three miles above its junction with the Kankakee. There are large settlements on this stream at Walker's grove and Fountaindale.

Dutch Church Creek, in Pike county, takes its name from a bluff of a singular shape resembling one of the antiquated buildings of New York in Knickerbocker's days. It rises in the interior, and enters Snycartee.

Dutchman's Creek, a small branch of Cash river, in Johnson county. The land on this creek is excellent, and the settlement extensive.

Dutch Hill, a settlement in the southeast part of St. Clair county, and east of the Kaskaskia river. The land is good, and a mixture of timber and prairie.

Dutch Settlement, in Union county, lies south and in the vicinity of Jonesboro'. The land is good, rolling, and well timbered. The settlement contains probably 200 families and is watered by Clear creek.

Eaton's Mill, is noticed as the name of a settlement in Jasper county, near Crawford, on the west side of the North Fork of the Embarras.

Eagle Creek, a small stream in Gallatin county. It rises in the interior, runs south, and enters the Saline creek near its mouth. Some broken, and some good land, and a large settlement are on this stream.

Eagle Creek, or *L'Aigle creek,* in Monroe county, see *Fountain Creek.*

Eagle Point, a post office in Macoupin county, 16 miles northwest from Carlinville.

East Fork of Cash River rises in Johnson county, twelve south, three east, runs south, by Vincennes, and enters the main stream below the "*Scatters of Cash.*" The land on this stream is excellent. The timber consists of cypress, cedar, walnut, oaks of various species, etc.

East Fork of Kaskaskia River rises on the north side of Marion county, near the waters of the Little Wabash, runs west along the north part of Marion, crosses the northeast corner of Clinton, and enters the Kaskaskia, in the southwest corner of Fayette county. It has a heavy body of excellent timber on its banks; the prairies adjoining are undulating and rich, and the settlements along this water course are extensive.

17

East Fork of Shoal Creek, a stream and a settlement in the eastern part of Montgomery county. The stream rises in a large prairie in the northern portion of the county, runs southwestwardly, and enters the main creek near the south side of Bond county. The settlement extends along the timber which lines its banks and the land is tolerably level and fertile.

East Fork of Silver Creek rises in the northeastern part of Madison county, and unites with the West or main fork a short distance below the Marine settlement.

Edinburg, a town site in Sangamon county, in thirteen north, two west, 28 miles southeast from Springfield. Three stores, one grocery, one tavern, and a dozen families, surrounded with an excellent country along the south fork of Sangamon river.

Edmonson's Prairie, in McDonough county, six miles southwest from Macomb, is from one to two miles wide, ten miles long, and contains twenty-five or thirty families.

EDWARDSVILLE, the seat of justice for Madison county, is situated on sections two, three, and eleven, of township four north, in range eight west of the third principal meridian, twenty-one miles northeast from St. Louis, on the Springfield road, and twelve miles southeast from Alton. It has a court house and jail of brick, a land office for Edwardsville district, seven stores, two taverns, two physicians, four lawyers, a castor oil factory, various mechanics, and about seventy families. Here is also an academy and a commodious building. The Baptists and Methodists each have houses of worship. The inhabitants are generally industrious, intelligent, moral, and a large proportion professors of religion.

The location of Edwardsville is pleasant, on high ground, healthy, and in the centre of a fertile, well watered, and well timbered country, settled with enterprising farmers. It is in latitude thirty-eight degrees forty-five minutes north.

Edwards's Settlement is in the north part of Pike county, on McRaney's creek.

Edwards River rises in the prairies of Henry county, fifteen north, four east, runs west through Mercer county, where it turns south and enters the Mississippi near the Upper Yellow Banks. The country on this river is undulating, the timber in skirts and groves, the prairies large, and a supply of good water.

Eight Mile Prairie, in the southwest corner of Franklin county, eighteen miles southwest from Frankfort, level, and has a dense population. It is from one to two miles in diameter.

Elbridge Post office, in Edgar county, 10 miles from Paris, on the road to Terre Haute.

Elgin, a town site on Fox river, in the south part of McHenry county.

Ellisville, in Fulton county, on the west side of Spoon river, near the north side of seven north, two east. It has three stores, one tavern, a mill and a dozen families.

A large prairie lies west. The land on the river is rather broken and timbered.

Situation twenty miles northwest from Lewistown.

Ellison, a small stream that rises in the prairies of Warren county, runs west, and enters the Mississippi six miles below Henderson river. It has a fine settlement, and a rich body of land on its banks.

Elkheart Grove, in Sangamon county, north of Sangamon river, and about twenty miles northeast from Springfield, in eighteen north, three west. It is a beautiful grove of timber, containing six or seven hundred acres, on the right hand of the great road leading to Peoria, Ottawa, and Chicago. The timber is oak, walnut, linden, hickory, sugar tree, etc.

The prairie adjoining is rich soil, rather wet, and furnishes fine summer and winter range for cattle.

Several families are settled here.

Elkhorn, a stream that rises in Washington county, south of Nashville, runs northwest, and enters the Kaskaskia river. The country on its borders is tolerably level, and has a large settlement. A post office is here.

Elkhorn Grove is in Jo Daviess county, west of Buffaloe grove. It is nine miles long, and from one to three miles wide. A beautiful prairie surrounds it, and Elkhorn creek passes through it.

Elkhorn Creek, in Jo Daviess county. It rises near Red Oak grove, passes through Elkhorn grove, runs southwest, and enters Rock river twenty miles below Dixon's ferry.

Here is a beautiful country, and the timber in groves.

Elk Prairie lies between the little Muddy and Beaucoup creeks, in Perry county, and is about five miles in extent. It is dry and tolerably level; soil second rate, and the settlement contains about twenty-five families.

Elm River, a branch of the Little Wabash. It rises in two heads, in the Twelve Mile prairie, in Clay county, north of the Vincennes road, and taking a southeastern direction, enters the Little Wabash in Wayne county. The west branch of Elm river bears the name of Racoon creek.

Embarras River, (pronounced *Embroy* in Fr.) a considerable stream in the eastern part of the state. It rises in Champaign county, eighteen north, nine east, near the sources of the Kaskaskia, the two Vermilions, and the Sangamon rivers. It runs south through Coles county, receives several smaller streams, enters Jasper, turns southeast across a corner of Crawford, passes through Lawrence county, and enters the Big Wabash, about six miles below Vincennes. The country on the Embarras is various, though there is much good land. Towards its head the prairie greatly predominates, the timber being in groves, and narrow strips along its banks. In Coles county, north of Charleston, the timber is from two to six miles wide. Below that place it gradually widens to the distance of eight or ten miles.

It consists of the various qualities common on this side of the state. Generally the prairies through which it flows are second rate for more than half its length from its mouth. Its bottoms are inundated in very high floods. The main stream and its branches afford many good mill seats. From the vicinity of Lawrenceville to

Vincennes, in high freshets, the Embarras and Big Wabash unite their waters and spread over the country for seven or eight miles in extent. Hence, from this occasional obstruction to travelling on the old " *Vincennes trace*," as the obscure path through the prairies to Kaskaskia was then called, the early French explorers gave the name "*Embarras*" to this stream.

Embarras, a town site in Coles county, one half mile east of the Embarras river, at the junction of the *national road* and the road from Palestine to Shelbyville, twenty miles south of Charleston, and fifty-two miles east of Vandalia. Good springs of water, high, rich, undulating prairie, and abundance of fine timber are said to belong to the conveniences of this location.

Embarras Settlement, in Coles county. I have given this name to an extensive tract of country thinly populated, extending along the west side of the Embarras, and north of Charleston. The quality of the land is on a medium with the rest of Coles county. South of Charleston, and on the same side, the country is thinly settled.

Eminence, a town site near Sugar creek in Tazewell county.

Emmettsburg, a Roman Catholic Irish and German settlement, or hamlet, on the line of the canal, eight miles above Juliet.

English Settlement is in Morgan county, west of Jacksonville, on Cadwell's, Walnut and Plum creeks. There are about one hundred families, mostly from Yorkshire, England, and farmers. They appear to be well pleased with the country, and to be accumulating property.

English Settlement, in the east part of Monroe county, is on Prairie de Long creek, in township three south, eight west. It contains about forty families, amongst whom are a number of English Catholics.

EQUALITY, the seat of justice for Gallatin county, situated on the north side of Saline creek, on section fifteen, nine south, eight east. It has nine stores, four groceries, two taverns, a brick court house forty feet square, two stories high, and neatly finished, a number of mechanics of different trades, and about seventy or eighty families. It is situated in the vicinity of the salt manufactories, fourteen miles south of Shawneetown.

The adjacent country south and west is broken and rough; north and east is much good land.

Elvira Settlement, in Johnson county, on *Lick creek*, a branch of Cash river. It is about fifteen miles northwest from Vienna, and contains thirty or forty families. The land is rich and level.

Essex's Settlement, in the forks of Spoon river, in the western part of Putnam county, townships twelve and thirteen north, in range six east from the fourth principal meridian. The surface is undulating, excellent timber, rich prairie, good water, stone quarries, a saw and grist mill, and about fifty families. The post office is called *Wyoming*.

Estes's Prairie, in Franklin county, fourteen miles north of Frankfort, is level, dry, and has a thin population on its borders.

Evan's Settlement, on the north side, and near the head of Cash river, and on the eastern border of Union county. It has about forty families.

EWINGTON, the seat of justice of Effingham county, is situated on the national road, twenty-nine miles from Vandalia, in a northeastern direction, on the west bank of the Little Wabash river, and on section five, seven north, five east. The site is elevated, and surrounded with timber. Opposite is the bottom land of the Little Wabash, about one fourth or a mile wide, and in high floods occasionally inundated. Ewington will probably become a pleasant village, though but little improvement is yet made.

Ewing's Fork, a branch of the Middle Fork of the Big Muddy river, in Franklin county.

Exeter, a town site and post office on the Mauvaiseterre, in Morgan county, fourteen miles west of Jacksonville. It has a large flouring mill, two or three stores, and about fifteen families, and is surrounded with a large settlement.

Eyman's Settlement, in St. Clair county, four miles southwest of Belleville—a mixture of timber and prairie.

FAIRFIELD, the seat of justice for Wayne county, is on the border of Hargrave's prairie, on section six, township two south, range eight east. It contains three stores, one tavern, a handsome brick court house, and about twenty-five families. Large quantities of castor oil are manufactured at a press located here, belonging to Messrs. Leech & Turney.

Fairfield is a small but pleasant settlement in the northwestern part of Hancock county, in seven north, eight west.

Fairfield a town site in Adams county, on section eleven, township one north, range eight west, and has 10 or 12 families surrounded with a large settlement called Bear creek.

Fair Mount, a pleasant siuation in the Macoupin prairie, Greene county, sixteen miles a little west of south from Carrollton.

Fall Creek is a small stream in Adams county, eight miles long, which enters the Mississippi a few miles below Quincy.

Fancy Creek, a small branch of the Sangamon river. It rises in the prairies, takes a westerly course, and enters the river below the junction of the North and South Forks. The country is level, and the population considerable.

Fancy Farm, a post office in Franklin county, 9 miles east-southeast from Frankfort.

Fanning's Creek, a small branch of Apple creek, eight or ten miles long, in Morgan county, and has a dense population of about two hundred families.

Farm Creek, a small stream in Tazewell county, that runs west and enters the Illinois river opposite Peoria. Its bottoms are rich, bluffs broken, with white oak timber, and occasionally cedar. It is a mill stream.

Farmington, a town site and post office in the northeast corner of Fulton county, on the road from Canton to Knoxville. Elegant, rich, and rolling prairie around.

Fayette, a town site and post office in Greene county, adjoining Macoupin county, on sections twelve and thirteen, township ten north, ten west, and on the road from Alton to Jacksonville. It has two stores and several families.

Fayetteville, a town site on the west side of the Kaskaskia river in St. Clair county, 16 miles southeast from Belleville, long known as Pulliam's ferry. It is on elevated ground and a good situation for a town site.

Fever River, in Jo Daviess county, rises near the Platte Mounds in two branches, the East and West forks, runs a southwesterly course past Galena, and enters the Mississippi seven miles south of that place. It is navigable at all times to Galena by steamboats of any size, and in high water, two miles above. For this distance it is deep and sluggish.

The stream above Galena runs with a swift current over a rocky and gravelly bottom, is full of fine fish, and, like all the streams in this region, it is fed with perennial springs.

In the East Fork settlement, which is twelve miles east from Galena, the timber is scarce, but there is much excellent prairie, and the lead mines are the best in Illinois. Population of farmers and miners about fifty families.

On the West Fork or main creek is a considerable settlement, and some good farms. The alluvion on the stream is fine, and a tolerable supply of timber. This settlement is eight miles in a direct course, and twelve miles the travelled way, northeast from Galena.

Fever river has been incorrectly called *Bean* river (Riviere au Feve, Fr.) We have given its proper name from two traditionary accounts.

The first is, that in early times the Indians were carried off by a mortal sickness, supposed to be the *small pox*. This circumstance gave rise to the name of another creek now called *Small Pox*. The other tradition, and the correct one is, that it derived its name from a French trader by the name of *Le Fevre*, who settled near its mouth.

Finch's Settlement is on a branch of the South Fork of Spoon river, in the southwestern part of Knox county.

Five Mile Grove is in the south part of Cook county, on the road from Hickory creek to Kankakee and Danville.

Flag Creek, a trifling stream in Cook county, that rises in the prairie between Du Page and Des Plaines, runs easterly, and enters Des Plaines below the road from Plainfield to Chicago. The land on its borders rather wet.

Flat Branch rises in Shelby county, runs northward, and empties into the South fork of Sangamon, in the northwest corner of the county. The country prairie and timber, and a settlement of seventy or eighty families. The bed of the stream is rocky.

Flat Prairie, a well cultivated prairie and large settlement in Randolph county, twenty miles east of Kaskaskia, settled chiefly by Reformed Presbyterians, or Covenanters, who have a resident minister and a respectable society.

Flora, a post office in Edgar county, 8 miles east of Paris.

Floria, a town site and settlement in Putnam county, 5 miles east of Hennepin—a delightful situation.

Ford's Ferry, in Gallatin county, on the Ohio, twenty miles below Shawneetown, and twenty-five miles south of Equality. It is on the great road from the southern parts of Kentucky and Tennessee to Illinois and Missouri.

Forked Creek, a small creek in Will county, and branch of the Kankakee.

A post office of the same name is on it.

Forks of Sangamon is the name given to the settlement near the junction, and between the North and South forks of the Sangamon river. It is eight or ten miles south of Springfield. The surface is rather wet, level, considerable prairie land, with large bodies of timber on both streams. Here is a large settlement, and a town has been laid off, called Bolive.

Fork Prairie, in Bond county, between the forks of Shoal creek, and from two to eight miles north of Greenville. It is gently undulating, and surrounded with settlements.

Fork Settlement, in Clinton county, between Shoal creek and the Kaskaskia river, twelve miles southwesterly from Carlyle.

Forks of Spoon River. These are two principal branches that form the heads of this stream, and which for distinction I shall call the *East* and *West* forks.

The *East Fork* rises in fifteen north, six east, runs south, through townships fourteen, thirteen, and twelve, of the same range, where it turns west, and meets the West fork, receiving in its course a number of smaller streams. There is much excellent land on this fork and its branches; prairie predominates, but it is generally dry and rich, with groves and points of timber, and many fine springs.

The *West Fork*, rises in the southeast part of Henry county, in township fourteen north, five east, runs a southeasterly course, and unites with the East fork near the township line between four and five east. The country adjoining is similar to that on the East fork, except that the surface is more undulating. The timber is good, and in considerable bodies. Near the junction of these streams is much excellent timber, with a strip of fertile prairie between. Here is a considerable settlement, a grist and saw mill, and a post office. It is sometimes called *Essex's Settlement*.

Fort Chartres was a large stone fort, built by the French, while in possession of Illinois. It is situated half a mile from the Mississippi, and three miles from Prairie du Rocher, in the northwestern part of Randolph county.

It was originally built by the French in 1720, to defend themselves against the Spaniards, who were then taking possession of the country on the Mississippi. It was rebuilt in 1756. The circumstances, character, form and history of this fort are interesting, but I have not room in this place to give them. Once it was a most formidable piece of masonry, the materials of which were brought three or four miles from the bluffs. It was originally an irregular quadrangle, the exterior sides of which were 490 feet in circumference. Within the walls were the commandant's and commissary's houses, a magazine for stores, barracks, powder magazine, bake house, guard house and prison.

This prodigious military work is now a heap of ruins. Many of the hewn stones have been removed by the people to Kaskaskia. A slough from the Mississippi approached and undermined the wall on one side in 1772. Over the whole fort is a considerable growth of trees, and most of its walls and buildings have fallen down and lie in one promiscuous ruin.

Fort Edwards is situated on the Mississippi in the southern part of Hancock county, five miles below the foot of the Lower rapids, and directly opposite the mouth of the river Des Moines. This was a military post till within a few years past, situated on a high rocky bluff of sand stone, which does not show itself on the surface.

The country back is well timbered for a short distance, is of good soil and is now partially settled. Native *alum* is said to be found in considerable quantities near this site. Opposite the water is deep, the current gentle, and affords a good landing. When the river is low this will be the place to which the produce of the interior will be brought. A town called *Warsaw* is near this place.

Fort Massac, formerly a military post, situated on the Ohio river, on the dividing line of Johnson and Pope counties, eight miles below *Paducah* at the mouth of the Tennessee. " A fort was erected here by the French when in possession of the western country. The Indians, then at war with them, laid a curious stratagem to take it. A number of them appeared in the day time on the opposite side of the river, each of whom was covered with a bear skin and walked on all fours. Supposing them to be bears, a party of the French crossed the river in pursuit of them. The remainder of the troops left their quarters to see the sport.

"In the mean time a large body of warriors, who were concealed in the woods near by, came silently behind the fort, entered it without opposition, and very few of the French escaped the massacre. They afterwards built another fort on the same ground and called it *Massac*, in memory of this disastrous event."*

In 1750 they abandoned the position. After the revolutionary war the Americans repaired or rebuilt it, and kept a garrison here for several years. The buildings are now destroyed. According to Ellicott, the latitude of Fort Massac is 37 degrees 15 minutes north.

Foster's Settlement, in the southeast corner of McDonough county, on the head of Sugar creek.

Foster's Settlement, of sixty or seventy families, lies on Mounse's creek, five miles south of Decatur.

Fountain Creek, a small stream in Monroe county. It rises in New Design settlement, running first northeast, then northwest, and finally bending round to the southwest it enters the Mississippi river in section seven, three south, eleven west. It is also called *Eagle*, and by the early French explorers, *L'Aigle* creek.

Fountain Bluff, frequently called the "*Big Hill*," in Jackson county. It is a singularly formed eminence, or rocky bluff on the Mississippi, six miles above the mouth of the Big Muddy river. It is of an oval shape, eight miles in circumference, and with an elevation of 300 feet. The western side is on the river, and the top is broken, full of sink holes, with shrubs and scattering timber. The north side is nearly perpendicular rock, but the south side is sloping, and ends in a fine rich tract of soil, covered with farms. East is an extensive and low bottom with lakes and swamps.

Fine springs of limpid water gush out from the foot of this bluff on all sides.

North, and along the bank of the Mississippi, is dry and rich alluvion with a line of farms, known by the name of the "Settlement under the Bluff."

---

* See Beck's Gazetteer, Art. *Fort Massac;* and Stoddard's Sketches of Louisiana.

Fountaindale, a flourishing settlement in the forks of the Du Page, Cook county, thirty miles west of Chicago. Here are perennial springs, beautiful timber, rich soil, extensive prairies, and good society of industrious and enterprising farmers. The Methodists and Presbyterians have congregations and constant preaching.

Fountain Green, a town site and post office in Hancock county, on section twenty-eight, township six north, range five west, ten miles northeast from Carthage. A flourishing settlement.

Four Mile Prairie, in Perry county, adjoining Pinckneyville, is seven miles long, and four miles wide. It is an elevated, dry, undulating, and fertile tract, with a dense settlement, and lies between the Big Beaucoup and Little Elm creeks.

Fourteen Mile Prairie, in Effingham county, receives its name from its distance along the national road. It lies east of Ewington, is generally level, but has some dry land and good points of timber.

Fox River, one of the principal branches of the Illinois. It rises in the Wisconsin territory, passes through a series of small lakes about the boundary line, and enters the Illinois river at Ottawa.

Its general course is south. At the boundary line its width is forty-five yards.

Several bodies of fine timber line its banks, especially about the mouth of *Indian Creek* and the *Big Woods*. At the rapids, five miles above its mouth, are most extensive water privileges.

Here the river is from eighty to one hundred yards wide, with the bed and banks of coarse grained sand stone. The rapids are sixteen feet descent, and both sides of the river will admit of mills and machinery for three-fourths of a mile, with inexhaustible supplies of water.

The deficiency of timber near this spot is the only drawback upon it; but inexhaustible bodies of coal are to be found but a few miles distant.

It furnishes a vast amount of water power, and can be

easily made navigable by dams and slack water. From the town of Elgin near the south part of McHenry county, it is a deep sluggish stream, connected with a string of lakes, and is navigable within fifteen miles of Milwaukee. Hence, with small expense, a navigable communication may be opened from Lake Michigan by Milwaukee and Fox river.

Fox River, a tributary of the Little Wabash, dividing the counties of Clay and Lawrence. It rises in Jasper county, runs south, and enters the Little Wabash near the line of Edwards county. The land along its course is about second quality for this portion of the state.

Fox River, in the northeastern part of White county. It is a bayou that puts out from the Big Wabash, runs a few miles, and again enters that river. The late Morris Birbeck, Esq., known as one of the English emigrants to Edwards county, and author of " *Letters from Illinois*," was unfortunately drowned in attempting to swim this stream on horseback.

Fox River post office, is near Fox river in White county.

Frakers, a small settlement between the forks of Spoon river, and the borders of Henry county, thirteen north, four east.

Franklin Grove, in Ogle county, lies between Grand Detour and Winnebago inlet with seven or eight families settled around it.

FRANKFORT is the seat of justice for Franklin county, on section twenty, seven south, three east of the third principal meridian.

It is situated on elevated ground, and has five stores, two groceries, one tavern, with a blacksmith, wagon-maker, saddler, and tanyard, together with a horse mill, a distillery, and 150 inhabitants.

Franklin, a town site and post office in Morgan county, thirteen miles southeast from Jacksonville. It has two stores, one grocery and twenty families.

Frazier's Creek rises near the base line, in Adams county, runs west, and falls into the south prong of Bear creek. Along it are fine farms and a beautiful country.

Free's Settlement is on the borders of a handsome prairie, in the southeastern part of St. Clair county, between the two Mud creeks, eighteen miles from Belleville.

French Grove, in Putnam county, sixteen north, seven east—a small grove settled around; prairie dry and undulating.

French Grove, a small settlement in the northwestern part of Peoria county, on the branches of Spoon river. It contains three or four sections of excellent timber in groves, with abundance of rich, dry rolling prairie around it.

French Settlement, in the southeastern part of Lawrence county, ten miles from Lawrenceville, is a timbered tract, and rather broken. Of the population, which consists of sixty families, about one half are French.

French Village, in St. Clair county, called formerly Little French Village, was formed by settlers from Cahokia about forty years since. It lies on the bottom, near the bluffs, on the road from Belleville to St. Louis, and contains fifteen or twenty families.

Friends Creek, a branch of the North fork of Sangamon, in Macon county, sixteen miles northeast from Decatur. The land is good, and the settlement large.

Funk's Grove, a settlement in McLean county, twelve miles southwest from Bloomington. The grove is roundish in form, contains about eight square miles; and lies on the main branch of Sugar creek. It has an excellent soil, fine water, and is monopolised by a family connection of the name of Funk, from Ohio, who raise large numbers of cattle.

Fulfer's Creek, near the south border of Effingham county, enters the Little Wabash below Brockett's settlement. There is a considerable quantity of good land on its banks, and a settlement of twelve or fifteen families.

Fulton, a town site at the mouth of the Ohio river, where it is contemplated to erect a monument to the memory of Robert Fulton, whose inventive powers in the application of steam to navigation is fast transforming the immense regions of the valley of the Mississippi into the garden of the world.

Mercantile enterprise will undoubtedly yet triumph over the obstructions of nature, and erect a spacious city at the mouth of the Ohio river.

Gagnie, a sluggish stream that runs southwest into the Mississippi, and forms the boundary line between Randolph and Jackson counties.

GALENA is the seat of justice for Jo Daviess county, and the principal town in the lead mine country. It is pleasantly situated on Fever river, and on the fourth principal meridian. It has eighteen or twenty stores, a dozen groceries, four taverns and hotels, a printing office that publishes the "*Gazette,*" a weekly paper, four lawyers, three physicians, two schools, two preachers, a pipe and sheet lead manufactory, a flour and saw mill, a gunsmith, silversmith, saddler, tailor, several carpenters, blacksmiths, brick and stone masons, etc.

There are about three hundred families and ten or twelve hundred inhabitants. Fever river is navigable for steamboats to the town.

Gap Grove, lies in Ogle county, to the north of the road from Dixonville to Buffaloe grove. Three sections of timber.

Garden Prairie, between Richland and Rock creeks, in Sangamon county, is a level, rich, beautiful prairie, two miles wide, and six or eight miles long, fourteen miles northwesterly from Springfield, and contains a population of one hundred and fifty families.

Germany, a settlement of Pennsylvania Germans, in Sangamon county, four miles northeast from Springfield, and near the mouth of Sugar creek.

Geneva is a post office and town site in Morgan county, about ten miles southwest from Jacksonville.

George's Creek heads in the interior of Johnson county, runs south, and enters the ponds between the Big Bay creek and Cash river. The land is tolerably rich, and the settlement contains twenty-five or thirty families.

Georgetown, a post town and village, containing about twenty families and three stores, situated on the north side of the Little Vermilion, in eighteen north, eleven west, in Vermilion county, ten miles south of Danville. A fine country, and flourishing settlements around it.

Georgetown, a town site in Sangamon county, twenty miles northeast from Springfield, between Lake fork and Salt creek, in section nineteen, eighteen north, two west.

Georgetown, in the eastern part of Randolph county, contains one store, two groceries, a mill, and seven or eight families. The post office is called " *Steele's Mill.*"

Gilead, the former seat of justice of Calhoun county, is situated at the foot of the bluffs, three-fourths of a mile from the mouth of Salt Prairie slough, on section eight, eleven south, two west.

It has two stores, and a dozen families.

Gilham's Settlement is in Bond county, nine miles east of north from Greenville.

The land is of inferior quality, consisting of both timber and prairie.

Gilmore's Settlement is on Crooked creek, in Clinton county, on the road to Shawneetown, twelve miles southeast of Carlyle.

Girard, a town site in the northeast part of Macoupin county, on the road from Alton to Springfield.

GOLCONDA is situated on the south side of Lusk's creek and north bank of the Ohio. It is the county seat of Pope, and has three stores, one grocery, two taverns, and about twenty dwelling houses, chiefly framed and brick. The court house is of brick, thirty-six feet square, two stories, with a neat cupola. It is situated on the fractional township thirteen south, in range seven east of the third principal meridian.

Goose Creek enters the North fork of Sangamon, in Macon county, twenty-five miles northeast from Decatur.

Goshen is the oldest settlement in Madison county, along the bluffs, west and southwest of Edwardsville.

Grable's Settlement, in Gallatin county, is sixteen miles west from Equality, on the road to Frankfort.

18*

It is a large settlement, with considerable tracts of good farming land.

Graham's Settlement, in Alexander county, on the north side, twenty-five miles northwest from America. The upland is thin soil, but there is a rich bottom on a branch of Cash river, which runs through this settlement.

Grafton is a town recently laid off, two miles below the mouth of the Illinois, in Greene county. It is situated on a strip of elevated land, under the bluffs, and on the banks of the Mississippi, and has a good landing. It is on fractional section fifteen, township eight north, in range twelve west from the third principal meridian.

Several Islands in the Mississippi make this point the real junction of the Illinois and Mississippi rivers, as to navigation.

The country a few miles back is rich, and becoming densely populated.

Grafton is twenty-four miles from Carrollton, and ten miles from St. Charles, in Missouri, and must soon become a thoroughfare for travelling from the Sangamon country across the Mississippi to St. Charles, and the regions along the Missouri river. It has a post office, several stores and warehouses, 400 or 500 inhabitants, and promises to be a place of considerable business. A charter for a rail road from this place through Carrollton to Springfield has been obtained, the company organised and a portion of the stock taken. A chartered company are about to erect a splendid hotel, and a printing office is to be established here in a few weeks and a weekly paper issued.

Grand Cote, an eminence in a large prairie, in the eastern part of Randolph county.

Grand Detour, a singular bend in Rock river, in Ogle county, five miles above Dixonville. Here a town of the same name has been laid off, and by cutting a canal across the neck of the bend for a short distance, a valuable hydraulic power will be gained. An enterprising company are engaged in the project.

Grand Marais, called also *Clear Lake,* in St. Clair county in the bottom, between the French Village and Cahokia.

Grand Passe, two lakes in the Illinois bottom, at the southwest corner of Greene county, so called by the French explorers of Illinois, from the successive flocks of geese seen flying from the one to the other. They are connected with Apple creek by a stream called Fishing creek.

Granger's Prairie is in the northwest part of Adams county, and is three miles long and from one and a half to mile wide. Very rich land.

Grand Point, a small stream and settlement in Washington county, six miles northeast from New Nashville, and contains about twenty families. The creek runs north and enters Crooked ceek.

Grand Prairie. Under this general name is embraced the prairie country lying between the waters which fall into the Mississippi, and those which enter the Wabash rivers. It does *not* consist of one vast tract, boundless to the vision, and uninhabitable for want of timber; but is made up of continuous tracts, with points of timber projecting inward, and long arms of prairie extending between the creeks and smaller streams. The southern points of the Grand prairie are formed in the northeastern parts of Jackson county, and extend in a northeastern course between the streams of various widths, from one to ten or twelve miles, through Perry, Washington, Jefferson, Marion, the eastern part of Fayette, Effingham, through the western portion of Coles, into Champaign and Iroquois counties, where it becomes connected with the prairies that project eastward from the Illinois river and its tributaries. A large arm lies in Marion county, between the waters of Crooked creek and the East fork of the Kaskaskia river, where the Vincennes road passes through in its longest direction. This is frequently called *the* Grand prairie.

Much the largest part of the Grand prairie is gently undulating; but of the southern portion considerable tracts are flat, and of rather inferior soil. No insurmountable obstacle exists to its future population. No portion of it is more than six or eight miles distant from timber, and coal in abundance is found in various parts. Those who have witnessed the changes produced upon a prairie surface within twenty or thirty years, consider these extensive prairies as offering no serious impediment to the future growth of the state.

Grand Prairie, in Crawford county. The tract of prairie between the Embarras and Wabash rivers, commencing in Crawford county, and running northward through Clark and Edgar into Vermilion county, is called Grand prairie, by the citizens of those counties. It is not of great width, interspersed with long points of timber on the streams, and frequently throwing out arms of prairie land between those streams.

The prairie soil in this region is not equal in quality to that further north and west. With the exception of the sand prairies along the Wabash, the soil is thinner, less undulating, and more inclined to be wet.

Grand Tower, a perpendicular sand rock rising from the bed of the Mississippi, near the Missouri side, and a short distance above the mouth of Big Muddy river. The top is level, seventy or eighty feet high, and supports a stratum of soil on which are found a few stunted cedars and shrubs. Here are indications that a barrier of rock once extended across the Mississippi, and formed a grand cataract. The bed of the river, at a low stage of water still exhibits a chain of sunken rocks. The "*Devils Tea Table*," "*Back Bone*," etc. are names given by the boatmen of the Mississippi to the singularly formed, abrupt, and romantic precipices that line the banks of that river in the vicinity of the Grand Tower.

Grand View, a village in the southwestern part of Edgar county, ten miles from Paris, and on the state road to Vandalia. It is on, and surrounded by a beautiful, rolling rich prairie, near the head waters of Big creek. A post office is here.

Grassy Creek, in Franklin county, a branch of Crab Orchard. Good land.

Graysville, a town of fifteen or twenty families and a convenient landing on the Big Wabash, in the northeast corner of White county, and at the mouth of the Bon Pas creek.

It has 3 stores, 1 grocery, 2 taverns, one steam saw and grist mill and 100 inhabitants. Exports about $100,000; imports, $30,000 per annum.

This is a convenient place of deposit for Edwards county.

Gregory's Settlement, in Clinton county, fifteen miles northwest of Carlyle.

Green Plains, a post office and settlement, in Hancock county 8 miles southeast of Warsaw.

Greenfield, a town site near Lick creek, in Sangamon county, fifteen miles southwesterly from Springfield on sections three and ten, fourteen north, seven west, Heredith's mills are in the vicinity.

Greenfield, a town site in Green county, in String prairie, 10 miles east from Carrollton. It has two stores, a carding machine and a dozen families.

Greenfield, a town site in Putnam county, near the head of the Bureau timber, on section twenty-four, eighteen north, ten east. It has half a dozen houses.

Greenup, a town site and post office, on the National Road east of the Embarras, in Coles county. It has 2 stores, 2 saw and one grist mill and about 20 families.

GREENVILLE, the seat of justice for Bond county, is a pleasant village on the East fork of Shoal creek, on section ten, township five north, in range three west of the third principal meridian.

It has 4 stores, 3 taverns, 3 physicians, 1 lawyer, various mechanics, and 200 inhabitants. The court house is a two story frame building, unfinished.

Green's Settlement, in Bond county, seven miles southwest from Greenville. The country around is proportioned into timber and prairie.

Green River has its rise in the Winnebago and other

swamps in Ogle and Henry counties, runs a west course through Henry county, and enters Rock river in township seventeen north, one west. It is a deep sluggish stream well adapted to navigation and below the swamps has much fine land both timber and prairie.

Griggsville, a town site and post office in Pike county, eight miles northeast from Pittsfield, on sections fifteen and twenty-two, four south, three west. It is four miles west of Phillip's ferry on the Illinois river, on high ground, and on the border of a large, undulating prairie, and surrounded with good settlements.

Grindstone Fork, a branch of Crooked creek, in the south part of McDonough county.

Griswold's Post Office is in Lockwood's settlement, Hamilton county, twenty miles north of Equality.

Gros Point is a promontory that puts into Lake Michigan, twelve miles above Chicago. It is twenty feet high, projects two hundred yards into the lake, rich, timbered land, and settled around.

Groveland, a post office and town site, in Tazewell county, on section twenty-seven, township twenty-five north, range five west, and on the road from Springfield to Peoria.

GUILFORD, the new county seat of Calhoun county, is situated on the west side of the Illinois river, in fractional township eleven south, two west, one mile below and opposite the mouth of the Macoupin. It has been recently laid off and is said to be well situated for business purposes.

A company has been chartered to cut a canal from the Mississippi near Gilead, the former seat of justice, to the Illinois river at Guilford. The distance does not exceed three miles, and by tunneling a short distance under the bluff, it is said the work can be accomplished, and a steamboat canal constructed at comparatively small expense. This communication would save fifty miles navigation from the Illinois river to the Upper Mississippi, and, as the latter is elevated considerably above the former, create an immense water power, which is the object of the company.

Gum's Fort. See *Henderson's Settlement*, Knox county.

Gun Prairie, in Jefferson county, six miles south of Mount Vernon, two miles long, and one mile wide. The land is good, and the settlement contains twenty families.

Hadley's Creek rises in the north part of Pike county, in four south, three west, and enters the Snycartee slough. The land is undulating but good.

Hadley, a post office and settlement, in Will county, eight miles northeast of Juliett, and on the road to Chicago.

Hamburg, a landing on the Mississippi, in Calhoun county, and the residence of John Shaw, Esq., ten miles northwest of Gilead. The landing is said to be good, and the bank high. Here is a post office of the same name.

Hammet's Settlement, in Coles county, on the east side of the Embarras, twenty-two miles north of Charleston. The land is good, generally rolling, and the settlement has twelve or fifteen families.

Hancock Prairie commences above Bear creek, in Adams county. This is an extensive tract of rich prairie, tolerably level, which runs through Hancock county, enters Warren, and stretches between Henderson and Spoon rivers indefinitely north. Its width is various, being from ten to twenty miles.

A principal road to Rock river and northward passes through this prairie.

Hanover, a town site in Tazewell county, on sections seventeen and twenty, township twenty-seven north, range two west, and on the road from Springfield, via Tremont, to Ottawa. A steam mill and several buildings are in process of erection. A charter has been obtained for a college, which is contemplated to be brought into operation by the Baptist Reformers.

Harden's Settlement, in the southeast part of Hancock county, on the head and along the North fork of Bear creek. The land is excellent and well watered, with a tolerable supply of good timber.

Hargrave's Prairie, in Wayne county, adjoining Fairfield. It is about seven miles long and two wide: rolling, and thin soil. Population about one hundred families.

Harkness's Settlement is on the west side of Peoria county, adjoining Fulton, twelve miles west from Peoria.

Harris's Creek rises in the bluffs of the Ohio river, in Gallatin county, runs a north course, and enters Saline creek, fifteen miles below Equality. Much of the land on its borders is rough and broken, interspersed with tracts of good soil.

Harrisonville, the former seat of justice of Monroe county, situated on the east bank of the Mississippi, and nearly opposite Herculaneum. It is a place of very little account, having not more than half a dozen families.

Havanna, a town site and landing on the Illinois river, directly opposite the mouth of Spoon river.

It has an eligible situation on a high sand ridge, fifty feet above the highest floods of the river. It is on section one, township twenty-one north, in range nine west of the third principal meridian.

Havanna is well situated to receive the produce and direct the trade of a pretty extensive country on both sides of the Illinois river, and is on the great thoroughfare from Indiana, by Danville and Bloomington to the counties that lie to the west and north.

Haw Creek is a branch of Spoon river, twenty miles long, that rises in the middle part of Knox county, runs east, and enters Spoon river.

The country on its borders is first rate for settlements, which are forming fast.

It has some good mill seats.

Hawkins Prairie, in Greene county, on the south side of the Macoupin, and nine miles east of south from Carrollton.

Hazel's Settlement is in Pope county, on the road to Vienna.

Head of Apple-Creek is an extensive settlement in the

southeastern part of Morgan county, eighteen miles from Jacksonville.

It is a fertile tract, tolerably level, and has about three hundred families.

Head of Apple River is a settlement in Jo Daviess county, southeast of Galena.

Head of Richland is a fine settlement of fifty or sixty families in Sangamon county, seventeen north, seven west, on Richland creek, fourteen miles northwest from Springfield.

The land is high, dry, undulating and rich.

Here is an excellent flouring mill by ox power, and a carding machine and clothier's works, for dressing cloth.

Head of Silver Creek, a settlement in the northeastern part of Madison county, surrounded with large prairies.

Head of Wood River, a settlement in the south part of Macoupin county. It is a good tract of land, and the settlement is considerable.

Henderson River rises in Knox county, takes a southwestern course through Warren, and after receiving several branches, enters the Mississippi in ten north, five west, through a low and inundated bottom.

It is a beautiful stream, furnishes some good mill seats, and has a fine body of timber on its banks. The country on Henderson is considered one of the finest bodies of land in Illinois.

Its principal branches are South fork, and Cedar fork. The timber is oaks of various species, hickory, walnut, ash, elm, sugar maple, linden, etc.

South Fork of Henderson river rises in ten north, five west, runs through an excellent body of land and fine settlements in Warren county. The heads of all the streams in this part of the state are in rich and dry land.

Henderson Settlement lies in Knox county, on Henderson river, ten miles north of west from Knoxville. Here is a large body of rich timbered land, surrounded with dry, fertile, first rate prairies. The settlement is sometimes called Gum's fort.

Henderson's Creek, in Greene county, a small stream

that rises near the line of Morgan county, runs a south course, and empties into Apple creek.

HENNEPIN, the seat of justice for Putnam county, is situated in the great bend, and on the east bank of the Illinois river, and the border of De Pru prairie, on section nine, township thirty-two north, in range two west of the third principal meridian. Its situation is elevated, the surface gently ascending from the river, with an extensive body of rich land adjacent.

The bottom opposite is about one mile and a half wide, and overflowed in high water.

This town was laid off in 1831, and contains ten stores, 4 groceries, 3 taverns, 3 lawyers, 4 physicians, Presbyterian and Methodist congregations, court house and jail, a good school, and 475 inhabitants. Steamboats ascend to this place at a moderate stage of water.

Herron's Prairie is in the southwestern part of Franklin county.

Herrington's Prairie, eleven miles northwest from Fairfield, in Wayne county, is eight miles long, from two to four miles wide, surface rolling, soil second rate, and has a settlement of fifty families.

Hickory Creek, in Coles county, rises in the Grand prairie, runs southeast, and enters the Embarras five miles below Charleston. It is a good mill stream, and the land through which it passes is undulating and rich; the settlements contain 120 families.

Hickory Creek rises in Cook county, runs a westerly course, and enters the Des Plaines nearly opposite Mount Joliet. On its banks are large bodies of excellent timber, intermixed with good prairie land. The settlements are extensive.

Hickory Creek, a small stream in Fayette county. It rises about nine miles east of Vandalia in the prairies, runs southwest, and enters the Kaskaskia five miles below Vandalia. The soil is thin, timber post and other species of oak.

Hickory Creek Post Office, is in Fayette county, in the

centre of a large settlement, four and a half miles southeast from Vandalia, and on the road to Salem.

Hickory Grove, in Champaign county, on the north branch of salt fork, and 12 miles east of Urbanna. The timber is from half a mile to one and a half miles wide, and the soil and prairie round first rate.

Hickory Grove, a post office, and large settlement, on the borders of Shoal creek prairie, in Bond county, nine miles south of west from Greenville. The prairie is large undulating, and rich. The timber adjoining is excellent and abundant. The settlement contains seventy or eighty families and a store. Many European Germans are settling in the prairie.

Hickory Grove, a settlement near a point of timber in the Macoupin prairie, Greene county, twelve miles south of Carrollton, and on the road to Alton. The settlement is spreading over a fine, rich, prairie, moderately undulating.

Hickory Grove, in McDonough county, in seven north, two west, is a small and beautiful tract of timber, on the head of Camp fork. This is sometimes called *Walnut grove*. The prairie around it is undulating and rich.

Hickory Hill Settlement, in Wayne county, eighteen miles west from Fairfield, and on the west side of the Skillet fork. It is a mixture of timber and prairie, soil second quaility, and population about fifty families.

Higgins's Creek, a small stream in Fayette county, that enters the Kaskaskia from the west, three miles above Vandalia.

Higgins's Settlement, in Crawford county, is five miles south of Palestine.

Highland, a town site in the Looking-Glass prairie, Madison county, 16 miles southeast from Edwardsville.

An extensive settlement of Germans is in its vicinity.

Highland post office and settlement is in Pike county between Pittsfield and Atlas.

High Prairie, a beautiful prairie and fine settlement in St. Clair county, eight miles south of Belleville.

Highsmith's Settlement, in Crawford county, ten miles

south of Palestine. Here are considerable barrens, the timber is oak, hickory, etc., the soil a medium quality, the population twenty or twenty-five families.

HILLSBORO', the seat of justice for Montgomery county, is situated twenty-eight miles northwest from Vandalia. It has six stores, two taverns, three blacksmiths, three carpenters, one cabinet maker, two physicians, two tanneries, one shoemaker, two tailors, one tinner, a post office, 70 families, and about 350 inhabitants.

It is situated in an elevated region, near middle fork of Shoal creek.

The Presbyterian society in this place has built a neat brick edifice, in the modern style, for a house of worship.

Hillsboro' is a healthy and flourishing town. The principal road from Vandalia to Springfield, and another from Shelbyville to Alton, pass through this place.

Hitesville, a town site and post office on the east border of Coles county, 12 miles from Charleston.

Hittle's Grove, in Tazewell county, lies between little Mackinau and Sugar creek. It is four miles long and two miles wide, and surface level; the adjoining prairie undulating.

Hodge's Creek, in Greene county, rises in Pratt's prairie, runs southwesterly, and enters Grand Passe. It is also called *Hurricane*.

Hodge's Fork, a branch of the Macoupin from the north side, which unites with the main stream twelve miles east from Carrollton, and near the line of Greene county. Towards its head it is called Otter creek. See *North fork of the Macoupin*.

Hog Prairie is in Hamilton county, a few miles west of McLeansboro'. It is about two miles in diameter, level, and rather wet.

Holderman's Grove, in La Salle county, is sixteen miles northeast from Ottawa, containing about 500 acres of timber, and a settlement of several families. Here is a town site and post office called Lisbon.

Holland's Grove, a settlement on Farm creek, in Tazewell county. The timber and prairie are first rate. It adjoins Peoria lake.

Holland's Grove post office is in the town of *Washington*, which see.

Honey Creek is a stream that rises in the prairies of Warren county, runs west twenty miles, giving name to a low bottom, and enters the Mississippi, below Ellison.

Horse Creek rises near the centre of Monroe county, runs a southeasterly course into Randolph county, and enters the Kaskaskia river, in five south, eight west; several settlements lie along this creek where there is good timber and prairie land.

Horse Creek, in Sangamon county, rises in the prairies towards the head of Macoupin, and enters the South fork of Sangamon about section twenty, fifteen north, four west.

Horse Prairie, in Randolph county, on Horse creek, a rich undulating tract, and contains forty or fifty families.

Horse Shoe Lake, in Alexander county, eight or ten miles long, and from half a mile to one mile wide. Its name indicates its form, and its outlet is into Cash river.

Horse Shoe Prairie, is in the Virginia settlement, Mc Henry county, 7 miles west of Fox river.

Howard's Settlement, in Pope County, on Big creek, fifteen miles northeast from Golconda, comprises excellent land, and about seventy or eighty families.

Howard's Settlement, in Madison county, on the borders of the Looking Glass prairie, thirteen miles southeasterly from Edwardsville.

Howard's Settlement, near Potatoe creek, in Fulton county, twelve miles south of west from Lewistown. The soil is good, of the description called barrens.

Hoxey's Settlement, in Madison county, on the West fork of Silver creek, nine miles northeast from Edwardsville. The prairie is undulating and rich.

Hudson, a settlement of New England people in Mc Lean county, ten miles north of Bloomington, south side and in the bend of Mackinau river.

Hutson's Creek is a small stream in Crawford county, that flows into the Wabash.

Hutsonville, a small town and post office, on Hutson's creek, nine miles north of Palestine, in Crawford county.

Huey's Settlement, on the west side of the Grand prairie, in Clinton county, three miles east of Carlyle. A rich tract of prairie, bordered with heavy timber.

Hugh's Settlement, in Alexander county, on the west side of Cash river, seventeen miles north from America. Mill creek, a branch of Cash river, runs through it.

The bottom and the upland are both good, and the settlement has forty or fifty families.

Huron, a town site in Sangamon county, on the south side of the Sangamon river, about thirty miles north northeast from Springfield, on the road to Fulton county.

It is a good situation for a town, and where the Beardstown canal is projected to unite with the Sangamon river. It was formerly called Miller's ferry.

Hurricane Settlement, in the eastern part of Montgomery, and western part of Fayette counties. It extends along the timber of Hurricane fork, has a rolling surface, which is broken near the creek; the timber is post oak, and the soil rather thin.

Hurricane, an extensive settlement along the creek of that name and on the eastern side of Bond county. The prairie is rather wet, the timber excellent, and in large bodies.

Hurricane Post Office is in Hurricane settlement, Montgomery county, on the road from Vandalia to Hillsboro', and equidistant from these places.

Hurricane Fork, a branch of the Kaskaskia river, rises near the line of Montgomery and Shelby counties, runs south near the western line of Fayette county, and enters the Kaskaskia on the right side, twelve miles below Vandalia. The banks of this stream are well timbered, and the low bottoms occasionally inundated.

Hutchens's Creek, a branch of Clear creek, in Union county, ten miles from Jonesboro'.

Hutchens's Settlement, in Perry county, five miles north

of Pinckneyville. The surface is undulating, the soil of a middling quality, and the settlement small.

Illinois Prairie, formerly called *Wolf prairie*, commences near the mouth of the Illinois river, in Calhoun county, and extends twenty miles along the foot of the bluffs, adjoining the alluvion of the Illinois. Its average width is one mile and a half, the soil is good and thirty families are settled here.

Illinois River, a beautiful stream of water that passes diagonally through the state, and enters the Mississippi twenty miles above the mouth of the Missouri.

It commences under its proper name at the junction of the Kankakee and Des Plaines. From thence it runs nearly a west course, (receiving Fox river at Ottawa, and Vermilion near the foot of the rapids,) to Hennepin, in township thirty-three north, and in range two west of the third principal meridian. Here it curves to the south, and then to the southwest, receiving a number of tributaries, the largest of which are Spoon and Sangamon rivers, till it reaches Naples. Here it bends gradually to the south, and continues that course till within six miles of the Mississippi, when it curves to the southeast, and finally nearly to an east course. Its length, (without reckoning the windings of the channel in navigation,) is about 260 miles. It is navigable at a moderate stage of water to the foot of the rapids, 210 miles; and to Ottawa, nine miles further, in high water, for steamboats.

In going up the river at a low stage of water the following bars and impediments to the navigation exist:

1. French bar, gravel, twenty miles above the mouth, near Smith's ferry—three feet deep at low water.

2. A bar fourteen miles further up—channel close to an island—two and a half feet at low stage.

3. At Hodge's warehouse, seven miles above the mouth of Apple creek, there is difficulty in getting a point, but no bar.

4. Six miles below Naples is a centre bar—channel near the side of the river.

5. At Meredosia, is a narrow channel on the opposite side, but no getting to the landing at very low water.

6. Three fourths of a mile below Beardstown is a bar, extending, like a wing dam, nearly across the river, excepting a narrow passage near the west shore. Any boat that can pass this bar will reach the port of the rapids.

From this imperfect sketch of the obstructions to the navigation of this river at low water, it will be seen that with the comparatively trifling expense of 100,000 dollars, which the legislature has provided, the navigation of the Illinois may be made good at all stages of water.

At high floods this river overflows its banks and covers its bottoms for a considerable extent. The Mississippi, at extreme high water, backs up the Illinois about seventy miles to the mouth of the Mauvaiseterre.

Besides several villages and commercial towns, which are springing up on the banks of the Illinois, there are many landings for goods, and deposits for produce, where temporary warehouses have been erected.

The commerce of this river now is extensive, and increasing with a rapidity, known only in the rich, agricultural regions of the western states. Several steamboats are constantly employed in its trade, and many others make occasional trips. About thirty-five different boats passed and landed at Beardstown in 1836, making the arrivals and departures 450.

The following account of arrivals of steamboats at Naples, from 1828 to 1831, will show the increase during those years.

  1828, the first year of steamboat
    navigation . . . . . 9 arrivals
  1829 . . . . 3 "
  1830 . . . . 24 "
  1831 . . . . 186 "
  1832, from March 4, to June 19, 108 arrivals by
    nineteen different boats.

Illinois Town, a small village of a dozen families, in St. Clair county, on Cahokia creek, opposite St. Louis.

Illiopolis, a town site, laid off on a magnificent scale in Sangamon county, twenty-two miles east of Springfield, on the road to Decatur. It is a handsome elevated site in the prairie.

Indian Creek, a branch of Fox river from the northwest. It enters the main stream ten miles above Ottawa, and five miles above the rapids.

Large bodies of fine timber lie on this stream; the surface of the country is undulating, and the soil good.

On the 20th of May, 1832, fifteen persons belonging to the families of Messrs. Hall, Daviess, and Pettigrew were barbarously massacred by the Indians near this creek. Two young ladies, Misses Halls, were taken prisoners, and afterwards redeemed, and two young lads made their escape.

The bodies of men, women, and children were shockingly mutilated, the houses of the settlers burned, their furniture destroyed, and their cattle killed—all in day light, and within twenty miles of a large force of the militia! This was done by the Indians under the infamous *Black Hawk!* A portion of that band were exterminated during the same season by the combined forces of United States troops and Illinois militia, and the remainder dispersed over the prairies west of the Mississippi.

Settlements are now rapidly forming on Indian creek and Fox river, and much excellent country remains to be possessed in that quarter.

Indian Creek, a stream in Morgan county, near the borders of Sangamon, runs a westerly course, passes through a string of Lakes in the Illinois bottom, until its waters mingle with the Illinois, near the corner of the base line and the fourth principal meridian.

It passes through a beautiful and fertile country, diversified with timber and prairie.

The French explorers called it *La Ballance.*

Indian Creek, in Lawrence county, rises in the prairies west, runs southeast, and enters the Embarras five miles below Lawrenceville. It has much good land in its vicinity, both timber and prairie, and a settlement of 150 families.

Indian Creek, a small stream in Madison county, between Edwardsville and Alton, that enters Cahokia creek.

Indian Creek, a small stream and post office in Gallatin county 11 miles northwest from Equality.

Indian Creek a branch of the Des Plaines, rises in Mc Henry county, runs southeasterly, and enters the Des Plaines in Cook county. The land along its course very excellent.

Indian Creek, a small stream that rises in the east part of Sangamon county, and enters the Sangamon river above Salt creek. The timber adjoining is excellent, and the prairie is undulating and rich.

Indian Creek a small stream in the northern part of Bond county. It runs west and enters Shoal creek.

Indian Creek a name of one of the forks of Spoon river. It rises in Henry county, runs across the northeast corner of Knox, and enters Spoon river in twelve north, six east.

Indian Creek, in Coles county, and a branch of the Embarras. It rises in the Grand prairie, runs southeast, and enters the principal stream eight miles below Charleston. The land is good, both timber and prairie, and the population forty or fifty families.

Indian Prairie, in Wayne county lies ten miles northwesterly from Fairfield; surface level, soil of an inferior quality, with a scattering settlement of fifteen or twenty families.

Inlet Grove, in Ogle county, lies on the road from Dixonville to Chicago, 16 miles from the former place. The inlet is a stream that rises near the heads of the south fork of the Kishwaukee, runs a southwestern course for 50 miles, part of that distance through swamps, until it is lost in the Winnebago swamp.

Irish Grove, in Sangamon county, on the road from Springfield to Peoria, eighteen miles from the former place. It is two miles from Salt creek, and is three miles long and one mile and a half wide, and contains a settlement of about fifty families. The land is good, and the timber is chiefly oak of various kinds.

Irish Settlement in Randolph county, six miles northeast of Kaskaskia, on Plum Creek.

Irish Settlement, on the Ohio river, in Pope county, about fifteen miles above Golconda, is on a rich alluvial soil, and contains about one hundred families.

Iroquois, a town site and post office, on the south side of the Iroquois river, in Iroquois county, in twenty-seven north, eleven west. It has 3 stores, 2 groceries, 1 tavern and twenty families. Montgomery joins it.

Iroquois (*Riviere des Iroquois*, Fr.) a considerable river which rises in the northwestern part of Indiana, and taking a northwest course, flows into the Kankakee river, and thus forms one of the heads of the Illinois. It received its name from the circumstance of a large party of the Iroquois Indians being surprised and massacred on its banks by the Illinois nation.* The Kickapoos called it *Mocabella*. Others have called it *Canawaga*. It is probably the same stream that the Commissioners for settling the boundary between Illinois and Indiana called *Pickaminck*. It crosses the boundary line in township twenty-seven north, where its width is 175 links. The country through which it passes will soon be covered with settlements, the surface being fine and undulating, the soil rather inclined to sand, dry and rich, and the timber abundant. Sugar creek is a principal branch.

Iroquois City, a town site laid out in Iroquois county, on section twenty-five, township twenty-seven north, range twelve west, but contains no houses.

Irvin's Settlement lies in the western part of Hamilton county. The surface is undulating, the soil second rate, and timbered.

Island Grove, a large body of excellent timber, surrounded with rich prairie, in Sangamon county, sixteen

* Charlevoix.

miles west of Springfield, and on the road to Jacksonville.

Island Grove, a body of timber near the west side of Montgomery county, containing about 600 acres.

Jackson's Grove, a post office in Fulton county, on the road from Lewistown to Canton equidistant from the two places. Here is a considerable tract of barrens.

Jackson Grove, in Will county, six miles south of Juliet.

JACKSONVILLE is one of the largest inland towns in the state, and the seat of justice for Morgan county. It is situated on elevated ground, in the midst of a most delightful prairie, on sections twenty and twenty-one, township fifteen north, in range ten west of the third principal meridian.

The plat of this town was laid off in 1825, but its rapid growth did not commence in three or four years.

Few towns exhibit a finer prospect than does Jacksonville, from whatever side the traveller approaches. The surrounding prairie country, now in a state of cultivation is beautifully undulating, and uncommonly rich. The timber in sight is either in groves, or spread along the waters of the Mauvaiseterre and Sandy.

Jacksonville has 16 stores, 6 groceries, 2 druggist's shops 2 taverns or hotels, several respectable boarding houses, 1 baker, 2 saddlers, 3 hatters, 1 silversmith, 1 watchmaker, 2 tinners, 3 cabinet makers, 1 machinist, 1 house and sign painter, 6 tailors, 2 cordwainers, 4 blacksmiths, 3 chair makers, 1 coach maker, 1 wagon maker, 1 wheelwright, 11 lawyers and 10 physicians.

It has 1 steam flour and 1 saw mill, a manufactory for cotton yarn, a distillery, 2 oil mills, two carding factories a tannery, and 3 brick yards, with a proportion of various mechanics in the building line, and other trades.

The public buildings are, a spacious court house, of brick, a neat framed building for the Presbyterian house of worship, a large brick building for the Methodist society, and a handsome edifice, also of brick, for the Episcopalian denomination, another of wood for Congregationalists, a lyceum, a mechanics' association, a male and a female academy, a brick market house, and a county jail. The college edifices are one mile west from the town.

There are two printing offices that publish weekly papers, the "*Patriot*," and the "*News*," and also a book and job printing office, with a book bindery attached, and a monthly religious periodical.

The present population of Jacksonville is about 2,500; exclusive of the college students.

Situated near the centre of the county, and in the midst of one of the finest tracts of land, densely populated with industrious and enterprising farmers, with the advantages of good water, health, and good society, Jacksonville must continue to prosper, and doubtless will attract many emigrants who are seeking an agreeable home in the "far west."

The railroads projected and now working from this place to the Illinois river, have been noticed under the head of " Internal Improvements."

Jacksonville, a settlement in St. Clair county, on the bluffs, eight miles northwest from Belleville.

Jarvis's Settlement is near the head of Ellison, in Warren county. Here are about two townships of valuable timber, surrounded with immense tracts of fertile prairie.

Jersey Prairie is a beautiful and rich prairie, in Morgan county, ten miles northerly from Jacksonville.

The land is rich, timber adjoining excellent, the people moral and industrious, the settlement extensive and populous, and decidedly healthy.

Jerseyville, a town site and post office in Greene county, fourteen miles south of Carrollton; a beautiful situation in the prairie, containing twenty or twenty-five families.

Job's Creek is a small stream in part of Cass county, runs north, and passes through several small lakes into Sangamon river.

Job's Settlement, called also *New Hope*, in the northwest part of McDonough county, in townships six and seven north, range four west. The timbered land in the several forks of Crooked creek, and the intervening tracts of prairie, are all of first rate quality. Houston's, Bagby's, and Dicken's forks, are small streams north of Job's fork, and are heads of Crooked creek.

Johnson's Creek, a small stream in the south part of Jo Daviess county. Its head is towards Rock river, its course west, and it enters the Mississippi, thirteen miles above the Marais d'Ogee, and twenty-five miles below Plum river. The land towards its mouth is low and marshy; towards its head it is gently undulating, occasional groves of timber, and well adapted to farming.

Johnson's Settlement, on Sugar creek, in Clinton county, twenty miles south of west from Carlyle.

Jonathan's Creek is a tributary of the Kaskaskia, in Shelby county.

JONESBORO', the seat of justice for Union county, is situated on section thirty, twelve south, one west, in a high, rolling tract of country, nine miles from the Mississippi, twenty-five miles south-southeast from Brownsville, in latitude thirty-seven degrees, twenty-five minutes north. It has about twenty-five families, seven stores, one tavern, one lawyer, two physicians, two ministers of the gospel, one carding machine, and various mechanics. The court house is a framed building, two stories high, and finished; and a brick jail. The surrounding country is undulating and healthy, and contains several good settlements.

Jones's Creek post office. (See Liberty, Randolph county.)

Jordan Creek rises in the interior of Wabash county, and enters Bon Pas creek near the northwestern corner of the county. It passes through a fertile tract, both timbered and prairie, and has a considerable settlement ten or twelve miles northwest from Mount Carmel.

Jordan's Prairie, in Jefferson county, six miles north of Mount Vernon, is five miles long, and one mile and a half wide. The land is second rate, and the settlement contains about fifty families.

Jordan's Prairie post office is on section thirteen, one

south, two east, eight and a half miles north of Mount Vernon.

Jordan's Settlement, in Jasper county, on the west side of the Embarras river. In the centre of this settlement is the contemplated county seat.

JULIETT, the seat of justice for Will county, located on both sides of the Des Plaines, and at the crossing place of the Illinois and Michigan canal.

It has fourteen stores, two groceries, one drug store, three taverns, a saw and grist mill, and the benefit of great water power, various mechanics, six lawyers, five physicians, a Methodist and an Episcopal society, and about 600 inhabitants. This should have been called *Joliet*, from one of the earliest French explorers.

Kane Post Office, in Macoupin settlement, Greene county, nine miles south of Carrollton.

Kankakee, one of the principal streams that form the Illinois river. It rises in the northern part of Indiana, near the south bend of the St. Joseph's river, runs a westerly course into Illinois, where it receives the Iroquois, and forms a junction with the Des Plaines, in section thirty-five, township thirty-four north, and in range eight east from the third principal meridian. Here is a large body of fine timber, but along the Kankakee there is very little timber. It runs swiftly, and has a lime stone bed.

At the ford of the Vincennes and Chicago road it is two-hundred yards wide. This is 178 miles north of Vincennes, and forty-seven miles south of Chicago. The prairie country through which it passes is generally of good soil, gently undulating, and interspersed with sand ridges. Navigation for small craft can be effected through the Kankakee and St. Joseph.

This river was discovered by the French at a very early period, and was one of the principal routes to the Illinois country. Its aboriginal name was *Theakiki*, or as pronounced in French, Te-au-kee-kee, which by the fatality attendant upon many of the aboriginal names carried through French into English, has become fixed in the sound and orthography of *Kan-ka-kee*.

Kankakee, a town site in the forks of the Kankakee and Des Plaines rivers, with one store and three or four houses, saw mills, &c. Near the point the land is overflowed at high water. Further back is fine bottom and rolling prairie. Calculations are made for a city here at some future time.

KASKASKIA, the seat of justice for Randolph county, and formerly the seat of government of the Territory of Illinois. It is situated on the right bank of the Kaskaskia river, seven miles above its junction with the Mississippi.

The early French explorers made one of their first settlements at this spot, shortly after the visit of La Salle, in 1683; and so long as the French continued in possession of the Illinois country, Kaskaskia was its capital, and was flourishing and populous. In 1721, when Charlevoix visited it, there existed a Jesuit college. Its ruins are now scarcely visible. In 1763, when the country east of the Mississippi was ceded by France to Great Britain, it contained about one hundred families. Of late years its population and trade has been much reduced. It numbers now about fifty or sixty families, a majority of whom are French.

The court house is of brick. A Roman Catholic chapel, and a nunnery and female boarding school are here. Kaskaskia is the location of the land office for this district.

Kaskaskia River, a large and navigable stream. It rises in Champaign county, in township twenty north, range eight east, near the waters of the Sangamon and the Vermilion of the Wabash, and running in a south-western direction through Coles, Shelby, Fayette, Clinton, St. Clair, and Randolph counties, enters the Mississippi, in sections fourteen and fifteen, nine south, seven west, about 120 miles above the mouth of the Ohio.

It is four hundred miles in length, following its meanderings, and receives a large number of tributaries, which are noticed under their respective names. An extensive body of timber from two to ten miles wide, is found along this stream, generally of a good quality, consisting of oaks of various kinds, as overcup, burr, water, white, black, red or Spanish, and post oak, walnut, hickory, ash, hackberry, elm, white and sugar maple, honey locust, cotton wood, sycamore, pecaun, mulberry, sassafras, box elder, etc. The country through which it passes is undulating, and fertile, adapted to the growth of corn, wheat, oats, tobacco, and some cotton. The latter is not a sure crop in all seasons; but with proper care, a sufficient quantity may be raised for home consumption. The bottoms of this stream are from half a mile to two or three miles in width, and subject to inundation in high floods.

The legislature in its system of internal improvement, appropriated $50,000 to improve the navigation of Kaskaskia river. The chief obstructions are logs, sand banks and short bends. A steamboat went up as far as Carlyle in April, 1837.

Kellogg's Grove, in Jo Daviess county, thirty-five miles east-southeast from Galena, and on the road from Dixon's ferry. It is a small grove of three or four hundred acres, with several small groves near it.

Kellogg's Grove, a small tract of timber in La Salle county seventeen miles northeast from Ottawa.

Keltner's Fork, in Morgan county, is a small branch of Indian creek. It rises near Jersey prairie.

Keys's Creek rises in the interior of Pike county, and enters the Snycartee slough. The bottom is excellent land proportioned into timber and prairie. About the bluffs very uneven, towards the head of the creek moderately undulating.

Kickapoo, a stream that rises near Spoon river in two forks denominated East and West forks.

East Fork rises in sections eleven and twelve, eleven north, seven east, runs a southwestern course.

West Fork rises in ten north, four east, runs a southeasterly course and unites with the east fork in section thirty-four, ten north, six east.

The Kickapoo then takes a southern course, and enters

the Illinois river two miles below Peoria. On the forks there is much excellent land, with groves and points of timber, interspersed with barrens. The country bordering on the main creek has considerable bodies of fine timber, but the land is generally too uneven for convenient cultivation.

Kickapoo, a branch of Salt creek in Sangamon county. It rises in Dawson's grove, McLean county, in twenty-three north, four east, runs a southern course and enters Salt creek in Sangamon county, in the north part of nineteen north, three west. It furnishes good mill seats, when the water is not too low; and the soil and timber on each side of the creek are first rate.

Kincaid Creek, is a small branch of Big Muddy river, which heads in Randolph county, runs southeast, and enters that stream twenty-four miles from its mouth. The land along this creek is rocky, broken, heavily timbered with poplar, oak, etc. and the settlement is small.

Kinsawl's Settlement, near the northern side of Gallatin county, on the road from Carmi to Equality. The land is rather inferior, and the settlement considerable.

Kishwaukee or *Sycamore*, a branch of Rock river. It is divided into North, East and South forks, and these again have numerous branches.

The branches of North Fork head in Winnebago, Boone and northwest corner of McHenry counties, and in the Wisconsin Territory, of which the Beaver, Piskasau and Pappoose creeks are best known.

The East Fork has several heads in the northern parts of Kane county.

The South Fork originates in several heads in the interior of Kane, and southeastern corner of Ogle counties. One of its heads is near the Paupau grove. The East and South Forks unite in township forty-one north, range three east, where is a large body of timber, twelve sections or more of various kinds, and the prairies adjoining undulating and rich. Along the East Fork the prairie is flat and rather wet. Ohio, Norwegian and Big groves are found in this region.

The North and South Forks unite in township forty-three north, range two east, and the main Kishwaukee enters Rock river on section twenty-two, township forty-three north, range one east, of the third meridian. The country in general has an undulating surface, a rich, deep, black, sandy, calcareous soil, and abounds with lime and free stone, coal, and fine perennial springs, while the different streams produce good mill sites.

There is a deficiency of timber as there is through the northern part of Illinois. Much of it is in groves, many of which equal in appearance English parks. There are also extensive tracts of barrens or oak openings, as they are called by the people, and the whole country gives most unequivocal promise of health.

Kite river, in Ogle county, rises in the prairie north of Paupau grove, runs a west-southwest course and enters Rock river one and a half miles, below Oregon. Soil rich and sandy, timber scattering, surface tolerably level. Besides other timber, here is yellow and white poplar, or aspin.

Knight's Prairie lies west of McLeansboro', in Hamilton county, with a settlement around it.

Knob Prairie, fifteen miles northwest from Frankfort, in the corner of Franklin county, is low and wet, and has a small settlement.

KNOXVILLE is the county seat of Knox county, and is pleasantly situated on an elevated and rich prairie on the north side, and adjoining the timber of Haw creek. It is on section twenty-eight, eleven north, and two east of the fourth principal meridian. It was laid off about 1832, contains now 40 families and bids fair to become a thriving inland town. The surrounding country is rich, and settling fast with industrious farmers.

Knox's Grove, in the northeastern part of Putnam and extends into La Salle and Ogle counties. It is at the head waters of the Bureau.

Knox Settlement, in Putnam county, on Sandy, thirteen miles southeast from Hennepin, is a large and flourishing settlement.

Lacon, (formerly Columbia) is on the left bank of the

Illinois river in Putnam county, 20 miles below Hennepin surrounded with a populous and rich settlement. It has 3 stores and 15 or 20 families.

La Fox, a post office on Fox river in Kane county, near the Big Woods.

La Harpe, a town and post office in Hancock county, in seven north, five west, with a beautiful country, interspersed with timber and prairie around it.

Lake Fork, a main branch of Macoupin creek, which rises in the prairie between the heads of Shoal creek, and Sangamon waters, and near Macoupin point, which see. Below the *point* it passes through a small lake, or pond.

Lake Fork, a branch of Shoal creek, that rises in seven north, five west, runs a northeastern direction, and enters the west fork of Shoal creek in Montgomery county.

Lake Fork of Salt Creek is formed by a long lake in the northeastern part of Sangamon county, runs a north course and forms one of the heads of Salt creek. It is in township seventeen north, and range two and three west.

Lake Joliet is an expansion of the River Des Plaines, two miles below Mount Joliet, and opposite Mount Flat Head, in Will county. It is about five miles long, 60 or 70 rods wide, and deep water.

La Marche, a small stream and branch of the Kickapoo in Peoria county. Excellent land and a fine body of timber, especially near its mouth.

Lamaster's Settlement is in Schuyler county, on Crane creek four miles south of Rushville.

Lamotte Creek rises in the interior of Crawford county, runs east and enters the Wabash below Palestine.

Lamotte Prairie is a sandy and rich tract of prairie, in Crawford county, eight miles long, and from one to five miles broad. The soil is well adapted to the growth of corn.

La Salle Prairie, a prairie and large settlement in Peoria county, adjoining Peoria lake. The southern part is sandy, rich and undulating; the northern portion is a mixture of clay and sand, elevated in the middle.

La Salle prairie is an elevated bottom, above the highest floods, ten miles long, and from three to four miles wide. At the shore of the lake the water is deep, and the landing good.

The settlement contains about 100 families and is fifteen miles distant from the county seat.

Laughton's, an old trading house and settlement on the Des Plaines, in Cook county, twelve miles west of Chicago.

LAWRENCEVILLE, the county seat of Lawrence county. It is situated on the west bank of the Embarras river, nine miles from Vincennes, on the St. Louis road, and on an elevated ridge. It contains three stores, two groceries, two taverns, and sixty or seventy families.

The court house is of brick, and is a respectable building. A saw and grist mill is on the Embarras, adjoining.

Its exports per annum $50,000; imports $30,000.

Leaf River, in Ogle county, rises in North Grove, near the source of Pine creek, runs east about 12 miles, and enters Rock river four or five miles below Stillman's run. It has several branches of four or five miles in length, fine groves of timber, and rich, calcareous soil on its borders.

Lebanon, a beautifully situated village in St. Clair county, twelve miles northeast from Belleville, and one mile east of Silver creek.

It is on elevated ground, surrounded with a beautiful, populous and well cultivated district of country and on the Vincennes and St Louis stage road.

Lebanon has a steam mill for manufacturing grain—an ox mill for flouring, on an inclined plane, a post office, two public houses, seven stores, one grocery, three physicians, mechanics' shops of various kinds, and about sixty families. The Methodist college, located in the immediate vicinity of Lebanon, has been noticed under the head of " EDUCATION" in the first part of this work.

The Methodist society embraces the largest proportion of the religious community about Lebanon. There is a large society of the Methodist Episcopal church, and a small society of the Methodist Protestant church.

Leesburgh, a town site in Montgomery county on sections seven and eight, township ten north, five west.

Lemarde Prairie, in Wayne county, seven miles northwest from Fairfield, about six miles long, and three wide, of inferior quality, with a small population.

Lester's Point, in Iroquois county in twenty seven north, eleven west;—a point of timber, surrounded with a rich, undulating prairie.

Lewis's Creek, a trifling stream in Jackson county, enters Big Muddy near the coal bank four miles east of Brownsville.

Lewis's Settlement, in the southern part of Pope county, above and opposite the mouth of Cumberland river. This is the oldest settlement in this part of the state, and contains sixty or seventy families.

LEWISTOWN, the seat of justice for Fulton county, situated on section twenty-two, five north, three east, four miles east of Spoon river, and twelve miles from the Illinois.

It has three stores, two taverns, a framed court house, painted white, and about forty families. Lewistown is surrounded with a heavy body of timber, chiefly of white and other oaks; the soil rather thin, and surface broken.

Lexington, a town site in the north part of McLean county, eighteen miles northeast of Bloomington, on the road to Chicago.

Liberty, a town and post office in Adams county, near Weigle's setlement.

Liberty a town site on the Mississippi, in Randolph county, on section seven, township eight south, five west. It has a steam saw and flouring mill, six stores, three groceries, two taverns, one minister, two physicians and 140 inhabitants. One house for public worship.

Lick Creek, a branch of Sugar creek, of Sangamon county. It rises on the western side of the county, takes an easterly course through a rich and populous tract, with good timber, and enters Sugar creek a short distance above its mouth. The settlements extend its whole length, and the borders of the prairie adjoining are well populated.

Lick Run is a branch of Indian creek, in Morgan county near the bluffs of the Illinois.

Lima, a town site and post office in Adams county, 18 miles north of Quincy, and has eight or ten families.

Paine's Grove is in Ogle county on Kite creek.

Lincoln, a post office and town site in Macoupin county, near the head of Wood river, and on the road from Edwardsville to Springfield. It is thought to be an eligible situation, and will soon be surrounded by a large settlement.

Linden Bottom, in Greene county, south of the Macoupin called also the "Richwoods." It is a fine tract of timbered land, elevated and rich, yet in appearance its surface resembles alluvion.

It has a large settlement extending from the Macoupin river to Otter creek.

Linden Grove, a small body of excellent timber in the northeast part of Morgan county, surrounded with rich, undulating prairie.

Lisbon, a post office and town site at Holderman's grove, in La Salle county, sixteen miles northeast from Ottawa.

Little Beaucoup Creek, a small stream in Perry county, and a branch of Big Beaucoup creek, between that stream and Little Muddy.

Little Crooked Creek rises in Washington county, near Nashville, runs a north course, and enters Crooked creek near its mouth. Land good, surface undulating, and a mixture of timber and prairie.

Little Detroit is the French name for the "*Strait*" or narrows in Peoria Lake.

Little Indian Creek, in Morgan county, rises in Silvan grove, runs southwest, and enters Indian creek.

Little Mackinau is a stream in Tazewell county, that

runs westward, and enters the Mackinau. The settlement here is extensive.

Little Missouri Creek, a branch of Crooked creek, in the western part of Schuyler county and eastern part of Adams county, twelve miles from Rushville. *Green's settlement* is on the southern, and *Brown's Settlement* on the northern side of this creek. The country is a mixture of timber and prairie.

Little Mount Prairie is in Wayne county, three miles southwest from Fairfield, about two miles long, and one wide.

Here is a small but high mound, covered over with the graves of the aboriginal people.

Little Muddy is one of the four heads of the Big Muddy river. It rises in the southeastern corner of Washington county, crosses the line into Jefferson, then into Franklin and finally into Jackson, where it enters the parent stream on the right side, in section thirteen, eight south, one west. A post office.

It has good timber and prairie on both sides.

Little Piasau, called also Cave Spring branch, rises in a large spring among the bluffs of Lower Alton, and passes through the town into the Mississippi.

Little Rock River, rises in Jo Daviess county, runs south into Whiteside county and enters Rock river in township nineteen north, four east. There is much good land along its course.

Little Rock Creek rises in the interior of Kane county, and runs south into Fox river.

Little Saline, in Gallatin coutny, rises in the bluffs of the Ohio river, runs a north course, and enters the South fork of the Saline creek, eighteen miles above Equality. It waters a tolerably good country, with a scattering population.

Little Sandy, a small creek that heads in Sweet's prairie, in the south part of Morgan county; and enters Sandy creek, about the bluffs of the Illinois. A large tract of timbered land is on it.

Little Silver Creek rises in the Looking Glass prairie,

in the northeastern part of St. Clair county, runs southwest past Lebanon, and enters Silver creek two miles below that village.

Little Vermilion rises in the prairies west of Fox river, runs south, and enters the Illinois near the foot of the rapids. Just below is the termination of the canal, and the site of a great commercial town.

Its Indian name is *Pe-cum-sauk-in*, or *Tomahawk*.

Little Wabash River rises in township eleven north, range six east, in the large prairies towards the head waters of the Kaskaskia, and running south through the counties of Coles, Effingham, Clay, Wayne, Edwards, and White, enters the Big Wabash, in the northeast corner of Gallatin county, seven south, ten east. It is about one hundred and ten miles in a direct line from its heads to its mouth, though about one hundred and fifty miles to follow its meanderings.

Its principal tributaries are Skillet fork, Fox, and Muddy. It is navigable for flat boats and small craft, at a full stage of water—about forty of the former leaving it annually, from Wayne and White counties, with beef, pork, corn, cattle, and some tobacco, for the New Orleans market.

The timber upon the banks of the Little Wabash is generally heavy, and of a good quality, and is several miles in width. In Clay county is some poplar.

The country adjoining is generally fertile, but the bottoms are subject to inundation at high floods. The country between the Little Wabash and the Skillet fork, is generally flat, and in some places inclined to be wet.

Several valuable mills have been erected on this stream in White county.

Little Woods is a tract of timber on Fox river, in Kane county above the "Big Woods." The land of excellent quality, but swampy in places.

Liverpool, a town site on the right bank of the Illinois river, in Fulton county, six miles above the mouth of Spoon river. The site has been called Bailey's Island, from being surrounded in the rear by a slough at high water, over which a causeway or leveè is about to be constructed. It is the landing place for Canton, and the termination of the Liverpool, Canton and Knoxville rail road.

Livingston, a village on the national road, in Clark county. It is in the timber of Big creek, fourteen miles from Terre Haute, in Indiana and ten miles west of north from Darwin. It has three stores, three groceries, three taverns, one physician, two ministers, various mechanics, and 150 inhabitants.

Lockport, a town site on the Illinois and Michigan canal, at the termination of the lake level, thirty-four and a half miles from Chicago. Here will be two locks established, each ten feet lift, which will give twenty feet fall for the immense quantity of surplus water that can be brought from Lake Michigan, equal to 10,000 cubic feet of surplus water per minute, after supplying the canal, and making full allowance for leakage, evaporation, &c., enough to drive 234 pairs of mill stones, four and a half feet diameter. A large town and extensive manufacturing operations will be here as soon as the canal is completed. Near this place the Des Plaines has fifteen feet fall.

Lockwood's Settlement, near the south fork of Spoon river, on the border of Warren county, township ten north, range one west. An excellent tract of country.

Lockwood's Settlement is in the south part of Hamilton county. The surface is rolling, timbered, and the soil second rate.

Locust Creek, a branch of Elkhorn creek, in Washington county, and has a settlement on it three miles south of Nashville; country chiefly prairie.

Locust Grove, a post office and settlement in Shelby county, five miles east of Shelbyville.

Logan's Settlement is in a good tract of country, in Gallatin county, eighteen miles northwest from Shawneetown.

Lollard's Settlement is ten miles northwest from Shawneetown, in Gallatin county, and contains much good land.

Long Creek, a branch of Big creek, in Macon county.

Long Grove lies west of Au Sable grove, in the eastern part of La Salle county.

Long Prairie, thirteen miles northwest from Mount Carmel, in Wabash county, is undulating, second rate land, with twenty-five or thirty families.

Long Prairie, in Edwards county, north of Albion, nine miles long, and from one mile to one and a half wide, interspersed with groves and points of timber.

Long Prairie, a branch of the Twelve Mile prairie of Clay county, projecting into Wayne. It is eight or ten miles long, three miles wide, level, poor soil, and has a population of twenty-five or thirty families.

Long Prairie, in Jefferson county, five miles west of Mount Vernon, is four miles long, and one mile and a half wide.

It lies between the Middle and West forks of Big Muddy river, is tolerably good land, and contains a settlement of forty families.

Looking Glass Prairie, a large, rich, beautiful, and undulating prairie lying between Silver and Sugar creeks, and on the eastern border of St. Clair county. It commences near the base line, in range six west, and extends northward about twenty miles into Madison county, and is from six to ten miles in width. Few prairies in the state present more eligible situations for farms than this.

Extensive settlements are on its borders, and project into its interior.

Lorton's Prairie, on the north side of Apple creek, in the upper part of Greene county. It is a tract of excellent land, has good timber, and contains about eighty families.

Lost Creek, in Marion county, rises in the Grand prairie, runs southwest, and enters the Kaskaskia river, near the mouth of Crooked creek.

Lost Grove is seven miles east of Sidney, on the eastern border of Champaign county.

Lost Prairie, in Perry county, seven miles west of Pinckneyville, is three miles long, and one mile and a half wide. It has a rich soil, high undulating surface, and a good settlement. There are two prairies between this and Pinckneyville, called Eaton and Conant prairies.

Loup Creek, an insignificant branch of Silver creek, in St. Clair county, in township one south, range seven west.

Luken's Prairie is on the south side of Lawrence county, with a settlement of fifty or sixty families.

Lusk's Creek, a small stream, running southwardly through Pope county, and entering the Ohio at Golconda.

Lynn Grove, in Champaign county, is four miles south of Sidney, from seventy-five to one hundred acres of timber, mostly linden and honey locust.

Lynnville, a town site and post office in Morgan county, and a point on the rail road from Jacksonville, by Winchester to the Illinois river. It has three stores, three groceries, and fifteen or twenty families. It is in the prairie at the head of Walnut creek, in an English settlement, and eight miles southwest from Jacksonville.

Lyons, is a town site on the Des Plaines at Laughton's old trading house, twelve miles west of Chicago. It now has a sawmill, three houses and a tavern.

Mackinau, (Michilimacinac) a navigable stream in Tazewell county. It rises in the prairie near the centre of McLean county, and after receiving several small branches, runs southwestwardly through Tazewell county, and enters the Illinois three miles below Pekin.

It is a clear stream, and has Little Mackinau, Rock, Walnut, and Panther creeks for its branches. The Mackinau bottoms are rich, but its bluffs are very broken, thin soil, from one to two miles in width, and the timber chiefly white oak, and some cedar. The prairies adjoining are rolling, dry, and tolerably good. Towards its head the land is less broken, timber various, and soil rich. It has a number of mill seats.

Mackinau, a small village, and formerly the county seat of Tazewell. It is situated on the Mackinau creek, in twenty-four north, two west, sixteen miles north of east from Pekin, surrounded with a large setttement. It is located in the prairie, on the southeast side of Mackinau.

Macon County Prairie, an extensive tract, from twelve to twenty miles in width, lying north of Decatur, and betwixt the North fork of the Sangamon and Salt creek. Some parts are level and wet—other portions dry and undulating.

Macoupin Creek, a considerable stream that rises in the north part of Macon county; runs southwesterly, passes through Greene county, and enters the Illinois river twenty-six miles above its junction with the Mississippi, in section twenty-four, eight north, fourteen west of the third principal meridian.

Its branches are Phill's, Dry fork, Bear, and Hodge's creeks, and Lake fork.

The country along its banks is generally fertile, suitably proportioned into timber and prairie, and has a line of settlements through Macoupin and Greene counties.

Macoupin is aboriginal, and in all the French authors, spelled *Ma-qua-pin*, but it has become legalised on the statute books of the state in the uncouth form given at the head of this article, and usually pronounced by the people, *Ma-goo-pin*.

This word is said to be the Indian name of a vegetable with a large round leaf, growing in the lakes and ponds of Illinois, called by some people "splatter-dock," and found plentifully near this stream.

The large roots of this plant, if eaten raw, are very deleterious. The Indians, in early times, dug holes in the earth, which they walled with stone, and after heating them with large fires, put in the roots, covered them with earth, and in two days the rank poisonous taste was gone. They were then put on poles and dried for food. In this form they were eaten by the natives.*

Macoupin Prairie, a large prairie in Greene county, between the Piasau and Macoupin, moderately undulating, rich, and rapidly settling. The road from Alton to Carrollton passes through this prairie.

Towards the Illinois river, on the west, and the Macoupin creek on the east, are extensive bodies of fine timber. Emigrants from Vermont, and other northern and eastern states, are covering over this part of the county with fine farms. The settlement in the south part of this prairie is sometimes called *South Greene*.

Macoupin Settlement lies near the timber bordering upon the Macoupin creek and prairie, in Greene county, nine miles south of Carrollton. This settlement was commenced in December, 1816, by Daniel Allen, and John and Paul Harriford, and was then the most northern white settlement in the Illinois Territory. The prairie land is rich, but rather level, and the timber adjoining good. *Kane* post office is in this settlement.

Macoupin Point, a noted stand at the junction of the roads from Edwardsville to Springfield, and from Hillsboro' to Morgan county and Beardstown, sometimes called Henderson's stand.

It is in the northwest corner of Montgomery county, at the head of the timber, on the South fork of the Macoupin. South, along the roads to Edwardsville and Hillsboro', the surface of the prairie is flat and wet. North, towards Sugar creek, it is dry and undulating.

Maddux Settlement is in Clinton county, near the mouth of Crooked creek, eight miles south of Carlyle.

Manchester, a post town in Morgan county, on section twenty-eight, thirteen north, eleven west of the third principal meridian. It is on the main road leading from Carrollton to Jacksonville, eighteen miles from each place on the north side of Mark's prairie, and surrounded with a body of excellent timbered and prairie land.

* See Charlevoix's Voyage to North America, 1721.

Mantua, a large settlement in a timbered tract, in the southwestern part of White county, ten miles from Carmi. Duncanton is the post office.

Marais d'Ogce (*Ma-re-do-she*) is a sluggish stream, and a series of swamps, extending from Rock river to the Mississippi, and constituting the present boundary between the counties of Rock Island and Whiteside.

It is about twenty miles long, and in some places one mile, and in other places twenty or thirty yards wide. Near the Mississippi, where the road crosses, it is a clear stream of water, twenty yards wide, and sandy bottom. It is supposed that a canal might be cut, at very little expense, through this swamp into Rock river.

Marchant's Settlement, on the north side of Fulton county, twenty-four miles east of north from Lewistown.

Marine Settlement, a flourishing settlement in Madison county, between the east and west forks of Silver creek, and twelve miles east of Edwardsvslle.

This settlement was commenced by Captains Blakeman and Allen, in 1819. The settlement is large, and spread over an undulating, rich, and beautiful prairie, and is healthy and well watered. A post office.

Markham's Settlement, in Macoupin county, on Taylor's creek, twelve or fifteen miles west of Carlinville.

The land is good, surface undulating, and equally divided into timber and prairie.

Marrow Bone, a small creek in the north part of Shelby county. It rises in Macon county, runs southeast through Bone's settlement, into the west fork of the Kaskaskia.

Marseilles, a projected manufacturing town, on the north side of the Illinois river, at the Grand rapids, eight miles above Ottawa. A chartered company are engaged in constructing dams, mills, &c. Flour and lumber are made here, and the water power is immense and easily commanded. A post office has been established here. The canal will pass through it, and it already assumes the aspect of a bustling, enterprising village.

Marshall, a town site in Clark county, on the national

road, on sections thirteen and twenty-four, township eleven north, twelve west. It is a pleasant, healthy situation, and bids fair to become a place of some importance.

Marshall's Prairie, north of Cox's prairie, fourteen miles northeast of Brownsville, in Jackson county, is rich, undulating land, and the settlement contains a dozen families.

Martin's Creek and *Settlement*, in Wayne county, on Elm river, five miles north of Fairfield. The settlement consists of fifty or sixty families, and the creek is a branch of Elm river.

Martinsville, a town site and post office on the national road, in Clark county.

Mason, a small stream that enters the Illinois river from the south, twelve miles below the junction of the Kankakee with the Des Plaines. It is called also *Nettle creek*.

Mason Grove, in La Salle county, lies eighteen miles northeasterly from Ottawa. It lies on the Little Mason, is five miles long, and one mile wide, a tract of excellent land. It is called also *Virginia Grove*.

Mason's Prairie and settlement is in the southwestern part of Lawrence county, from twenty to twenty-five miles from Lawrenceville, with seventy or eighty families.

Mauvaiseterre, a stream in Morgan county, that rises in the prairie on the borders of Sangamon county, in several branches, runs a west course near Jacksonville, and flows into the Illinois river two miles below Naples.

Above Jacksonville, it is divided into *North*, *South*, and *Brier* or Middle forks.

For beauty of situation, fertility of soil, salubrity of climate, a due proportion of timber and prairie, good water, and almost every other advantage for agricultural purposes, no country in the wide spread valley of the west exceeds this, and yet by a most singular misnomer, the French, who explored the Illinois river, called it "*Mauvaise terre*"—poor land.

MAYSVILLE, the seat of justice for Clay county, is situated on the borders of the Twelve Mile prairie, and near the Little Wabash river, on the stage road to Vincennes.

It has three taverns, three stores, and about twenty families. The adjacent prairie is undulating, and second rate.

McAdam's Settlement is in Bond county, four miles south of Greenville; the land level, and tolerably good, and the settlement large.

MACOMB, the seat of justice of McDonough county, is situated on elevated ground, in a delightful prairie, between Drowning fork and Town fork, near the centre of the county. It is on the southwest quarter of section thirty-one, six north, two west, and was laid off in 1831. In 1832 it contained three stores, one grocery, about twenty families, and promises soon to become a pleasant inland village, with a considerable population around it.

McCord's Settlement, in Bond county, on the east side of the west fork of Shoal creek, eight miles northwest of Greenville.

The land is good, and there is a due proportion of timber and prairie.

McCormack's Settlement, lies towards the southwestern part of Pope county.

McCreery's Settlement, in Franklin county, ten miles east of Frankfort, in a timbered tract of country. The timber consists of oaks of different kinds, hickory, some poplar and other varieties. The soil is good, rather undulating, and the settlement large.

McEaver's Settlement is six miles southeast of Carlyle, in Clinton county, on the waters of Crooked creek.

McFatridge's Settlement, in Johnson county, eight miles northeast from Vienna, on the old road from Golconda to Kaskaskia, and on the waters of Cedar creek. The surface is rather broken, the soil thin, and the settlement contains sixty or seventy families.

McHenry, a town site in McHenry county, twelve miles south of the state boundary, and on the west side of Fox river. Surrounded with excellent prairie, and timber in groves and bur oak openings or barrens.

McKee's Creek, in the military tract, enters the Illinois river, in the northeast part of Pike county, in township three south, in range two west of the fourth principal meridian. It is made up of three principal branches, known by the names of *North*, *Middle*, and *West* forks.

North Fork, which is the longest branch, rises in Adams county, near the base line, in range five west, runs a devious course into Schuyler county, and receives a number of small tributaries. Its general course to the Illinois river is southeast.

Middle Fork originates near the boundary of Pike and Schuyler counties, and enters the west fork a few miles above its junction with the main stream.

West Fork rises in the northern part of Pike county, where it interlocks with the waters that fall into the Mississippi, and after running an eastern course, joins the main stream a few miles above its mouth. The land on McKee's creek and branches is excellent, suitably proportioned into timber and prairie, which is gently undulating and rich. The settlements already are large, and population is increasing from emigration. The same obstruction to rapid settlement exists here as in all portions of the military tract. Much good land is held by non residents. Could the land all be had at a reasonable price, this tract of country would soon be overspread with large farms.

McKee's Branch, a fork of Sugar creek, in Schuyler county, is a mill stream, three miles north of Rushville.

McLeansboro', the county seat of Hamilton county, situated on high ground, in township five south, and in range seven east from the third principal meridian. The settlement around is pretty extensive and the town contains twenty or twenty-five families, and five stores.

McRaney's Creek is a small stream that heads in Adams county, passes into Pike, and enters the Snycartee slough. The land is proportionably divided into timber and prairie, and of a good quality.

Meacham's Grove, now called *Salem*, is in Cook county, near the head of Salt creek, and contains about three sections of timber, of sugar maple, walnut, oaks, linden, ash, elm, hickory, &c. The prairie is undulating and rich. Around that and other small groves are about twenty-five families.

Mechanicsburg, a town site in the prairie near Clear creek, fifteen miles east of Springfield, on the road to Decatur. Post office *Clear creek*.

Melrose, a town site and post office, situated in Clark county, twelve miles southwest from Darwin. It has eighteen or twenty families.

Menomone, a stream in the northwest corner of the state. It rises in Iowa county, Wisconsin territory, runs southwest, and empties into the Mississippi three miles below the boundary line. The surface near its mouth is broken, and towards its head are rich prairies, and rich mines of lead. The timber is scarce, in groves and patches for six or eight miles up. Length about fifteen or twenty miles.

Meredosia, a town site, landing, and place of considerable business on the Illinois river in Morgan county, six miles above Naples. It is situated on an elevated sand ridge, with a good landing when the water is not too low. Here are two steam mills, several stores, and fifty families: and to be a point in the Northern cross rail road from Quincy by Springfield, to Indiana.

Meredosia can be approached from the bluffs and table land, without crossing any lakes or sloughs, which is not the case with other towns on the river in Morgan county. Much of the mercantile business of Jacksonville passes through this place. Above the town is a singular bayou, from whence its name, which, in French orthography, would be, *Marais d' Ogee.*

Exports for pork, lard, flour, beef, corn, whiskey, butter and potatoes, $ 200,000.

Imports in various kinds of merchandise landed at Meredosia, $ 450,000.

Meredosia Bay, is a body of water connected with the Illinois river, above Meredosia. It is seven miles long; its width varies from one half to one mile.

Middle Fork of Big Muddy River, one of the four heads of Big Muddy river, in Franklin county. It rises on the borders of Hamilton county, runs a southwestern course, and enters the main stream a few miles west of Frankfort. The country along its borders is divided into timber and prairie; the surface tolerably level, and the soil good second rate.

Middle Fork Settlement, in Jefferson county, lies between Mount Vernon and Long prairie; a timbered tract, good sugar tree groves, and a pleasant settlement.

Middle Fork of Shoal Creek rises in the prairies of Montgomery county, eight north, four west, passes Hillsboro', and enters Shoal creek about four miles above Bond county line.

Middle Fork of Silver Creek rises in the prairies northeast of the Marine settlement, in Madison county, runs south and enters the East fork.

Middle Grove, a post office and settlement on the north side of Fulton county, on section six, township eight north, four west and on the road from Canton to Knoxville.

Middleton's Ferry, on the Kaskaskia river, twenty miles east of Belleville, and fourteen miles southeasterly from Lebanon.

Middletown, in Sangamon county, is laid off in the prairie, between the timber of Salt creek and Irish grove, near Musick's station. Several families, &c.

Miers's Settlement is in Bond county, on the west side of Beaver creek, and two miles south of Greenville.

Milan, a post office and town site in the south part of Calhoun county, fractional section twenty-eight, township thirteen south, one west.

Mill Creek, a small stream that rises in the southwestern part of Edgar county, runs diagonally through Clark, and enters the Wabash near York.

Mill Creek, a small mill stream, in Randolph county. It enters the Kaskaskia river on the east side, one mile above the town of Kaskaskia.

Miller's Settlement adjoins the Mississippi, on the west

side of Alexander county. Here is some bottom, and rolling upland, generally good. Population about thirty families.

Miller's Settlement, near the centre of Mercer county. A good tract of country.

Miller's Settlement, in Macon county, four miles west of Decatur, in the south side of Macon county prairie. Soil rich with good timber adjoining.

Mills's Prairie, in Edwards county, eleven miles northeast from Albion, four miles long, and two and a half wide—a fine and well settled tract.

Milton was once a town site, situated on Wood river, in Madison county, two miles southeast of Alton.

Mitchell's Settlement, in St. Clair county, six miles east of Belleville—a fine tract of country.

Monk Hill is situated on the American bottom, in the borders of Madison county, eight miles northeasterly from St. Louis.

The circumference, at the base, is about six hundred yards, and its height about ninety feet. On the south side, about half way down, is a broad step, or apron, about fifteen feet wide.

This hill, or mount, was the residence, for several years, of the monks of the order of La Trappe, the most rigid and austere of all the monkish orders.

Their monastery was originally situated in the district of Perche, in France, in one of the most lonely spots that could be chosen. They fled from the commotions of that kingdom to America, lived for a time in Kentucky, and came to Illinois in 1806 or '07, and settled on this mound.

They cultivated a garden, repaired watches, and traded with the people, but were generally filthy in their habits, and extremely severe in their penances and discipline. In 1813, they sold off their personal property, and left the country, for France.

MONMOUTH, the seat of justice for Warren county, is in the prairie, and, on the south side of the timber of Henderson river. It is located on section twenty-nine, eleven north, two west has a flourishing settlement, and a first rate tract of country around it.

It has four stores, two groceries, one tavern, two physicians, no lawyers, and about twenty families.

Montebello is a town site, post office and settlement in Hancock county, on the bluffs of the Mississippi, one and a half miles above the foot of the Lower rapids.

There is a considerable settlement along the river, the whole length of the rapids.

Montecello, the site of the Alton Female Seminary, a delightful situation on the borders of Scamet's prairie, four and a half miles north of Alton.

Montezuma, a town site, post office, and landing on the right bank of the Illinois river in Pike county, thirteen miles southwest from Pittsfield.

Montgomery, a town site in Adams county, in section twenty-seven, township two south, six west, with four families.

Moore's Prairie, in Jefferson county, is eight miles long, from two to three miles wide, and from six to twelve miles southeast of Mount Vernon. A post office.

Some portions are flat and wet, other parts dry and gently undulating, and the settlement along its borders consists of seventy-five families.

Moore's Prairie, in St. Clair county, is five miles east of Belleville, and about the same in extent. It is tolerably level, of good soil, and spread over with fine farms.

Moore's Settlement, in Monroe county, near Waterloo, is an extensive settlement.

Morgan's Creek, in Kane county, rises in Ausauble grove, runs west, and enters Fox river, one mile above the south boundary of Kane county.

Moss's Settlement, in Pope county, near the heads of Big Bay and Lusk's creeks; twenty miles from Golconda. It is a good tract of country.

Mounse's Creek, a small stream, and branch of the North fork of Sangamon, in Foster's settlement, Macon county.

Mount Carbon, a coal bank on Muddy river, four miles

above Brownswille, in Jacksou county. Large quantities are exported from this place down the river. Here is a large steam saw and grist mill.

MOUNT CARMEL, the seat of justice for Wabash county, is situated on high ground, on the Wabash river, and on section twenty, in fractional township one south, and in range twelve west from the second principal meridian.

This town was laid off in 1818, by Rev. Thomas S. Hinde, of Ohio, on the project of establishing a moral, temperate, and industrious village.

The prospective improvement of the rapids of the Wabash near this place, is thought to give it peculiar importance as a place of business. The country around is high, undulating, healthy, and contains an extensive settlement of industrious farmers. The court house and jail are brick. The Methodist society, which is large, has a house of worship.

In Mount Carmel are ten stores, two groceries, (or "doggeries," as our correspondent calls them, and further states, " the keepers are getting ashamed of them,")— two taverns and a third in course of preparation, one stationed preacher, and four local preachers, of the Methodist Episcopal Church, one German Reformed preacher, two physicians, one steam doctor, three lawyers, and from one thousand to twelve hundred population.

The religious denominations, are Methodists (Episcopal,) numerous, evangelical Lutherans, associated with the German Reformed, Presbyterians, some Baptists and Episcopalians—three steam mills, one ox tread mill, mechanics and trades of various descriptions, a foundry for castings for machinery, etc. The commerce of this place is considerable, and from the 31st of March to the 12th of April, 1837, 26 steam boats arrived and departed.

Mount Flat Head, on the west side of the Des Plaines, and two miles below Mount Joliet. It extends two miles; the north end is rounded—the south end irregularly shaped—its contents sand, gravel, and coarse pebbles, worn smooth by water friction.

Mount Joliet, a mound situated on the west bank of the

Des Plaines, about sixteen miles above its junction with the Kankakee. It is in the southwestern part of Cook county, in township thirty-five north, in range ten east from the third principal meridian. It is in the midst of a large plain, covered in summer with short, thin grass, and which bears striking marks of having been once inundated.

Its size is variously estimated. Beck, in his Gazetteer, states, "It is three or four hundred yards in length, north and south, and two or three hundred in breadth, east and west. It is in the form of a pyramid, and is evidently the work of art."

From the last position I entirely dissent. From all the facts I have gathered from those who have visited it, I have no doubt, but like similar eminences in every part of the globe, it is a natural production. Several gentlemen, who have passed this mound without stopping particularly to measure it, have estimated its length one mile, its breadth, at the base, half a mile, and its height one hundred and fifty feet. It appears to be an immense pile of sand and pebbles, similar to the sand ridges along the Illinois river.

This name was given by the companions of Joliet, who visited this country in 1673.

Mount Pleasant, in St. Clair county, and four miles northeast of Belleville, the residence of William Kinney, a former lieutenant governor of the state, and now president of the "Board of Public Works."

Mount Pleasant, a post office in Union county, east of Jonesboro', on the road to Vienna. (See Stokes's Settlement.)

Mount Pulaski, a town site in Sangamon county, on an elevated prairie, in township eighteen north, range two west.

Mount Sterling, a post office and town site in Six's prairie, Schuyler county, seventeen miles west of Rushville, on the mail road to Quincy. It has four stores, one minister and a small Presbyterian church, organised, various mechanics, and about 150 inhabitants.

Mount St. Charles, in Jo Daviess county, twelve miles

east of Galena. The surrounding country becomes elevated to the height of seven or eight hundred feet above the mining country generally. This mount, like a pyramid, rises from the centre of this elevation one hundred and fifty feet. The base of the whole mount includes two or three square miles;—the base of the pyramid is one fourth of a mile in length, and two hundred and fifty yards in breadth. Its top is long and quite narrow. The whole mound, as is the case with many smaller ones, is a natural formation.

MOUNT VERNON, the seat of justice for Jefferson county, situated on the stage road from St. Louis, by Carlyle, to Shawneetown, on section twenty-nine, township two south, in range three east of the third principal meridian, and near the centre of the county.

It has six stores, three groceries, one tavern, two physicians, two ministers, a court house and jail, a Methodist Episcopal and a Baptist society, and various mechanics, and 140 inhabitants, and is pleasantly situated on the north side of Casey's prairie, and surrounded with a considerable settlement. It is in latitude thirty-eight degrees twenty minutes north, forty-seven and a half miles a little east of south from Vandalia.

Mouth of Ohio. The importance of a good town site, at the junction of the Ohio and Mississippi rivers, has, for many years, excited the attention of the enterprising. It is a feature in our western rivers, with few exceptions, that at and near their junction, the land is alluvion, of a recent formation, and at the high annual floods, usually inundated to the depth of several feet. This is the case, particularly at the mouth of the Ohio. For twelve miles along that river, above its mouth, and a farther distance along the Mississippi, and across the point to Cash river, the country is subject to annual inundations. Had the author of nature formed here an elevated situation, nothing could have prevented this spot from becoming the central commercial emporium of the great western valley. The immense trade of the Ohio and Mississippi, at some future day, will warrant the expense of forming a site here for a commercial town. The termination of the great central railroad will greatly facilitate this object, and, with the commerce of these great rivers, build up a splendid city. In due time, art, enterprise, and perseverance will triumph over nature at this place, and a large commercial city will exist where now the waters of the Ohio and Mississippi occasionally spread.

Mud Creek, a small stream in the southwestern part of Washington and southeast part of St. Clair counties. It rises in the northwestern part of Perry county, takes a northwestern direction, and enters the Kaskaskia river opposite an island in township two south, six west. A smaller creek, in the same region, is called Little Mud creek.

Mud Creek, a branch of Vermilion river in Livingston county. It rises in the prairie, runs southwest, and enters Vermilion, twelve miles below Otter creek. Weed's settlement is on it near the head of the timber.

Muddy, a small stream and branch of the Embarras, in Lawrence county, ten miles west from Lawrenceville.

Muddy, a branch of the Little Wabash that flows into it on its eastern side, in Clay county, just below the Vincennes road. Between the two streams for some distance, is a swamp, which overflows in high water.

Muddy Creek, in Lawrence county, rises in the prairie, runs north of east, and enters the Embarras, five miles above Lawrenceville. Land, second rate; population forty or fifty families.

Muddy Fork, a branch of the Embarras river, in Coles county, that enters the Embarras, three miles below the national road.

Muddy Point, in the southwestern part of Coles county, and one of the heads of the Little Wabash. The timber is excellent, prairie adjoining is rolling and rich, and the settlement consists of eighty or one hundred families.

Mud Prairie is on Mud creek, a small branch of Big Beaucoup creek. It lies in Washington and Perry counties, fourteen miles northeast from Pinckneyville, and is level and rather wet.

Mud Prairie, in Wayne county, eight miles northwest from Fairfield, is a low, wet tract, rightly named.

Mulberry Grove, a small grove at the head of Apple creek, near the boundary line of Morgan and Sangamon counties.

Mulberry Grove Post Office, the eastern side of Bond county, on the road to Vandalia.

Muskeeto Creek, rises in the large prairie of Macon county, and enters the North fork of Sangamon, in Sangamon county.

Muscooten Bay, a large body of water in the northwest part of Morgan county, that unites with the Illinois river just above Beardstown. In high water it becomes connected with the Sangamon river.

Napierville, a town in Cook county, on the east side of the west fork of the Du Page, and has four stores, a saw and grist mill, a school, twenty-five families, and two-hundred and fifty inhabitants. The country around is dry, undulating surface, and rich soil, with a tolerable supply of timber on the Du Page.

Naples, a commercial town in Morgan county, situated on the Illinois river, two miles above the mouth of the Mauvaiseterre, on section twelve, township fifteen north, in range fourteen west from the third principal meridian.

It is laid off on a level prairie, at the foot of a sand ridge, and above ordinary high water. Very occasionally, extreme floods will come over a portion of the town site.

Here are several stores, three taverns, a medical and drug shop, two physicians, a number of mechanics, three steam mills, and one hundred families.

Its commerce is considerable. In 1835, the arrivals and departures of steamboats amounted to 302. Exports in produce, 1835, $965,000. Imports in merchandise and sold wholesale and retail, 25,000. A railroad to Jacksonville is now in progress of construction; distance, via Bethel, 20 miles.

Narrows, or *Little Detroit*, a place so called, on Peoria lake five miles above Peoria. The bluffs from the west side here touch the lake, and the Galena road runs at the foot.

Narrows. Two places in Morgan county bear this name. One is now *Sweet's Settlement,* five miles east of Jacksonville. The other is on the road from Springfield to Beardstown, ten miles from the latter place. Here is a fine settlement, good prairie, with points and groves of timber. The settlement receives its name from two points of timber approaching.

NASHVILLE, the seat of justice for Washington county, is situated on a beautiful and elevated prairie, near the head of Little Crooked creek, and two and a half miles south of east from the centre of the county.

It is situated on section twenty-four, township two south, range three west of the third principal meridian. It contains three stores, several mechanics, a steam mill, and fifteen or twenty families. It is on the borders of an arm of the Grand prairie, elevated, rich and undulating.

Nettle Creek, a trifling stream in Morgan county, near Winchester. The settlement contains one hundred families.

Nettle Creek, in La Salle county. (See *Mason.*)

Newbern, a post office in Greene county, seven miles northeast from Grafton.

NEW BOSTON, the seat of justice for Mercer county, situated on the Mississippi, two and a half miles above the mouth of Edwards river. It is a small but growing place.

New Castle, a town site in the southwest part of McLean county in township twenty-one north, range one east.

New Design is in Monroe county, four miles south of Waterloo. This is one of the oldest American settlements in Illinois. The land was originally a mixture of timber and prairie.

New Haven, a post town, two miles above the mouth of the Little Wabash, on the line between Gallatin and White counties. Here is a large saw and flouring mill, with several stores, and about fifteen or twenty families.

New Lexington, a town site and post office eight miles northwesterly from Jacksonville, in Morgan county. It has two stores, two groceries, and fifteen or twenty families.

Newlin's Settlement, in Crawford county, ten miles northwest from Palestine, on the borders of a prairie, with fifty or sixty families.

Newman's Branch, a trifling stream in Morgan county, that runs southwest, and enters the Mauvaiseterre north of Jacksonville.

Newport, a town site and landing at the mouth of Apple creek, in Greene county. It contains two or three stores, and half a dozen families.

New Salem, a post office and town located in Sangamon county, on the southwest side of Sangamon river, on a bluff and surrounded with a large settlement. It has three or four stores, and thirty families. A grist and saw mill is here, erected on Sangamon river.

It is on section twenty-five, eighteen north, seven west.

NEWTON, the seat of justice for Jasper county, situated on the west side of the Embarras, on the road from Palestine to Vandalia and about the centre of the county.

It has one store, one grocery, a Baptist society, and 100 inhabitants.

New Virginia, a settlement and tract of country in Bond county, two miles east of Greenville, and on the head waters of Beaver creek. Here are several fine groves, and good prairie.

Nine Mile Creek, in Randolph county. It rises northeast of Kaskaskia, takes a western direction, and enters the Kaskaskia river ten or twelve miles above the town.

A branch of it is called Little Nine Mile creek.

Nine Mile Prairie, in Perry county, lies ten miles east of Pinckneyville, and a post office of the same name.

It is about nine miles in diameter, tolerably level, and considerable population around it.

North Arm, a prairie and a settlement, in Edgar county, six miles east of Paris. The prairie is good land, about three miles wide. Its east end runs to the state line, and its west end unites with the grand prairie. The settlement is large and dense.

North Fork, a post office, in section twenty-five, township twenty-two north, twelve west in Vermilion county.

North Fork of the Embarras rises in the southwest part of Clark county, runs south near the line between Crawford and Jasper, and enters the Embarras at the southeast corner of the latter county. The country is a level, timbered tract, in some places rather wet.

North Fork of the Macoupin. This stream is the same as Hodges's or Otter creek, but the settlement, which is extensive and flourishing, is known by the name of *North Fork*.

North Fork of Salt Creek. It rises in McLean county, and, with Lake fork, forms the head of one of the principal branches of the Sangamon river.

North Grove, in Cass county, is at the head of Clear creek, twelve miles east from Beardstown. It has fine timber.

North Grove at the head of Leaf river in Ogle county.

North Prairie, in Morgan county, twelve miles north easterly from Jacksonville, is a delightful tract of rich, dry, undulating prairie. A large settlement surrounds it, and several families from Virginia have recently made locations in it.

North Prairie, on the south side of the Mauvaiseterre in Morgan county, and adjoining Walnut creek. It is level.

Norris's Settlement in Greene county, twelve miles northeasterly from Carrollton, with a proportion of timber and prairie, rather level, but good soil.

Norwegian Grove is on the east fork of the Kishwaukee in Boone county.

Oakland, a post office and settlement in Coles county,

14 miles northeast from Charleston, and on the road from Springfield to Paris and Terre Haute.

Ogle's Creek, a small stream in St. Clair county that rises in the west end of Ogle's prairie, runs a northeast course and enters Silver creek.

Ogle's Prairie, a beautiful, undulating prairie, in St. Clair county, five miles north of Belleville. It is five miles long, and from one to two miles wide, surrounded, and partly covered, with a flourishing settlement and fine farms.

Ohio Settlement, in Fork prairie, Bond county, five miles north of Greenville, is of considerable extent. The land is second rate.

Ohio Grove is in the east fork of the Kishwaukee four miles from its mouth, near the corners of Winnebago and Boone counties.

Okau, (*Au Kas*, Fr.) a name frequently given to the Kaskaskia river.

It appears to have been originally a contraction, using the first syllable for the whole name, and prefixing the article—a practice common among the early settlers and explorers of Illinois.

Okau post office is in Washington county, section twenty-five, township one south, five west, on the road from Nashville by Middleton's Ferry to Lebanon.

Okau Settlement, in the southeastern part of Macon county, twenty miles from Decatur, lies on the West fork of the Kaskaskia, and contains twenty or thirty families.

Olmsted's Mound, an eminence in the prairie in Morgan county, eight miles south of west from Jacksonville. It was the temporary seat of justice for this county previous to 1825.

Oldman's Creek, a small stream in the country attached to La Salle county, that enters Rock river eighteen miles above Dixon's ferry.

Oliver's sometimes called *Allen's Prairie*, in the corner of Hancock, Adams, and Schuyler counties. It is twelve miles long, and from two to four miles broad.

Old Town Timber. (See *Dawson's Grove.*)

O'Neal's Creek, is a branch of Crooked creek, in Schuyler county, ten miles from Rushville.

Ono, a post office in Edgar county, on section four, township fourteen north, eleven west, six miles north-northeast from Paris.

Orendorff's Mill and settlement is on Sugar creek, in the south part of Tazewell county. The settlement is large, and the land good.

Oregon City, is the temporary seat of justice for Ogle county, situated on the north side of Rock river on a handsome elevated alluvion bottom, ten miles above Grand Detour, and fifteen miles above Dixonville. It has two stores and eight or ten families.

OTTAWA, the seat of justice for La Salle county, was laid off by the canal commissioners, in 1830, at the junction of Fox river with the Illinois, and is thought by many to be an important location for business.

It is laid off on both sides of the Illinois river, on the entire section numbered eleven, and in township thirty-three north, in range three east of the third principal meridian.

At the town site, the water of the Illinois is deep, and the landing convenient. Steamboats reach this place in the spring, and at other seasons when the water is high.

Below, for the distance of eight or nine miles, are rapids and shoals, formed by barriers of sand and lime stone rock. Ottawa has 8 or 10 stores, 2 taverns, 3 physicians, 5 lawyers, and 75 or 80 families. Large additions have been made to the town plat by laying off additional lots on lands adjoining. It is expected a lateral canal from the Illinois and Michigan canal will pass through the town to the Illinois river. This, by means of a feeder to the rapids of Fox river will open a navigation into Kane county. Fox river is susceptible of improvement by slackwater at small expense, into the Wisconsin territory, and from thence by a short canal of fifteen miles may become connected with Milwaukee. Hence Ottawa may be regarded as one of the most important sites for commercial business in the state. Near it dams are already projected across the Illinois river and immense water power thus created. The *Ottawa Republican* a weekly paper is published here.

The country around is pleasant, undulating, and well adapted to farming. The timber is in small quantities, chiefly in groves; the prairie land generally dry and rich soil.

Lime, and coarse free stone, in great abundance.

Otter Creek, a small stream that rises in the prairies in the southwestern part of Greene county, runs a westerly course, and enters the Illinois river about fourteen miles above its junction with the Mississippi.

Towards its head is fine, undulating prairie, but lower down the surface is timbered and broken.

Otter Creek rises in the southwestern part of Fulton county, runs east, then south, and enters the Illinois in section twenty-two, three north, three east. Large bodies of timber and good coal are on this stream.

Otter Creek, in Livingston county, rises in La Salle county, runs southwest, and enters Vermilion river in the southwest corner of thirty north, four east. Here is a valuable body of timber, rolling and rich prairie and a large settlement.

Out House Settlement, on Sugar creek, in Clinton county, twenty-two miles southwest from Carlyle.

Ox Bow Prairie is in Putnam county, ten miles south of Hennepin. It is a rich prairie, five miles long, and from one to two miles wide, shaped like an ox bow, and surrounded with excellent timber. The prairie is overspread with fine farms.

Paddock's Settlement is in Madison county, on the Springfiele road, seven miles north of Edwardsville. The prairie is undulating, fertile, and healthy.

Panky's Settlement is in the southeast corner of Pope county.

Panther Creek heads in McLean county, runs southeast, and enters the Mackinau near the county line.

Panther Creek, in Sangamon county, a trifling stream and branch of Sugar creek, in fifteen north, five west.

Panther Creek is in the northeastern part of Morgan county, and enters Sangamon river.

Panther Grove, a point of timber on Panther creek, in Morgan county.

Another grove, called *Little Panther*, lies east of it.

PALESTINE, the seat of justice for Crawford county, situated three miles from the Wabash river, on the borders of Lamotte prairie, and in sections thirty-three and thirty-four, township seven north, in range eleven west of the second principal meridian.

It is twenty-five miles north of Vincennes, in latitude thirty-eight degrees, fifty-eight minutes north, and eighty-two miles east from Vandalia.

It has 4 stores, 2 groceries, 3 taverns, 2 lawyers, 4 physicians, 2 ministers, about 450 inhabitants, 2 apothecaries' shops and a land office, and mechanics of various trades.

The religious denominations are Presbyterians, Methodists and Baptists. The Methodists have a house of worship.

Palmer's Settlement, above the south fork of Spoon river, in the county of Knox, and near the line of Fulton county.

Pappoose Creek rises in the swampy land in the eastern part of Boone county, runs a southwestern course and enters the North Fork of the Kishwaukee. Timber oak barrens, chiefly bur oak; soil sandy and gravelly.

Paradise, a post office at the head of the Little Wabash, in Coles county, on the road from Shelbyville to Charleston.

PARIS, the county seat for Edgar county, on section one, thirteen north, twelve west of the second principal meridian. It is a pleasant village, on the borders of a rich prairie, surrounded with good farms, and has a court house of brick, 7 stores, 2 groceries, 1 tavern, 4 physicians, 3 lawyers, and about 55 families, or 275 inhabitants.

Parker's Prairie is a large, level prairie, on the western side of Clark county, somewhat wet, soil second rate. A considerable settlement.

Parker's Settlement is ten miles southwest from Palestine, in Crawford county. A mixture of timber and prairie, and about forty families.

Parr's Settlement is in Bond county, seven miles north of Greenville, adjoining, and within the timbered tract, on the East fork of Shoal creek.

Paupau Grove is at the head of Indian creek, Kane county. It is a rich tract of country.

Peek-a-ton-o-kee, a large, navigable stream that enters Rock river, in Jo Daviess county, about six miles below the boundary line. It rises in two principal branches, near the Blue Mounds, in Wisconsin territory, called the *East* and *West forks*, which unite before they enter the state of Illinois.

The *East fork* rises north of the Blue Mounds, near the head of Grant river The *West fork* runs near the Blue Mounds.

After their junction, the Peek-a-ton-o-kee runs first a south course into Illinois, thence a southeast course, and finally winds round north of east, and enters Rock river. It is one hundred yards wide at the mouth, eighty yards wide at the boundary line, and is navigable for flat boats to Mineral Point, in the Wisconsin territory.

I have had no little trouble in determining the orthography of this name. Its aboriginal meaning is said to be "*Swift water.*" By many persons it is written and pronounced *Pik-e-tol-e-ka*. I have adopted the orthography and pronunciation of gentlemen from its vicinity.

PEKIN is situated on the east side of the Illinois river, twelve miles below Peoria, on fractional section thirty-three, twenty-five north, five west of the third principal meridian, on a sandy bluff, elevated and pleasant. The landing is tolerably good at a moderate stage of the river, but too shoal at the low stage.

Pekin contains twelve stores, three groceries, two taverns, (and a splendid hotel building by a company,) seven lawyers, four physicians, four ministers of the gospel, one drug store, three forwarding and commission houses, two houses for slaughtering and packing pork, one auction house, a printing office which issues the Tazewell Telegraph, and about eight-hundred inhabitants.

There is also one steam flouring mill that manufactures two hundred barrels of flour per day, a steam saw mill and two steam distilleries, an academy and a common school.

The religious denominations are Presbyterian, Methodist and Unitarian, which have houses of worship.

PEORIA, the seat of justice for Peoria county, situated on the west bank of the Illinois river, on section nine, eight north, eight east, and formerly called *Fort Clark.*

From a report made by Edward Coles, Esq. formerly governor of Illinois, to the Secretary of the treasury, it may be learned, "The old village of Peoria was situated one mile and a half above the lower extremity or outlet of the Peoria lake. This village had been inhabited by the French previous to the recollection of the present generation. About the year 1778 or 1779, the first house was built in what was then called La Ville de Maillet, afterwards the new village of Peoria, and which has recently been known by the name of Fort Clark, situated about one mile and a half below the old village, immediately at the lower point, or outlet of the lake. The situation being preferred on account of the water being better, and its being thought more healthy, the inhabitants gradually deserted the old village, and by the year 1796 or 1797, had entirely abandoned it, and removed to the new one.

" The inhabitants of Peoria consisted generally of Indian traders, hunters, and voyagers. and had long formed a link of connection between the French residing on the great lakes and the Mississippi river. From that happy felicity of adapting themselves to their situation and associates, for which the French are so remarkable, the inhabitants of Peoria lived generally in harmony with their savage neighbours. It appears, however, that about the year 1781, they were induced to abandon the village from an apprehension of Indian hostility; but soon after the peace of 1783, they again returned, and continued to reside there until the autumn of 1812, when they were forcibly removed from it, and the place destroyed by a captain Craig, of the Illinois militia, on the ground, it was said, that his company of militia was fired on in the night, while at anchor in their boats before the village, by Indians, with whom the inhabitants were suspected by Craig to be too intimate and friendly."

The inhabitants being thus driven from the place, fled to the French settlements on the Mississippi for shelter.

In 1813, Peoria was occupied by the United States troops, and a block house erected and called Fort Clark. The timber was cut on the opposite side of the lake, and with considerable labor transported across, and hauled on truck wheels by the men.

After the termination of the war, Fort Clark was abandoned, and the buildings soon after burnt by the Indians. The present town is near its ruins.

Without intending to do injustice to several other beautiful town sites along the upper parts of the Illinois river, amongst which is Pekin, Hennepin, the foot of the rapids, Ottawa, etc. I shall copy from Beck's Gazetteer the following description of Peoria.

"The situation of this place is beautiful beyond description. From the mouth of the Kickapoo, or Redbud creek, which empties into the Illinois two miles below the old fort, the alluvion is a prairie which stretches itself along the river three or four miles.

"The shore is chiefly made up of rounded pebbles, and is filled with springs of the finest water. The first bank, which is from six to twelve feet above high water mark, extends west about a quarter of a mile from the river, gradually ascending, when it rises five or six feet to the second bank. This extends nearly on a level to the bluffs, which are from sixty to one hundred feet in height. These bluffs consist of rounded pebbles, overlaying strata of lime stone and sand stone, rounded at the top, and corresponding in their course with the meanders of the river and lake. The ascent, although steep, is not perpendicular. On the bluffs, the surface again becomes level, and is beautifully interspersed with prairie and woodland.

"From the bluffs the prospect is uncommonly fine. Looking towards the east you first behold an extensive prairie, which, in spring and summer, is covered with grass, with whose green the brilliant hues of a thousand flowers form the most lively contrast. Beyond this, the lake, clear and calm, may be seen emptying itself into, or by its contraction forming the river, whose meanders, only hid from the view by the beautiful groves of timber which here and there arise, can be traced to the utmost extent of vision."

Peoria is now rapidly advancing in population and improvements. In the summer of 1833, it consisted of about twenty-five families. These more than doubled in a few weeks from emigration.

Peoria now has twenty-five stores, two wholesale and five retail groceries, two drug stores, two hotels and several boarding houses, two free schools and an incorporated academy, two Presbyterian houses of worship and congregations, one Methodist, one Baptist, one Unitarian and one Episcopal congregation, six lawyers, eight or ten physicians, one brewery, two steam sawmills, the usual proportion of mechanics, a court house and jail and a population from fifteen to eighteen hundred, and rapidly increasing. The "Peoria Register and Northwestern Gazetteer" is issued weekly, by S. M. Davis, Esq. The religious people of this place appear to have been uncommonly liberal, by contributing about *twenty-three thousand dollars* the past year for philanthropic purposes.

Peoria Lake, an expansion of the Illinois river, commencing at Peoria, and extending about twenty miles in a northeasterly direction. It is much wider than the river, and has very little current. The water is clear, and its bottom gravelly. It may be considered as two lakes, divided by the *Narrows*. It abounds with various kinds of fish, such as sturgeon, buffalo, bass of several species, perch, white fish, pickerel, etc., which can be caught with the seine in great abundance.

The Indian name for this lake is *Pin-a-ta-wee*. Some authors call it *Illinois Lake*.

Perkin's Settlement is in the northeast part of Hancock county, on the head waters of Crooked creek. The name of the post office is *Fountain Green*.

Peru, a post office, landing and town site, on the north side of the Illinois river, on section sixteen, township thirty-three north, one east, and one mile below the termination of the Illinois and Michigan canal. It has one warehouse and two or three families.

Perry, a town site in Pike county, on section twenty-one, township three south, three west. It has two or three stores, several families, and is a pleasant village, surrounded with a fine country, diversified with timber and prairie.

Petersburg, a town and post office, on the west side of Sangamon river, in Sangamon county, on fractional section fourteen, township eighteen north, seven west, and about seventeen miles northeast from Springfield. It has six stores, a steam saw and grist mill, and twenty families.

Phelps's Grove is on a small stream in Ogle county, that enters Rock river three miles above Oregon city.

Phelps's Prairie, in Franklin county on the waters of Crab Orchard creek, twelve miles south of Frankfort, is good land, and somewhat rolling.

In its neighbourhood is *Poor prairie*, a wet, level tract; and *Wright's prairie*, an undulating tract, with a considerable settlement.

Phigley's Settlement lies between the head waters of McKee's creek and Bear creek, in Adams county. It has about twenty-five families. The land is rather flat, but good,—about twenty miles east from Quincy.

Phil's Creek enters the Macoupin on the south side, about the middle of township nine north, eleven west. It heads in the prairies near the sources of the Piasau.

There is considerable timber, with excellent prairie on the borders of this stream.

Phillips's Settlement, in the northwestern part of Alexander county, on Sexton's creek, twenty-five miles from America, consists of eight or ten families.

Piankeshau Bend, on the Wabash river, in Wabash county, eighteen miles north from Mount Carmel. It is a fertile tract, timber rather scarce, with a mixture of prairie and barrens.

Piasau, a small stream that rises in a beautiful tract of country near the line of Greene and Macoupin counties, and enters the Mississippi about ten miles above Lower Alton.

Pigeon Creek is a stream that rises in Adams county, and runs westward near that and Pike county, which it enters, and passes into the Snycartee slough three miles below the county line.

In the bottom, the land is level, dry, and excellent—on the bluffs, somewhat broken.

Pilot Knob, in the western part of Washington county, a singular eminence and point of observation on the old Vincennes and Kaskaskia trace.

PINCKNEYVILLE, a small village, and the seat of justice for Perry county. It is situated on the west side of Big Beaucoup creek, at the head of the four mile prairie, and on section twenty-four, five south, three west. It has four stores, one tavern, one grocery, and fifteen or twenty families, and is surrounded with a large settlement of industrious farmers.

Pine Creek, in Ogle county. It rises in the prairie between Rock river and White Oak grove, runs a southeast course and enters Rock river at Grand Detour, and is a good mill stream. Its timber is shrubby pine, white, black, red and bur oaks, hickory, linden, sugar maple, elm, &c. One-sixth part of the land on its borders is timbered. The prairie adjoining is elevated, rolling and rich, and the country abounds with fine springs.

Pinus, a post office in Jackson county, on section thirty-four, township ten south, two west, twelve miles south-southeast from Brownsville.

Piper's Point, a settlement in Greene county, sixteen miles northeast from Carrollton, adjoining String prairie, and the timber of Apple creek. The land is tolerably level, rich, and proportionably divided into timber and prairie. There are sixty or seventy families in this settlement.

Piskasau, a branch of Kishwaukee. It rises in Boone county, and some of its head branches probably over the boundary line, runs a southwestern course, and enters the north branch of the Kishwaukee, in section twenty-five, township forty-four north, range four east. Near its head the soil is wet, but further down, dry and undulating.

PITTSFIELD, the new seat of justice for Pike county, was laid off in April, 1833, on the southwest quarter of section twenty-four, five south, four west. It is a high and healthy situation, in an undulating prairie, and on the dividing ridge nearly equidistant from the Illinois and Mississippi rivers. The country around is fertile, and proportionably distributed into timber and prairie, and is rapidly settling.

Pittsfield has three stores, two groceries, two taverns, three lawyers, one physician, several mechanics, and from 150 to 200 inhabitants.

Plainfield, a village and post town in Will county, on section nine, township thirty-six north, nine east, and nine miles north-northwest from Juliet.

It has two stores, two taverns, several mechanical trades, a Methodist and a Baptist congregation with houses of worship, and between four and five hundred inhabitants.

Plainfield is beautifully situated on an undulating prairie, east side of the Du Page, and adjoining Walker's grove.

Plato, a town site laid off on Iroquois river, four miles from the mouth of Spring creek, in Iroquois county. A steam mill is to be erected here.

Pleasant Grove, in Boone county, on the stage road from

Chicago to Galena, on the southeast side of the Kishwaukee, and twelve miles east of Belvidere. It is about four miles long and one mile wide, surrounded with a rich, undulating prairie. A considerable settlement around.

Pleasant Grove, three miles long and one wide, and a settlement of twenty-five or thirty families, in Tazewell county, eight miles east of Pekin, on the waters of Dillon's creek. The land is rich, and the timber consists of walnut, sugar maple, linden, oak, etc.

Pleasant Grove, in Morgan county, a settlement on the borders of Sweet's prairie, between Manchester and Winchester. The land in this quarter is good, with a due mixture of timber and prairie.

Pleasant Vale, a town site and post office in Pike county, on section nine, township five south, six west, seventeen miles northwest from Pittsfield. It is pleasantly situated under the bluffs, and surrounded with rich land, both timber and prairie.

Plum Creek, in Randolph county, enters the Kaskaskia river from the east side, eighteen miles above Kaskaskia.

Plum Creek rises in the prairie of Morgan county, west of Jacksonville, runs west, and enters the Illinois river below Phillip's ferry.

Plum Creek Prairie is near the boundary line of St. Clair and Randolph counties, ten miles long, and three broad; good soil, and scattering settlements along its borders.

Plum River, in Jo Daviess county, rises near Kellogg's grove, runs southwest, and enters the Mississippi ten miles below Rush creek. It is a good mill stream.

Above its mouth are rapids, The country along its borders is a mixture of timber and prairie. It is divided into *South*, *North*, and *Middle forks*, and here is some of the finest farming land in the country.

Point Republic, a post office and settlement, near the Vermilion river, in La Salle county, and on the road from Hennepin to Ottawa.

Polecat Creek, a stream in Coles county, that rises in the prairies towards Edgar county, runs southwest, and enters the Embarras east of Charleston. Near its head is a very fertile region, well timbered: further down the surface is broken. The settlement has thirty families.

Pond Slough, the name given to the outlet of a line of ponds in Johnson county, between Big Bay creek and Cash river. It is a deep, muddy channel. [See Cash river.]

Pope's River rises in the great prairies in the south part of Henry county, between Henderson's and Edwards's rivers, runs a west course through Mercer county, and enters the Mississippi, a few miles below Edwards's river. In Mercer county there are some fine tracts of timber on this stream, further up it passes through a prairie country. The land generally on Pope's and Edwards's rivers is abundantly rich, but there is a deficiency of timber.

Postville, in the northeastern part of Sangamon county, on section twenty-five, township twenty north, range three east, and on the north side of Salt creek. It has 2 stores, 1 grocery, and 3 or 4 families.

Potatoe Creek rises on the west side of Fulton county, near Table grove, runs a southeastern course, and enters Spoon river about four miles west of Lewistown. Excellent land, both prairie and timbered, adjoins it.

Prairie Creek in Sangamon county, a trifling stream that rises in the prairie between Spring and Richland creeks; makes a circuit in sixteen north, six west, and enters the latter before its junction with Sangamon river.

Prairie de Long Creek rises north of Waterloo, near the dividing line of St. Clair and Monroe counties, runs southeasterly through the eastern part of Monroe, receives Richland creek, and enters the Kaskaskia river in the southwestern part of township three south, range seven west. Along its borders is a considerable settlement, and the soil in some parts is good, in others inferior.

Prairie du Pont, [pronounced *Prairie du Po*, Fr.] a small stream in St. Clair county. It rises in the bluffs southwest of Belleville, passes through the American bottom, and enters the Mississippi in the southwestern part of the county.

———— ———— An old French village, with the appendage of commons and common fields to the same, located a short distance south of Cahokia.

Prairie du Rocher, an ancient French village, in Randolph county, on the American bottom, near the Rocky bluffs, from which it derives its name, fourteen miles northwest of Kaskaskia. It is a low, unhealthy situation, along a small creek of the same name, which rises in the bluffs, passes across the American bottom, and enters the Mississippi. The houses are built in the French style, the streets very narrow, and the inhabitants preserve more of the simplicity of character and habits peculiar to early times, than any village in Illinois. It has its village lots, common fields, and commons, the peculiarities of which are noticed under the article " *Cahokia.*"

Prairie du Rocher, in 1766, contained fourteen families; the population at present is estimated at thirty-five families.

Here is a Catholic church dedicated to St. Sulspice, but at present has no resident priest. American settlers have not yet disturbed the repose of this ancient community. The ruins of Fort Chartres are three miles north west from this village.

Pratt's Prairie, in the northeastern part of Greene county, fifteen miles northwesterly from Carrollton.

Prather's Settlement, on Apple creek, in the northeastern part of Greene county, sixteen miles from Carrollton.

Preston, a town site in Randolph county, east of the Kaskaskia river.

Prophet's village, a post office and town site on Rock river, in Henry county, and on the road from Rushville and Warren county to Galena.

On the south side of the river is a handsome town site, on a high, undulating bottom. The opposite side of the river is inundated at high floods.

Rock river can be forded at this place for two-thirds of the year. It is about two hundred yards wide.

The country around will admit of considerable settlements.

Prospect Hill, in St. Clair county, one mile south of Belleville, and the residence of Major Washington West. Spread out before this delightful situation is one of the most beautiful prairies in the state, about five miles in extent, and partially covered with well cultivated farms.

Prince's Settlement is on a branch of Spoon river, twenty miles northwest from Peoria, in ten and eleven north, ranges six and seven east. Here are three groves of timber, from which at least one hundred farms might be supplied. The soil is a rich clay, and undulating. The present population does not exceed fifteen families.

Princeton, a town site on the borders of Jersey prairie, in Morgan county, ten miles north from Jacksonville, in township seventeen north, in range ten west. The surface is undulating, and the surrounding country one of of the finest tracts of land in the state, and the settlement is large. The post office is called *Workman*.

Princeton, a town site in Putnam county, in Bureau settlement, ten miles north of west from Hennepin. It was laid off by colonists from Northampton, Massachusetts, in 1833, contains a post office of the same name, and is in the heart of a flourishing settlement and a rich body of land.

Puncheon Camp, a creek near the north side of Morgan county, that enters the Sangamon. It is divided into two branches. A grove of the same name is on this stream.

Putnam Creek rises towards Canton, in Fulton county, and taking a southwestern course, enters Spoon river.

QUINCY, the seat of justice of Adams county, is situated on the bluff of the Mississippi on section two, two south, nine west. It has seven stores, four groceries, one carding machine, one large flouring and saw mill by steam power, with four run of burr stones, two schools, seven lawyers, four physicians, several mechanics, about one hundred families and six hundred inhabitants.

24

The land office for the sale of Congress lands north and east of the Illinois river, is located at this place. The land in the vicinity is excellent. A low alluvion lies on the opposite side of the Mississippi river, which is overflowed in high waters.

Quincy must become a place of considerable business.

Quaker Settlement, near the Wabash, in the northeastern part of Crawford county, on Racoon creek. Here is a society of Friends who keep up regular meetings.

Racoon, a small stream in Greene county, that enters the Illinois river twelve miles above its mouth. The bottoms on this creek, and on the Illinois river at this point, are narrow, and the surface adjoining is much broken into bluffs and ravines.

Racoon Creek, a small stream that runs across the north end of Crawford county, and enters the Wabash.

Racoon Creek, in the northeastern part of Morgan county, and runs into Dickerson's lake.

Radcliff's Point, in Washington county, five miles west of Nashville, and a small settlement.

Ramsey's Creek rises near the line of Montgomery and Shelby counties, runs a southeastern course, and enters the Kaskaskia ten miles north of Vandalia. A considerable settlement lies along this creek. This is sometimes called *Booz Creek*.

Ramsey's Settlement, in the southwestern part of Madison county, on Sugar creek, twenty miles from Edwardsville.

Randleman's Settlement, in St. Clair county, twelve miles southwest of Belleville, and near the borders of Monroe county.

Randolph, a town site at the mouth of the Piasau on the Mississippi, on fractional sections twenty-five and twenty-six, township two north, eleven west and about equidistant between Alton and Grafton. It is laid out above the Piasau and betwixt that stream and the Mississippi, on table land, above the highest floods. Abundance of lime stone and good timber, water privileges and never failing springs, a good landing for steamboats and other advantages are found here.

Lots to the value of $20,000 have been sold this spring and buildings are in process of erection, especially a large hotel.

Randolph's Grove, on Kickapoo creek, above Big grove, above twelve miles south from Bloomington, in McLean county. In shape, it is almost circular, and is a valuable tract of land, containing lime stone, and a population of about forty families. The grove comprises about twelve sections of timbered land. A post office.

Rapids of Illinois. There is a succession of rapids in the Illinois, both above and below the mouth of Fox river, with intervals of deep and smooth water. From the mouth of Fox river to the foot of the rapids is nine miles—the descent in all eight feet. The rock soft sand stone mixed with gravel and shelly lime stone. Nine miles above Fox river the grand rapids commence, and extend ten or twelve miles. They are formed by ledges of rock in the river, and rocky islands.

The whole descent from the surface of lake Michigan, at Chicago, to the foot of the rapids, a distance of ninety-four and one-fourth miles, is 141 87-100 feet.

Rapids of the Mississippi. These are distinguished as the *Lower* and *Upper* rapids.

The *Lower*, or, as frequently called, the *Des Moines*, because opposite the mouth of that river, are twelve miles long, and formed by beds of rock. They injure the navigation in low water, and sometimes entirely prevent the passage of large boats.

The *Upper Rapids* commence at Rock Island, and extend eighteen miles up the river. The navigation of these rapids is about to be improved by the general government for which purpose an appropriation was made last congress.

Rattan's Prairie is in Madison county, seven miles northwest from Edwardsville. It is level, some portions rather wet, and surrounded with fine farms.

Ray's Settlement is on the east side of Hancock county,

in five north, five west—a fine tract on the waters of Crooked creek.

Readfield, a town site in Pike county on section thirty, four south, five west.

Rector's Fork, in Gallatin county, is a branch of the North fork of Saline creek, which it enters fifteen miles above Equality.

Rhoades's Settlement, in Greene county, south of the Macoupin, and fifteen miles southeast of Carrollton. A mixture of timber and prairie.

Richland Creek, a small stream and branch of Sangamon river. It rises in the prairies near the borders of Morgan county, runs a northerly course, and enters Sangamon river below Spring creek. The land on its borders is first rate.

Richland, a tributary of the Kaskaskia, in Shelby county, rises on the east side of the county, runs southwest, and enters the Kaskaskia river near the line of Fayette. A large settlement in the southeastern part of the county.

Richland, a small creek in St. Clair county, that rises in Ogle's prairie, runs south past Belleville, and unites with Prairie du Long creek, in the east part of Monroe county. The land upon its borders is proportioned into timber and prairie, and of excellent quality.

Richland Grove, on Camp creek in the eastern part of Mercer and western part of Henry county, is a valuable body of timber, five miles long, and an average width of two miles. It is principally in fifteen and six north and one east.

Richwoods. Three tracts of timbered land in Greene county are known by this name, one of which is also called *Linden bottom*.

The timbered tract north of Apple creek, and between Apple creek prairie and the Illinois bluffs, bears this name.

A tract of timber lying between Carrollton and Bluffdale, several miles in extent, has also received this name. The land is undulating, rich, well timbered, and is occupied by a large settlement. See Linden bottom.

Ridge Prairie is situated in Madison county, commencing near Edwardsville, and extending south to St. Clair county.

It is on the dividing ridge between the waters that fall into the Mississippi west, and those that flow to the Kaskaskia east. Originally this prairie extended into St. Clair county as far south as Belleville, but long since, where farms have not been made, it has been intersected by a luxuriant growth of timber. Its surface is gently undulating, the soil rich, and is surrounded and indented with many fine farms.

Ridge Prairie post office is at Troy, Madison county, seven miles southeast from Edwardsville, on the road to Carlyle.

Ridge Settlement, in Clinton county, from three to six miles south of Carlyle, is a large settlement and in a good tract of land.

Ridge Settlement lies in Union county, on the road to Brownsville, and extends into Jackson county. It is a high, hilly, timbered tract of good land, well watered, and has from one hundred to one hundred and fifty families.

River Precinct is the settlement which extends along the Wabash river opposite Vincennes, in Lawrence county. It is a rich bottom, heavily timbered, and contains sixty or seventy families.

Robinson's Creek rises in the northwestern part of Shelby county runs a south course, and enters the Kaskaskia river near Shelbyville. The country on its borders is proportioned into timber and prairie, and has a large settlement.

Rochester, a town site in Sangamon county, at the junction of the North and South forks of the Sangamon river, ten miles east of Springfield, on the principal road to Decatur. It has a steam and other mills, and twenty-five or thirty families, and a post office.

Rock Creek rises in Adams county, in one north, seven west, runs west, and enters the south prong of Bear creek. The land is timber and prairie, and excellent.

Rock Creek, a branch of the Mackinau, in Tazewell county.

Rock Creek, in Sangamon county, rises near Clary's grove, runs north and enters the Sangamon river, a few miles below Richland creek. The land adjoining is excellent.

Rockford, a town site in Winnebago county at the rapids of Rock river in township forty-four north, and on the stage road from Chicago to Galena. Here is immense power for hydraulic purposes, and mills are erecting.

Rock Island is in the Mississippi, three miles above the mouth of Rock river. It is three miles long, and from one half to one mile wide, with lime stone rock for its base. Fort Armstrong is on its south end. On two sides the rock is twenty feet perpendicular above the river, and forms the foundation wall of the fort. A portion of the island is cultivated.

Rock Island City is laid out on a magnificent scale, at the junction and in the forks between Rock river and the Mississippi. In connection a company has been chartered to cut a canal from the Mississippi, near the head of the upper rapids, across to Rock river, by which it is said, an immense hydraulic power will be gained. The town site as surveyed, extends over a large area and includes *Stephenson* the seat of justice.

Rock Port, a town site in Pike county, on the Snycartee Slough, and where it strikes the bluff and high grounds. Here the Atlas mills are in operation for sawing and manufacturing flour on an extensive scale. A charter has been granted and a company formed to open a steamboat canal from the Snycartee to the Mississippi rivers, at a point three miles above Rockport, where the Snycartee approaches within half a mile of the Mississippi, and thus furnish steamboat navigation direct to the town.

Rock River a large, navigable stream in the northern part of the state, that enters the Mississippi three miles below Rock Island. Its principal head is in a region of lakes and swamps, towards Fox river of Green Bay, its course south, and then southwesterly. Another head is Catfish, a stream in Wisconsin territory, that connects together the "*Four lakes,*" the head waters of which commence in a swamp a few miles south of fort Winnebago. The country towards the head of Rock river is made up alternately of swamps and quag mires, ridges, of sand and shrubby oaks, with tracts of rich, dry, undulating land. The *Terre Tremblant,* or trembling land, is in this region, so called from the shaking of the surface while passing over it. The militia of Illinois suffered much in passing their horses through this country in 1832 while pursuing the army of Black Hawk.

After Rock river enters the state of Illinois it receives the Peek-a-ton-o-kee, and several smaller streams, from the right; and from the left, Turtle river, Sycamore, Green river and several smaller streams.

Much of the country through which it passes in Illinois is prairie. About the mouths of Turtle river and Sycamore creek are large bodies of timber. It generally passes along a channel of lime and sand stone rock, and has several rapids of some extent that injure the navigation at low water. The first are three or four miles above its mouth. The second are twelve or fifteen miles below Dixon's ferry. The next are below the Peek-a-ton-o-kee.

The country generally along Rock river to the boundary line is beautifully undulating, the soil rich, and the timber deficient. This, however, will not prevent it from becoming an extensive agricultural region.

Rock Spring is situated in St. Clair county, on the Vincennes and St. Louis stage road, eighteen miles east of the latter place, and eight and a half miles northeast of Belleville. It is an elevated, and a healthy, and pleasant situation, in a tract of barrens, selected by the author of this work as a permanent residence in 1820. Its name is derived from a series of springs that issue from ledges of rock a few rods from the public road. Here is a post office, and daily mail.

Rockwell, a town site on the north side of the Illinois

river above the mouth of Little Vermilion river, on the line of the canal.

Rodgers's Creek, called also *Turkey fork,* a branch of Crooked creek, in McDonough county. [See *Vance's settlement.*]

Rollin's Prairie, in Franklin county, north of Frankfort, is six miles long and four miles wide. The land is level and good, the settlement small.

Rome, a town laid off on section five, ten north, nine east on the west side of Peoria lake, in Peoria county. Here the lake is one mile wide. Population about 150.

Round Grove is a small tract of timber described by its name in Warren county, in ten north, three west.

Round Prairie, in the northeastern part of Schuyler county, on Williams's creek twenty miles from Rushville. It is a rich, dry, undulating prairie, four miles in diameter, and surrounded with timber.

Round Prairie, in Wabash county, twelve miles northeast from Mount Carmel, four miles in diameter, very fertile, and has eighteen or twenty fine farms on it.

Round Prairie, in Bond county, six miles west of north from Greenville, is from one to two miles in diameter. It is undulating and rich, surrounded with a large body of good timber, and has a considerable settlement.

Round Prairie, in Perry county, on the east side of Beaucoup, eight or nine miles from Pinckneyville. It is one mile wide, and from one to two miles long, and has a good settlement.

Round Prairie, the forks of Sugar creek and the south fork of Sangamon river, in Sangamon county, a fine tract of country, seven miles southeast of Springfield.

Rush Creek, a small stream in Jo Daviess county, that rises between Plum and Apple rivers, runs a southwestern course, and enters the Mississippi six or eight miles below Apple river. The first six miles from the mouth is low, wet, bottom land; above are alternate bottoms and precipitous bluffs. At the head is a fine farming country, with considerable timber.

RUSHVILLE, the seat of justice for Schuyler county, is situated in the central part of the county, at the south end of a beautiful prairie, on section thirty, two north, one west, ten miles from the Illinois river at the nearest point, and twelve from Beardstown.

It has eight or ten stores, various mechanics and professional men, Presbyterian, Methodist, Episcopalian and Campbellite churches, and 1000 inhabitants. A charter for a railroad to the Illinois river opposite Beardstown has been granted.

The court house is of brick, two stories, and the people have erected a brick school house. Good building stone and plenty of coal are found in the vicinity.

The settlements around Rushville are large, and the village itself exhibits a quietness and neatness in its external appearance that is pleasing to the traveller.

Russell's Grove, in McDonongh county, north of west from Macomb, is a fine tract of timbered land surrounded with rich prairie, and a considerable settlement.

Russelville, a town site and post office on the Wabash river in the northeast corner of Lawrence county.

Sadorus, a small grove and settlement at the head timber of the Kaskaskia, on the road from Springfield to Danville.

SALEM, the seat of justice for Marion county, is situated on the eastern border of the grand prairie, on the Vincennes and St. Louis stage road, on section eleven, two north, range two east of the third principal meridian. It is a pleasant village of about thirty families.

Saline, a navigable stream in Gallatin county, that enters the Ohio river twelve miles below Shawneetown, on section five, eleven south, ten east. It is made by three principal branches distinguished as the *North*, *South*, and *Middle forks*, which unite near Equality.

The *North fork* rises near McLeansboro' in Hamilton county, and runs a southerly course.

The *South fork* rises on the borders of Johnson and Franklin counties, takes an easterly course, and unites with the North fork.

The *Middle fork* rises on the east side of Franklin county, takes a southeasterly course, and unites with the South fork a few miles above Equality.

Saline creek is navigable for steamboats to Equality, fourteen miles.

Salisbury, a village just commenced in the border of the timber of Richland creek, ten miles northwest from Springfield, in Sangamon county.

Salt Creek, in Effingham county, five miles east of Ewington, and on the west side of the Fourteen Mile prairie. It is large enough for a mill stream, and enters the Little Wabash river ten or twelve miles below Ewington.

Salt Creek rises in the prairies north of Du Page, runs an easterly course and enters the Des Plaines near the Chicago road. The timber is good and the prairie land dry, undulating, and rich soil.

The settlement contains fifteen or twenty families; the land is tolerably good, and the surface rolling.

Salt Creek Settlement, on the north side of Macon county, twenty miles from Decatur, of about one hundred families. The land is good, with plenty of prairie.

Salt Creek post office is in the the above settlement.

Salt Prairie, in Calhoun county, lying between the bluffs and Salt Prairie slough.

It is a dry, rich prairie, six miles long, and half a mile wide, densely settled with about sixty families. Fine springs break out from the foot of the bluffs, and a large saline rises at the head of the prairie, which furnishes abundant salt water for stock.

Salt Prairie Slough, a small arm of the Mississippi, in Calhoun county, six miles long, near the foot of which is Gilead. It is navigable for small boats, and affords an excellent harbor.

Sangamon River, a prominent branch of the Illinois. It rises in Champaign county, in the most elevated region of that portion of the state, and near the head waters of the two Vermilions and the Kaskaskia rivers. It waters Sangamon and Macon counties, and parts of Tazewell,

McLean, Montgomery, Shelby, and Champaign counties. Its general course is northwesterly. Besides a number of smaller streams, noticed in their alphabetical order, as Clary's, Rock, Richland, Prairie, Spring, Lick, Sugar, Horse, and Brush creeks, on the south side, and Crane, Cantrill's, Fancy, Wolf creeks, and other streams on the north side, its three principal heads are Salt creek, North fork, and South fork.

Salt creek rises in McLean county, twenty-two north, ranges four and five east, and runs a westerly course through the northwest corner of Macon into Sangamon county, where, after receiving Kickapoo and Sugar creeks, and several smaller ones, it enters the Sangamon river in the northwest part of township nineteen north, range six west. Its two principal heads are called the North fork of Salt creek, and Lake fork of Salt creek.

North fork, which may be regarded as the main stream, rises in Champaign county, near the heads of the Vermilion river of the Illinois, the Vermilion of the Wabash, and the Kaskaskia, in twenty-four north, seven east, in a small lake. It runs southwesterly through Macon, then south, then west into Sangamon county, where it receives South fork and Salt creek.

The South fork of Sangamon rises by several branches, in the northwestern part of Shelby, and the northeastern part of Montgomery counties, runs a southeastern course, and forms a junction with the North fork in sixteen north, four west, seven miles east from Springfield.

Sangamon river and its branches flow through one of the richest and most delightful portions of the Great West. Complaints are made of the extent of the prairies, but this offers no serious inconvenience for the present. These prairies for many years will afford range for thousands of cattle. The general aspect of the country on the Sangamon is level, yet it is sufficiently undulating to permit the water to escape to the creeks. It will soon constitute one of the richest agricultural districts in the United States, the soil being of such a nature that immense crops can be raised with little agricultural labor.

The Sangamon is navigable for steamboats of the smaller class to the junction of the North and South forks, and, with a little labor in clearing out the drift wood, each principal fork may be navigated with flat boats for a long distance. In the spring of 1832 a steamboat of the larger class arrived within five miles of Springfield, and discharged its cargo. At a small expense in clearing out the logs, and cutting the stooping trees, this river would be navigable for steamboats half the year. From a bend near the mouth of Clary's creek, fifty miles above the mouth of the Sangamon, the waters find a channel through the low grounds and sloughs to the vicinity of Beardstown, so that keel-boats can pass in this direction into the Sangamon. It is thought that with small expense, a communication might be opened in this direction. The improvement of the navigation of this river by slackwater, the connection with Beardstown by a canal, and the opening a navigable water communication across the state by this route have already been suggested.

Sangamon, a village and post office on the left bank of Sangamon river, 7 miles northwest from Springfield. It has a steam saw and flour mill and 10 or 12 families.

Sand Creek is a small stream in Shelby county, ten miles northeast of Shelbyville, and enters the Kaskaskia river.

Sand Creek Settlement, in Shelby county, eight miles northeast of Shelbyville. The land is good, and the settlement large.

Sandy, a small mill stream that rises on the west side of La Salle county, runs southwest, and enters the Illinois in Putnam county.

Sandy Creek post office is in La Salle county, on section ten, township thirty north, one west.

Sandy, a small mill stream in Morgan county. It rises near the South fork of the Mauvaiseterre, runs a southwesterly course past Winchester, and enters the Illinois river above Apple Creek.

Sandy, an insignificant stream, and branch of Cash

river, in Alexander county. The land near it is rolling surface and rather thin soil.

Sand Prairie, a prairie of some extent, and a settlement of eighty or a hundred families, in Tazewell county, four miles south of Pekin. A rich sandy soil.

Sau-ga-nas-kee Swamp, is a sloughed tract of inundated land in Cook county, about twenty miles southwest of Chicago. After perforating through a few feet of mud, the base is found to be lime stone. The canal commissioners are authorised to cause a survey of this route from the Illinois and Michigan canal to the Calumet, for a lateral canal.

Sauk village, in Rock Island county, was three miles above Rock river, and four miles east of Rock Island. This was formerly the chief village of the Sauk nation. Here were Indian fields fenced with poles, bark cabins, plats of blue grass pasture, and a large body of rich prairie land.

The white settlement here is large, with fine farms.

Savanna, a town and post office on the Mississippi, in Jo Daviess county, above the mouth of Plum creek, and a point for the central rail road from the mouth of Ohio to Galena.

Scatters of Cash. This name is given by the people of Johnson county to a succession of ponds in which Cash river "*scatters*" itself. They are in township thirteen south, two east.

Seminary Township, a settlement in the southwest corner of Fayette county, being five north and one west of the third principal meridian. It is a township of land, thirty-six miles square, granted by congress to Illinois for purposes of education. It has since been relinquished to the general government, and in place thereof, an equal quantity is to be selected from unsold lands within the state. The Kaskaskia river crosses its southeastern part, and the Hurricane fork runs through it near its western boundary.

It is proportioned into timber and prairie, contains much good land, and about thirty-five families.

Senatchwine, a stream in Peoria county, rises in thirteen

north, eight east, and runs a devious course, nearly parallel with the Illinois, which it enters in section eighteen, eleven north, nine east, twenty miles above Peoria.

There is much good land, both timbered and prairie, on this creek, and a settlement of twenty or thirty families.

It derives its name from a well known Indian chief who formerly resided at its mouth.

Senex, a post office in McLean county, fifteen miles east of Bloomington, on section twenty-seven, township twenty-three north, four east.

Seven Mile Creek, in Ogle county, rises near the Buffalo grove, runs an east course, and enters Rock river six miles above Dixon's ferry. The country for twenty or thirty miles above Dixon's ferry is generally prairie, interspersed with small groves of three or four hundred acres each, gently undulating, soil dry and very rich. From thence on the road to Galena the surface is hilly and broken.

Seven Mile Prairie, in White county, seven miles west of Carmi, contains a large and flourishing settlement and post office.

Sexton's Creek, a small stream in Alexander county, running westward, and emptying into the Mississippi a short distance below Cape Girardeau.

The bottom land is rich, but the upland near it is rolling and rather thin soil. This by mistake is called Seaton's creek, on some maps.

Shannon's Store, a post office and settlement, in Randolph county, eighteen miles northeast of Kaskaskia, on the road to Vandalia. Here is a town site called Columbus.

Shawneetown is the principal commercial town in the southern part of the state. It is situated on the Ohio river, about ten miles below the mouth of the Wabash, in section six, of township ten south, in range ten east of the third principal meridian, in latitude thirty-seven degrees forty minutes north.

The bank of the Ohio at this place has a gradual ascent, but is subject to inundation at the extreme floods. Between the town and the bluffs the surface is still lower, and more frequently submerged. Though no considerable sickness has prevailed in this town for some years past, it cannot but be regarded as less healthy than the more elevated portions of the state.

Considerable commercial business is transacted at this place, both in the wholesale and retail line. It has eight or ten stores, several groceries, two public houses, and six or seven hundred inhabitants.

The land office for the district is in Shawneetown. A printing office is here which publishes a weekly paper called the "*Illinois Advertiser.*" There is also a bank here which was chartered by the territorial legislature, and which has lately recommenced doing business, after a suspension of several years.

SHELBYVILLE, the seat of justice for Shelby county, is situated on the west bank of the Kaskaskia river, on elevated and timbered land, on section seven, eleven north, four east. It has six stores—three groceries—a brick court house, forty feet square, two stories, with a cupola—and forty-five or fifty families. The country around it is excellent land, a mixture of timber and prairie, and the settlements are extensive. There is a large sulphur spring in the town.

Shiloh, a settlement in St. Clair county, six miles northeast from Belleville. Here is a Methodist meeting house and camp ground.

Shipley's Prairie, a small prairie in Wayne county, five miles southeast of Fairfield, and has fifteen or twenty families.

Shoal Creek, a fine stream that rises in Montgomery county, runs southwesterly through Bond and Clinton, and enters the Kaskaskia river in section six, one south, four west. It is formed by the union of the East, West, and Middle forks, and might be made navigable for small craft to a considerable distance. Its branches are Beaver, East, and West forks. The timber on its banks is of various kinds, and from two to six miles in width, with prairies between each fork. The soil is second rate, and the surface in some places is rolling, in others level.

Shoal Creek Bridge and post office, in Clinton county, on the Vincennes and St. Louis road, nine miles west of Carlyle.

Shoal Creek Prairie, an extensive prairie lying to the west of Shoal creek, in Clinton, Bond, and Montgomery counties. Its average width is eight miles. It is slightly rolling, and contains much good land.

Shoal Creek Settlement, in Clinton county, twelve miles southwest from Carlyle.

Shockokon, a post office in Warren county, on section twelve, township eight north, range six east, and on the road from Commerce to Monmouth.

Shont's Settlement, in Mercer county, between Edwards river and the Mississippi, and seven miles above New Boston. Timber and prairie interspersed; rich, dry land, and uneven.

Shook's Settlement, in the American bottom, in Monroe county. The land around is rich prairie.

Shuey's Settlement is in the eastern part of Adams county, near the heads of Bear and McKee's creeks, and the land is less rolling than other portions of the same county.

Silvan Grove, a settlement and post office in Cass county, sixteen miles south-southwest from Beardstown. It is at the head of Job's creek, and both the timber and prairie are excellent land.

Sidney, a town site in Champaign county, on Salt Fork of the Vermilion river, on the south side of section nine, township eighteen north, range ten west, on the northern cross rail road from Springfield by Decatur to Danville.

Silver Creek rises in the northern part of Madison county, runs south into St. Clair, and enters the Kaskaskia in section twenty-eight, two south, seven west. It is about fifty miles in length, has several branches, and passes through a fertile and well populated country, diversified with timber and prairie. Its name was given from the supposed existence of Silver mines, not far from Rock

Spring, where the early French explorers made considerable excavations.

Sinsinaway, a stream in the northwest corner of the state. It rises in the prairies of Wisconsin territory, runs a southwest course, and enters the Mississippi six miles above Fever river, and nearly west from Galena. Timber scattering, some cedar and a few pines.

Sitgreave's Settlemeat, in Clinton county, twelve miles south of Carlyle.

Six's Prairie lies in the southern part of Schuyler county, seventeen miles west of south from Rushville, and seventeen miles northwest from Naples. It is a rich, undulating, dry tract, ten miles long, and three miles broad, and surrounded with excellent timber. The settlement commenced in 1829, and now contains seventy-five or eighty families. The post office is called *Mount Sterling*.

Six Mile is the name of a creek, and a settlement, in Pike county. The creek heads in the interior and enters Snycartee near the county line of Calhoun. The settlement on it is large.

Six Mile Prairie, in the American bottom, southwestern part of Madison county—a rich tract of alluvion, with fine farms, and surrounded with a heavy body of timber —rather unhealthy.

Six Mile Prairie, in Perry county, nine miles southwest of Pinckneyville, is nine miles long and six miles wide. It is level, tolerably good soil, and settled along its eastern border.

Skillet Fork, a large branch of the Little Wabash. It rises in the prairies east of Vandalia, and running a southern course, enters that river in the northern part of White county. Its banks are subject to inundation. The land adjoining it is fertile, but too level for convenience.

Skillet Fork Settlement, in the northeast corner of Hamilton county.

Skillet Fork, a settlement in White county, six miles

northeast of Carmi, in a timbered region, between the Skillet fork and Little Wabash.

Slab Point, a point of timber and a small stream in the border of Montgomery county, a few miles west of south from Macoupin point, on the road from Springfield to Edwardsville.

Small Pox River, in Jo Daviess county, rises southeast of Galena, runs west, and enters the Mississippi at the mouth of Fever river, in an acute angle with that stream. It is fifteen miles long, the county on its borders very broken, has some fertile and level bottom land, and considerable timber towards its mouth.

Smallsburg, a town site with mills, etc., on the Embarras, six miles below Lawrenceville.

Small's Settlement, in St. Clair county, six miles southwest from Belleville. The land chiefly timbered and barrens.

Smith's Lake, in the Illinois bottom, Morgan county. It is below Meredosia, and unites with the river.

Smith's Settlement is near Shoal creek timber in Bond county, four miles south of Greenville.

Smooth Prairie is in Madison county, in the forks of Wood river, eight miles east from Alton. It is three miles long and about two wide, level and rather wet.

Snake Creek, a branch of Indian creek, in Morgan county.

Snycartee, (in French, *Chenail-ccarte*, said to mean the "cut off," or "lost channel,") an arm of the Mississippi, in Pike county, commonly called a "slough," in the dialect of the country. It is a running water at all stages of the river, and for several months furnishes steamboat navigation to Atlas. It leaves the Mississippi in section nineteen, three south, eight west, in Adams county, enters it again in Calhoun county, section seven, eight south, four west, and runs from one to five miles from the main river. It is about fifty miles in length. The land on the island is of first rate alluvion, proportioned into timber and prairie, but subject to annual inundations.

Snider's Settlement is on the south side of Macon county.

Somonauk Creek rises in Kane county, runs a southern course, and enters Fox river in La Salle county. It is a mill stream.

South America is a settlement in Gallatin county, fifteen miles southwest from Equality, and near the corner of Pope and Franklin counties.

South Fork of Spoon River rises in Warren county, near the head of Ellison creek, runs a southeasterly course, and unites with the main stream in section four, township eight north, range two east.

Some of the best land in the state lies on this stream. This is frequently called *West Fork*.

South Prairie, in Morgan county, is on the south side of Walnut creek.

Spanish Needle, a trifling stream in Macoupin county that enters Macoupin creek, above Dry fork.

Spoon River, a large and beautiful river on the military tract. A description of its principal heads may be seen by reference to the articles, "*Forks of Spoon river*," and "*South fork of Spoon river*." After the union of these forks, the general course of this river is south till within a few miles of its mouth, when it takes a southeasterly course and enters the Illinois in section thirty-three, four north, four east, directly opposite Havanna.

This stream is navigated for several miles, and, at a trifling expense, in clearing out the trees and rafts of timber, it might be made navigable for one half of the year to the forks.

Large bodies of timber of the best quality line the banks of this stream, and the soil in general is inferior to none.

The main river and several of its tributaries furnish excellent mill seats. The prairies adjacent are generally undulating, dry and fertile.

Above the mouth of Spoon river is a large lake on the west side of the Illinois.

Spring Bay, a singular basin, about seventy-five rods

in diameter, adjoining the Illinois river, in the upper part of Tazewell county. In front it opens to the river, the waters of which enter and fill it at flood stage. When low, they retire and leave the basin dry, excepting a stream made by a number of springs which burst forth from the sand ridge on three sides of it. On this ridge are signs of an old settlement or fortification, A short distance below is the mouth of Blue creek, over which is a bridge of earth. Below this is a mound, forty-five yards in circumference at the base, and twenty feet in height. It is said to have been opened, and human skeletons found twenty feet from the top.

Spring Creek enters Sangamon river four miles from Springfield. The country bordering is rather level, very rich and densely populated. The timber is from two to five miles wide, and of excellent quality.

Spring Creek, in Putnam county, enters the Illinois four miles below the Little Vermilion.

Spring Creek, a branch of the Iroquois river, in Iroquois county, excellent timber, and level, rich prairie.

SPRINGFIELD one of the largest towns in Illinois, and the seat of justice of Sangamon county. It is situated on the border of a beautiful prairie on the south side of the timber of Spring creek, on sections twenty-seven and thirty-four, in township sixteen north, in range five west of the third principal meridian. This town was laid off in February, 1822, before the lands in this region were sold. At the land sales of November, 1823, the tract on which the older portion of the town is located, was purchased and duly recorded as a town. It then contained about thirty families, living in small log cabins. The surface is rather too level for a large town, into which it is destined to grow; but it is a dry and healthy location.

Springfield has nineteen dry goods stores, one wholesale and six retail groceries, four public houses, four drug stores, one book store, two clothing stores, eleven lawyers, eighteen physicians including steam doctors, one foundry for castings, four carding machines, mechanics and trades of various descriptions, and two printing offices from which are issued weekly the "*Illinois Republican*," and the "*Sangamon Journal.*" The public buildings are a court house, jail, a market house, and houses of worship for two Presbyterian churches, one Methodist, one Baptist Reformer, one Episcopalian, and one Baptist society, each of which have ministers, and respectable congregations.

The first house built in Springfield was erected fifteen years since. The town has increased more than half within the last three years. It has excellent schools for both sexes, and an academy. By a recent act of the legislature Springfield is to be the permanent seat of government after 1840, and an appropriation has been made of $50,000 and commissioners appointed to build a state house.

Spring Island Grove, in Sangamon county, from fourteen to twenty miles west of Springfield, on the road to Jacksonville. It lies at the head of Spring creek, and is an excellent timbered tract, surrounded with rich prairie, from six to ten miles long, and from two to three miles wide, and has a flourishing settlement. Many excellent springs are found in this tract of country.

Spring Grove post office, in Warren county, seven miles north of Monmouth.

Spring Point, in Jasper county, on the national road.

Squaw Prairie, in Boone county, lies between the Beaver and Piskasau creeks. It is round, rich, level, and contains about ten sections of land.

Starved Rock, near the foot of the rapids, and on the right bank of the Illinois, is a perpendicular mass of lime and sand stone washed by the current at its base, and elevated 150 feet. The diameter of its surface is about 100 feet, with a slope extending to the adjoining bluff from which alone it is accessible.

Tradition says that after the Illinois Indians had killed Pontiac, the French governor at Detroit, the northern Indians made war upon them. A band of the Illinois, in attempting to escape, took shelter on this rock, which they soon made inaccessible to their enemies, and where they were closely besieged. They had secured provisions, but their only resource for water was by letting down vessels with bark ropes to the river. The wily besiegers contrived to come in canoes under the rock and cut off their buckets, by which means the unfortunate Illinois were starved to death. Many years after, their bones were whitening on this summit.

Steam Point, a point of timber running into the prairie that adjoins Brulette's creek, in Edgar county.

Steel's Mill, a post office and settlement in Randolph county sixteen miles east of Kaskaskia, on the Shawneetown road. The soil is of a middling quality.

Steven's Creek rises in Macon county, and enters the North fork of Sangamon three miles below Decatur.

Stephenson, the seat of justice of Rock Island county, is situated on the Mississippi opposite the lower end of Rock Island. It has twenty or thirty families and is increasing.

Stillman's Run, in Ogle county, formerly called *Mud Creek*, a small stream that runs northwest and enters Rock river a few miles below Kishwaukee, where, on the 14th of May, 1832, a battalion of militia, consisting of about 275 men, under the command of Major Isaiah Stillman, of Fulton county, were attacked, defeated, and eleven men killed, by a portion of the Indian army under the celebrated Black Hawk.

Stinking Creek, see Beaver creek.

St. Marion, a town site in Ogle county, at Buffaloe grove.

St. Mary's River rises in Perry county, and enters the Mississippi six miles below the mouth of the Kaskaskia.

St. Mary's, a town and post office on the west side of crooked creek in Schuyler couuty, in four north, five west, on the mail route from Rushville to Carthage. It commenced in 1836, and has two stores, one grocery, and a dozen families.

Stokes's Settlement, in the eastern part of Union county, near the head, and on the south side of Cash river, contains one hundred families. The surface of the land is rolling, and the soil good.

Stone's Settlement is fifteen miles below Quincy, in three south, seven west.

Stout's Grove, a settlement in McLean county, on the Mackinau, in twenty-four and twenty-five north, one west, and twelve miles northwest of Bloomington. The north part is a large and heavily timbered bottom, principally oak, with some barrens. The south part is first rate timbered land.

Strawn's Settlement, in Putnam county, about twenty miles below Hennepin, was commenced in 1831.

String Prairie, in Greene county, lies between Macoupin and Apple creeks, commencing four miles west of Carrollton, and extending fifteen miles east, and from half a mile to three miles in width. It is a rich, level tract, and much of it in a state of cultivation.

String Town, on the Embarras, in Lawrence county, sixteen miles north of Lawrenceville, has 100 families.

Stubblefield's Branch is a trifling stream that rises in the northern part of Bond county, runs southwest, and enters the East fork of Shoal creek, two miles above Greenville. A considerable settlement is near it.

Sugar Creek, in Sangamon county, rises in the prairies towards the southwestern part of the county, where its waters interlock with the heads of the Macoupin and Apple creeks, runs a northeasterly course, and enters the Sangamon river a short distance below the forks. Its main branch is Lick creek. The land is good, surface rather level, and the timber of various kinds, from one to two miles in width. The settlements are large, and extend from the mouth to the head of the timber.

The lands situated between Lick and Sugar creeks, are said to be of a superior quality for grazing, etc.

Sugar Creek, in the northeastern part of Schuyler county. It rises in the southeast corner of McDonough county, takes a southeastern course, near the boundary line of Fulton, and enters the Illinois above Beardstown, on section four, two north, one east. A large body of excellent timber lies on this stream. Red and yellow ochre are found in its banks.

Sugar Creek, a small stream that rises in the interior of Edgar county, takes an eastern course and passes through a corner of Indiana into the Wabash.

Sugar Creek, a small stream in Clark county, that passes near Palestine and enters the Wabash.

Sugar Creek, in Iroquois county, a branch of the Iroquois river. There is considerable timber along its borders.

Sugar Creek, a small stream rising in township four north, in range five west of the third principal meridian, and running a southerly course through the eastern borders of Madison into Clinton county, enters the Kaskaskia near the base line, in five west. It passes through a fine country of land.

Sugar Creek, in McLean county, rises in twenty-four north, two east, and runs through Blooming grove in a southwestern direction. It is a good mill stream, has firm banks, and gravelly bottom. It passes across the southeast part of Tazewell into Sangamon county, and enters Salt creek in township twenty north, range five west. It waters a rich body of land, and has an extensive line of settlements.

Sugar Creek Settlement, in the southeastern part of Tazewell county, on Sugar creek. It has seventy or eighty families, and is increasing.

Sugar Grove, in the north part of Sangamon county, twenty miles north of Springfield. It is a fine tract of timber surrounded with fertile prairie, about three miles long, and one mile wide, with a respectable settlement.

Sugar Grove, in Putnam county, in fifteen north, six east; a beautiful grove of timber with good prairie and barrens around it.

Sugar River, in Winnebago county. It rises in the Wisconsin territory, runs south across the boundary line about eleven miles west of Rock river, and enters the Peek-a-ton-o-kee. The country between it and Rock river is rather swampy, with ridges of bur oak timber. Along its course the land and timber are good.

Sugar Tree Grove, in Henry county, north of Edwards

river, in fifteen north, three east. Timber, various; prairie, undulating and rich.

Summit, a town site in Cook county, at the "Point of Oaks," on the canal, thirteen miles from Chicago.

Sweet's Prairie is in the south part of Morgan county, three miles west of Manchester. It is level and wet.

Swett's Prairie is in Madison county, four miles northeast from Edwardsville.

Swigart's Settlement, in St. Clair county, is under the bluffs seven miles east of St. Louis.

Swinnington's Point, a settlement in Morgan county.

Swanwick's Creek rises near the Grand Cote, and enters Beaucoup creek, in Perry county.

Sycamore Creek rises in the prairies near Fox river, and enters Rock river, thirty-five miles above Dixon's ferry. It is fifty yards wide at its mouth. The Indian name is *Kish-wau-kee*.

Table Grove is a beautiful and elevated tract of 150 or 200 acres of timber, on the west side of Fulton county, and has a delightful prospect.

Tamarawa, a town site on the right bank of the Kaskaskia river, and near the line of St. Clair and Monroe counties, and at the lower end of the Twelve Mile prairie. It is an elevated and pleasant situation.

Tarapin Ridge, a settlement four miles north of Lebanon, in St. Clair county.

Taylor's Creek rises in Macoupin county, and enters Macoupin creek, in Greene county.

Tecumseh, a town site on the Great Wabash river, in White county, at the Little Chain, (rapids,) on high ground, and well situated for business. It is on fractional section thirty-one, township six south, eleven east.

Tegarden's Mill, on Taylor's creek, in Greene county.

Ten Mile Creek rises in the Great prairie near Putnam county, runs through a broken but well timbered country, and enters Peoria lake five miles above Peoria.

Ten Mile Creek, in Hamilton county, is a branch of Muddy river, and runs through an undulating tract. Here is a settlement of forty or fifty families.

26

Thorn Creek rises in three forks in the northeast part of Will county, runs north and enters the Calumet in Cook county.

Thornton, a town site on Thorn creek, near the southeastern part of Cook county.

Three Mile Prairie, in Washington county, has an undulating surface. It is eight miles south of Nashville.

Timbered Settlement includes the northeast quarter of Wabash county, and is ten miles from Mount Carmel. it contains sixty or seventy families. The timber is excellent.

Tom's Prairie, in Wayne county, is six miles northeast of Fairfield, on Elm river, and has twenty or twenty-five families. The soil is second rate.

Totten's Prairie, in Fulton county, seven miles northwest of Lewistown, is from one to three miles wide and ten long. It is good land and has a large settlement.

Town Fork is a branch of Troublesome creek, in McDonough county.

TREMONT, the seat of justice for Tazewell county, is situated in a delightful prairie, between Pleasant grove and Mackinau, on section eighteen, township twenty-four north, three west, and was laid off by a company in the spring of 1835. It now contains six stores, four groceries, two taverns, two lawyers, two physicians, two ministers, one apothecary's shop, sixty-eight buildings, and about three-hundred inhabitants. The religious denominations are Baptists, Presbyterians, Methodists, Episcopalians, and Unitarians, all of whom, at present, worship in one house. It is contemplated to erect one or more houses of worship this year. It lies in the heart of a beautiful country of prairie and timber.

Trinity is on the Ohio six miles above its junction with the Mississippi, and at the mouth of Cash river, on sections one and two, seventeen south, one west. Steamboats from the Ohio and Mississippi rivers exchange cargoes here, repair, etc. It has one tavern and one store, and is inundated six feet at extreme high water.

Troublesome Creek, a branch of Crooked creek, in McDonough county.

Troy, a town site in Madison county, seven miles southeast from Edwardsville.

Troy Grove is in La Salle county, at the head of Little Vermilion, twelve miles above its mouth, through which the stage road passes from Ottawa to Dixonville and Galena.

Turkey Creek enters the Illinois river, in Morgan county, between Walnut and Sandy creeks.

Turkey Hill, in St. Clair county, four miles southeast of Belleville, the oldest American settlement in the county was commenced by William Scott, Samuel Shook, and Franklin Jarvis, in 1798. It is now populous. Formerly this name was used to designate a large tract.

Turney's Prairie, in Wayne county, eight miles south of Fairfield, is from one to two miles in extent. The soil is good, and the settlement contains about twenty-five families.

Turtle River rises in Wisconsin territory, and enters Rock river, forty rods below the boundary line.

Twelve Mile Grove is between the Kankakee and Hickory creek, in Cook county, and contains 600 acres.

Twelve Mile Prairie, in Effingham county, west of the Little Wabash, is level, and in many places wet. It extends through Effingham and Clay counties. The national road crosses it in the former, and the Vincennes in the latter county.

Twelve Mile Prairie, in St. Clair county, is moderately undulating, and good soil. Indian name *Tau-mar-waus*.

Twitchell's Mill, a post office on Big creek, Pope county.

Tyrer's Creek, a branch of the Mississippi, in Adams county, rises in two south, eight west.

Union Prairie, in the southeast part of Clark county, is five miles long and three broad. The settlement is large.

Union Prairie, in Schuyler county, four miles west of Rushville.

Union, a post office in Champaign county, twenty miles west of Danville.

Union Grove, in St. Clair county, is on the borders of Looking Glass prairie and on the east side of Silver creek. The land is excellent, and the settlement extensive. It is sometimes called *Padfield's Settlement.*

UNITY, the seat of justice of Alexander county, recently located, in the corners of townships fifteen and sixteen south, in ranges one and two west of the third principal meridian. It is on the east side of Cash river.

Upper Alton, a delightfully situated town, on elevated ground, two and a half miles back from the river and east from Alton, on section seven, township five north, range nine west. The situation of the town is high and healthy The country around was originally timbered land, and is undulating; the prevailing growth consists of oaks of various species, hickory, walnut, etc.

There are eight stores, five groceries, two lawyers, five physicians, mechanics of various descriptions, a steam saw and flour mill, and about 300 families, or 1500 inhabitants. The Baptists, Methodists, and Presbyterians, each have houses of worship. The Baptist and Presbyterian houses are handsome stone edifices, with spires, bells, &c. and provided with ministers. There are seven or eight ministers of the gospel, residents of this place, some of whom are connected with the college and the Theological seminary;—others are agents for some of the public benevolent institutions, whose families reside here.

Good morals, religious privileges, the advantages for education in the college, and in three respectable common schools, with an intelligent and agreeable society make this town a desirable residence.

Upper Alton was laid off by the proprietor in 1816, and in 1821, it contained fifty or sixty families. In 1827, it had dwindled down to a few from several causes. But since the commencement of Alton, the flourishing mercantile town on the river, it has experienced a rapid growth and will doubtless continue to advance, proportionate to the progress of the town and country around.

Upper Mackinau Settlements, a string of settlements towards the head of the Mackinau, in McLean county, about fourteen miles north of Bloomington. The timber is divided into several groves, and is about twenty-four miles in length from east to west, and from one to three miles in width. The old Kickapoo and Pattowatomie towns were on the north side of this timber, where the blue grass grows in wild luxuriance. Here are over 100 families, and the land is excellent.

URBANNA, the seat of justice for Champaign county, named by the last legislature.

Ursa, a post office in Bear creek settlement, Adams county, on section eighteen, township one north, eight west and ten miles north of Quincy.

Utica, a town site in Fulton county, two and a half miles from the Illinois river, on Copperas creek. It has one steam mill, one store, one distillery and ten or twelve families.

Utica, a town site and post office on the north side of the Illinois river at the Lower rapids, on the canal line, and 10 miles below Ottawa, on section seventeen, township thirty-three north, two east. It is four miles from the termination of the canal, and has two or three stores, and families.

Valentine's Settlement is in Bond county, on the west side of Shoal creek. The land is good.

Vandewenter's Settlement is on the Illinois river, in the south part of Schuyler county, twenty miles from Rushville.

Vancil's Settlement, in Union county, on a branch of Clear creek. The land is rolling.

Van Buren, a town site on the Mississippi in Whiteside county, 42 miles above Rock Island, and 50 miles below Galena. It has two steam saw mills, a post office, (name unknown) and ten or twelve houses building.

Van Buren, a post office in Big Grove, in Champaign county, four miles north of Urbanna.

Vance's Settlement, in McDonough county, is in five north, two and three west, six or eight miles southwest, from Macomb, and on the waters of Crooked creek. The land is excellent.

VANDALIA is the present seat of government for the state, the seat of justice for Fayette county, and was laid out in 1818, by commissioners appointed for that purpose, under the authority of the state. It is situated on the west bank of the Kaskaskia river, on sections eight, nine, sixteen and seventeen, of township six north, in range one east of the third principal meridian. The site is high, undulating, and was originally a timbered tract. The streets cross at right angles and are eighty feet in width. The public square is on elevated ground. The public buildings are, a state house of brick and sufficiently commodious for legislative purposes, unfinished, a neat framed house of worship for the Presbyterian society, with a cupola and bell, a framed meeting house for the Methodist society, another small public building open for all denominations, and for schools, and other public purposes.

There are in the town two printing offices that issue weekly papers, the "*State Register*," and the "*Free Press*,"—four taverns, eight stores, two groceries, one clothing store, two schools, four lawyers, four physicians one steam and one water saw mill, one minister of the gospel, and about 850 inhabitants.

Near the river the country generally is heavily timbered, but a few miles back are extensive prairies. The "national road" has been permanently located and partially constructed to this place.

Vermilion River, of the Wabash, rises in the great prairies of Champaign and Iroquois counties and enters the Wabash in the state of Indiana. Its branches are, North, Middle and Salt forks.

North fork, rises in Iroquois county, and unites with the main stream below Danville.

Salt fork rises in Champaign county, near the head of the Sangamon river, runs a south course till it enters township eighteen north, in range ten east, when it makes a sudden bend and runs north of east to Danville. The Salt works are on this stream, six miles above Danville.

Middle fork rises in the prairie, forty miles northwest of Danville, and enters Salt fork.

The timber on these forks is from one to two miles wide and of a good quality. The adjoining prairies are dry, undulating and rich.

Vermilion (*Little*) rises in the south part of Vermilion county, and enters the Wabash river in Indiana. It is a mill stream, with a gravelly and rocky bottom, and has a fine body of timber on its banks. Large and flourishing settlements have been made on both sides ef the timber to its head.

Vermilion River of the Illinois, rises in Livingston county, through which it passes into La Salle county, and enters the Illinois near the foot of the rapids. Towards its head the surface is tolerably level, with a rich soil, large prairies, and but small quantities of timber. Towards the Illinois its bluffs become abrupt, often 100 feet high, with rocky banks and frequent rapids and falls. It is an excellent mill stream, about fifty yards wide, and runs through extensive beds of bituminous coal. Its bluffs contain immense quarries of lime, sand and some free stone excellent for grind stones. The timber upon its banks are oaks of various kinds, walnut, ash, sugar maple, hickory, etc.

Vermilionville, a town site and post office north of the Vermilion river in La Salle county, on section nine, township thirty-two north, two east. It is a pleasant situation, a thriving village, and surrounded with an excellent country.

Near it on the Vermilion river, is *Lowel*, a manufacturing town in embryo, with abundance of water power. Great quantities of bituminous coal exist in this vicinity.

Versailles a village of twelve or fifteen families on the west side of McLean county, 20 miles northwest of Bloomington.

VIENNA, the county seat of Johnson county, contains twenty-five or thirty families, and three stores. It is situated on the east fork of Cash river, in sections five and six, thirteen south, three east. The main road from Golconda to Jonesboro,' and Jackson, Mo., passes through this place. It is in latitude 37 deg. 25 minutes north.

Village Prairie, in Edwards county, two miles north of Albion, about three miles wide. A small stream called " *The Village*" runs through it to the little Wabash.

Vincennes Road passes from Vincennes to St. Louis, through Lawrence, Clay, Marion, Clinton, and St. Clair counties, 154 miles. A daily mail in post coaches passes this road.

Vinegar Hill, in Jo Daviess county, six miles north of Galena, is a prairie country, and contains one of the richest lead mines in this region.

Virginia Settlement, in McHenry county on the west side of Fox river, seven miles from it. It is on the old Indian trail from Chicago to the Wisconsin. The prairie and timber about equally interspersed, surface rolling, soil a black sandy loam and very rich.

Wabash Grove, in the east part of Shelby county, is on one of the heads of the Little Wabash. The timber and prairie are excellent and the settlement is large.

Wabash Point, in the southwestern part of Coles county is the principal head of the Little Wabash. The timber and adjoining prairie are good, and the settlement is large.

Wabonsie, a tributary of Fox river in Kane county. It rises in a large spring, runs southwest, and enters Fox river, 8 miles below the Big Woods. It is a fine mill stream.

Wait's Settlement, is in Bond county, nine miles west of Greenville and on the west side of Shoal creek. The prairie is good, and the timber abundant.

Wakefield's Settlement, in the south part of Shelby county, is a fertile tract well timbered. The settlement is large.

Walker's Grove, a post office in McDonough county, seven miles south of Macomb.

Walnut Creek, in Morgan county, enters the Illinois above Plum creek.

Walnut Creek heads in the northwestern part of Tazewell county, and enters the Mackinau in section sixteen, twenty-five north, one west. It has a free current, gravelly bottom, and runs through rich land.

Walnut, a branch of Beaucoup creek, in Perry county.

Walnnt Grove, a rich tract on Walnut creek, in Tazewell county, about one mile wide and nine long.

Walnut Grove, a settlement in the southwest corner of Edgar county.

Walnut Hill Prairie, on the line between Jefferson and Marion counties. Some parts are tolerably good, others rather flat and wet. It is four miles long, and three broad and contains seventy-five families.

Walnut Hill post office is in the southwest corner of Marion county, on the road from Carlyle to Mount Vernon.

Walnut Prairie, in Clark county, near the Wabash, about five miles long and two broad. It is tolerably level, has a rich sandy soil, and a fine settlement.

Walnut Point post office, is in Adams county, on section thirty-two, township one north, six west, eighteen miles northeast from Quincy.

Walker's Grove, on the Du Page, in Will county, forty miles from Chicago, is a beautiful tract surrounded by a rich prairie and a large settlement. It is about three miles long and one wide.

Wapelo, a town site at the falls of Apple river, in Jo Daviess county. Here are a saw and grist mill, several families, stores, etc.

Ward's Settlement is the oldest in Macon county, and is eight miles south of Decatur.

Warrenton, a town site in Cook county on the west fork of the Du Page, four miles above Napierville.

Warsaw is an important commercial position, on the Mississippi river, at the foot of the Des Moines rapids, 16 miles west-southwest from Carthage. It has a steam mill, several stores, and 200 or 300 inhabitants, and is to be the termination of the railroad from Peoria. It is near the site of old Fort Edwards.

Washington, a new village in the western part of Fulton county, twenty miles from Lewistown.

Washington, a town site and handsome village in Tazewell county, on section twenty-three, township twenty-six north, three west, and 14 miles north of Tremont. It is situated on the south side of Holland's grove, on the border of a delightful prairie, and contains 5 stores, 2 groceries, 4 physicians, various mechanics, a steam saw mill, and about 300 inhabitants. The post office is *Holland's Grove.*

Washington Grove is in the interior of Ogle county, and contains two or three sections of timber, surrounded with an excellent rolling prairie.

WATERLOO, the seat of justice for Monroe county, is situated on high ground, in township two south, ten west. It has a court house of brick, two stores, two taverns, and about twenty families.

Watt's Settlement, in Crawford county, is sixteen miles west from Palestine, and has about twenty families.

Waynesville, a town in the southwest corner of McLean county, on the road from Springfield to Bloomington, and on the south side of the timber of Kickapoo creek. It has 6 stores, 2 groceries, 2 physicians, a Methodist and a Presbyterian society, a good school, and a charter for a Seminary of learning. It has a fine body of timber on the north, and a rich, undulating and beautiful prairie south. Population in the village about 150.

Webb's Prairie, and settlement, in Franklin county, fifteen miles east of north from Frankfort. The land is good.

Weed's Settlement is on a branch of the Vermilion in Livingston county. Here is fine, rolling, rich prairie, lime and free stone, coal, and will probably be the location of the county seat.

Webster, a town site in the northwest corner of Livingston county on section ten, township thirty north, three east, on the south side of the Vermilion river, surrounded with great bodies of lime and free stone, coal, and extensive tracts of rich, undulating prairie.

Weigle's Settlement, in Adams county, has 600 or 700 industrious Germans, of the society of Dunkards, and is watered by the West fork of McKee's creek.

West Fork of Kaskaskia River rises in Macon county, in township sixteen north, four east, and enters the main stream, ten miles above Shelbyville. The land on its borders, in general, is excellent, and the timber good.

West Fork of Muddy Settlement, in the northwestern part of Jefferson county, is a well timbered tract.

West Fork of Shoal Creek rises in the north part of Montgomery county, in nine north, three west, runs south, and forms the main creek. The average width of the timber is two miles.

West Grove is a body of timber on Pine creek in Ogle county.

West's Settlement, in Johnson county, on the east side of Cash river, is a fine, fertile tract, and has thirty families.

Wet Grove, is a small body of timber in Ogle county near the head of Kite creek.

Whitaker's Creek, in Greene county, a branch of Apple creek on the south side.

While Hall, a village and post office in Greene county, 10 miles above Carrollton, on the road to Jacksonville. It has 9 stores, 2 groceries, 2 taverns, 3 physicians, one school, and an incorporation for a Seminary, a steam mill in the vicinity, framed houses of worship for Methodists and Baptists, and 600 inhabitants.

Whitley's Point is the head of Whitley's creek, in Shelby county, east of the Kaskaskia river, and fifteen miles northeast from Shelbyville. The timber and prairie are good.

Whitley's Settlement, on Whitley's creek, Shelby county, fifteen miles northeast from Shelbyville is a mixture of timber and prairie.

White Oak Grove, in Henry county, is a fine body of timber. Adjoining it is Andover settlement.

Whiteside's Settlement, in Pope county, is twelve miles west of Golconda on Big Bay creek and the state road, and has 100 families.

Whiteside's Station, in Monroe county, five miles north

of Waterloo, is one of the oldest American settlements in Illinois.

Wiggins's Ferry, on the Mississippi opposite St. Louis and the property adjoining, are owned by a company. Here are two good steamboats, a public house, livery stable, store, and post office.

Wilcoxen's Settlement, in Fulton county—good soil.

Williams's Creek rises in Hancock and enters Crooked creek in Schuyler county.

Willis's Settlement, in Putnam county, five miles east of Hennepin, was begun in 1827, in a rich tract of land.

Wilson's Grove is a beautiful eminence, one mile west of Jacksonville, and now called College Hill. The Illinois college stands on its eastern slope.

Winchester, in Morgan county, sixteen miles southwest of Jacksonville, on section twenty-nine, township fourteen north, in range twelve west of the third principal meridian, was laid off in 1831, on elevated ground, and is a thriving village, increasing rapidly, has several stores, mechanics of various descriptions, and a population of three or four hundred. The Baptists, Methodists and Congregationalists have societies here. It has excellent lime and free stone quarries in the vicinity and several mills.

Winchester, a town site on the Kankakee, 9 miles above its mouth, and containing half a dozen houses, one store, one tavern, two saw mills etc.

Windsor, a town, in fifteen north, nine east on the Bureau, and on the stage road from Peoria by Princeton to Galena. It has 2 stores, 2 groceries, one tavern, one lawyer, one physician, one minister and about 100 inhabitants. A grist and saw mill are near.

Winnebago Inlet, in Putnam county, passes through several ponds into the Winnebago Swamp, in Ogle county.

Winnebago Swamp is in Henry and Ogle counties, thirty miles long, and from one half to three miles wide.

Wolf Creek is a branch of the Sangamon river, in Sangamon county. The land is level but well settled.

Wolf Creek, in Effingham, enters the Kaskaskia river.

Wolf Run, in Morgan county, enters Dickerson's lake.

Wood River, in Madison county, enters the Mississippi nearly opposite the mouth of the Missouri. It rises in Macoupin and runs through a fine country.

Woodbury is a town site and post office on the national road, situated in Coles county, containing half a dozen families.

Wood's Prairie is a small tract of good land in Wabash county, ten miles from Mount Carmel.

Worcester post office is in McDonough county on the western side.

Workman post office in Jersey prairie Morgan county.

Wyoming, a town site and post office on the east side of Spoon river, on section two, township twelve north, six east, on the mail road from Hennepin to Knoxville.

Worley's Creek, in Adams county, enters Bear creek.

Yellow Banks are sand bluffs of the Mississippi, in Warren and Mercer counties, distinguished as Lower, Middle, and Upper, at the mouths of Henderson, Pope, and Edwards rivers—the first five miles long. They furnish convenient landings for steamboats.

Yankee Settlement, in the southwestern part of Cook and corner of Will county, a large settlement in a rich undulating prairie, between Hickory creek, and the Sauganaskee.

Yellow Creek, in Winnebago county, enters the Peek-a-ton-o-kee near its junction with Rock river. It rises near Kellogg's Grove.

York, a village in Clark county, on the Wabash, contains one steam saw and flouring mill, four stores, and about 300 inhabitants. Its exports amount to $40,000.

27

APPENDIX.

TABLE I.

A Table exhibiting the Name of each County, Date of Formation, number of Square Miles, Population according to the State census of 1835, (excepting certain new counties, marked thus *, of which the estimate is given,) and Seat of Justice.

COUNTIES.	DATE.	Square Miles.	Population 1835.	SEATS OF JUSTICE.
Adams,	1825	810	7,042	Quincy
Alexander,	1819	375	2,050	Unity
Bond,	1817	360	3,580	Greenville
Boone,*	1837	500	600	Not established
Cass,*	1837	256	6,500	Beardstown
Calhoun,	1825	260	1,091	Guilford
Champaign,*	1833	1008	1,250	Urbanna
Clark,	1819	500	3,413	Darwin
Clay,	1824	620	1,648	Maysville
Clinton,	1824	504	2,648	Carlyle
Coles,	1830	1248	5,125	Charleston
Cook,	1831	1330	7,500	Chicago
Crawford,	1816	426	3,540	Palestine
Edgar,	1823	648	6,668	Paris
Edwards,	1814	183	2,006	Albion
Effingham,	1831	486	1,055	Ewington
Fayette,	1821	720	3,638	Vandalia
Franklin,	1818	864	5,551	Frankfort
Fulton,	1825	874	5,917	Lewistown

APPENDIX.

TABLE I.—CONTINUED.

COUNTIES.	DATE.	Square Miles.	Population 1835.	SEATS OF JUSTICE.
Gallatin,	1812	760	8,660	Equality
Greene,	1821	912	12,274	Carrollton
Hamilton,	1821	432	2,877	McLeansboro'
Hancock,	1825	775	3,249	Carthage
Henry,*	1825	840	600	Not established
Iroquois,*	1833	1428	1,800	Not established
Jackson,	1816	576	2,783	Brownsville
Jasper,*	1831	508	375	Newton
Jefferson,	1819	576	3,350	Mount Vernon
Jo Daviess,*	1827	724	4,350	Galena
Johnson,	1812	486	2,166	Vienna
Kane,*	1836	1297	1,500	Not established
Knox,	1825	792	1,600	Knoxville
La Salle,	1831	1864	4,754	Ottawa
Livingston,*	1837	1040	750	Not established
Lawrence,	1821	560	4,450	Lawrenceville
Macon,	1829	1404	3,022	Decatur
Madison,	1812	750	9,016	Edwardsville
Macoupin,	1829	864	5,554	Carlinville
Marion,	1823	576	2,844	Salem
McDonough,	1825	576	2,883	Macomb
McHenry,*	1836	960	1,100	Not established
McLean,	1830	1675	5,311	Bloomington
Mercer,*	1825	550	800	New Boston
Monroe,	1816	360	2,660	Waterloo
Montgomery,	1821	960	3,740	Hillsboro'
Morgan,	1823	918	16,500	Jacksonville
Ogle,	1836	1440	1,200	Not established
Peoria,*	1825	648	4,500	Peoria
Perry,	1827	446	2,201	Pinckneyville
Pike,	1821	800	6,037	Pittsfield
Pope,	1816	576	3,756	Golconda
Putnam,	1825	1340	4,021	Hennepin
Randolph,	1795	540	5,695	Kaskaskia

APPENDIX. 317

TABLE I.—CONTINUED.

COUNTIES.	DATE.	Square Miles.	Population 1835.	SEATS OF JUSTICE.
Rock Island,*	1831	400	850	Stephenson
Sangamon,	1821	1234	17,573	Springfield
Schuyler,	1825	864	6,361	Rushville
Shelby,	1827	1080	4,848	Shelbyville
St. Clair,	1795	1030	9,055	Belleville
Stephenson,	1837	560	400	Not established
Tazewell,	1827	1130	5,850	Tremont
Union,	1818	396	4,156	Jonesboro'
Vermilion,	1826	1000	8,103	Danville
Wabash,	1824	180	3,010	Mount Carmel
Warren,	1825	900	2,623	Monmouth
Washington,	1818	656	3,292	Nashville
Wayne,	1819	720	2,939	Fairfield
White,	1815	516	6,489	Carmi
Whiteside,*	1836	770	350	Not established
Will,*	1836	1228	3,500	Juliet
Winnebago,*	1836	504	1,000	Not established.

The present population of Illinois (April, 1837) may be estimated at 375,000.

TABLE II.

A Table of the Public Officers in Illinois, both State and National, April, 1837.

GOVERNMENT OF THE STATE.

His Excellency JOSEPH DUNCAN, Governor; term of service expires December, 1838; residence, Jacksonville.

—————— —————— Lieutenant Governor, vacant. Hon. WILLIAM DAVIDSON, Speaker of the Senate, and ex officio lieutenant governor till December, 1838.

ALEXANDER P. FIELD, Esq., Secretary of State.
LEVI DAVIS, Esq., Auditor of Public Accounts.
JOHN D. WHITESIDE, Esq., Treasurer.
U. F. LINDER, Esq., Attorney-General.

UNITED STATES COURT.—*For the District of Illinois.*

NAMES.	OFFICES.	RESIDENCE.	SALARY.
Nathaniel Pope,	Judge,	Kaskaskia,	$1,000
David J. Baker,	U. S. Attorney,	do	200, fees
Harry Wilton,	Marshall,	Carlyle,	200, fees
——— ———,	Clerk,		fees, etc.

This court is held at Vandalia, the fourth Monday in May, and the first Monday in December, annually.

U. S. LAND OFFICERS IN ILLINOIS.

DISTRICTS.	REGISTERS.	RECEIVERS.
Kaskaskia,	Miles Hodgkiss,	Edward Humphries.
Shawneetown,	James C. Sloo,	John Caldwell.
Edwardsville,	Alex. M. Jenkins,	S. H. Thompson.
Vandalia,	Chas. Prentice,	William Linn.
Palestine,	Joseph Kitchell,	Guy W. Smith.
Quincy,	Samuel Leech,	Thomas Carlin.
Danville,	J. C. Alexander,	Samuel McRoberts.
Springfield,	S. A. Douglass,	John Taylor.
Chicago,	James Whitlock,	E. D. Taylor.
Galena,	James M. Strode,	John Demint.

MEMBERS OF CONGRESS.

SENATORS.

NAMES.	RESIDENCE.	TERM EXPIRES.
John M. Robinson,	Carmi,	March 3d, 1841
Richard M. Young,	Quincy,	March 3d, 1843

Representatives elect to the Twenty-Fifth Congress; their term commenced March 4, 1837.

DISTRICTS.	NAMES.	RESIDENCE.
First District,	Adam W. Snyder,	Belleville.
Second District,	Yadock Casey,	Mount Verno
Third District,	Wm. L. May,	Springfield.

No. III.

SUGGESTIONS TO EMIGRANTS.

Canal, Steam-Boat and Stage Routes.—Other Modes of Travel —Expenses—Roads, Distances, &c. &c.

1. Persons in moderate circumstances, or who would save time and expense, need not make a visit to the West, to ascertain particulars previous to removal. A few general facts, easily collected from a hundred sources, will enable persons to decide the great question, whether they will emigrate to the Valley. By the same means, emigrants may determine to what State, and to what part of that State, their course shall be directed. There are many things that a person of plain, common sense will take for granted without inquiry,—such as facilities for obtaining all the necessaries of life, the readiness with which property of any description may be obtained for a fair value, and especially farms and wild land, that they can live where hundreds of thousands of others of similar habits and feelings live; and above all, they should take it for granted, that there are difficulties to be encountered in every country, and in all business;—that these difficulties can be surmounted with reasonable effort, patience and perseverance, and that in every country, people sicken and die.

2. Having decided to what State and part of the State, an emigrant will remove, let him then conclude to take as little furniture and other luggage as he can do with, especially if he comes by public conveyances. Those who reside within convenient distance of a sea port, would find it both safe and economical to ship by New Orleans, in boxes, such articles as are not wanted on the road, especially if they steer for the navigable waters of the Missis-

sippi. Bed and other clothing, books, &c., packed in boxes, like merchants' goods, will go much safer and cheaper by New Orleans, than by any of the inland routes. I have received more than one hundred packages and boxes from eastern ports, by that route, within twenty years, and never lost one. Boxes should be marked to the owner or his agent at the river port where destined, and to the charge of some forwarding house in New Orleans. The freight and charges may be paid when the boxes are received.

3. If a person designs to remove to the north part of Ohio and Indiana, to Chicago and vicinity, or to Michigan, or Green Bay, his course should be by the New York canal, and the lakes. The following table, showing the time of the opening of the canal at Albany and Buffalo, and the opening of the lake, from 1827 to 1835, is from a report of a committee at Buffalo to the common council of that city. It will be of use to those who wish to take the northern route in the spring.

Year.	Canal opened at Buffalo.	Canal opened at Albany.	Lake Erie opened at Buffalo.
1827	April 21	April 21	April 21
1828	" 1	" 1	" 1
1829	" 25	" 29	May 10
1830	" 15	" 20	April 6
1831	" 16	" 16	May 8
1832	" 18	" 25	April 27
1833	" 22	" 22	" 23
1834	" 16	" 17	" 6
1835	" 15	" 15	May 8

The same route will carry emigrants to Cleaveland, and by the Ohio canal, to Columbus, or to the Ohio river, at Portsmouth; from whence, by steamboat, direct communications will offer to any river port in the Western States. From Buffalo, steamboats run constantly (when the lake is open,) to Detroit, stopping at Erie, Ashtabula,

Cleaveland, Sandusky and many other ports, from whence stages run to every prominent town. Transportation wagons are employed in forwarding goods.

Route from Buffalo to Detroit, by water.

	Miles.		Miles.
Dunkirk, N. Y.	39	Cleaveland, Ohio,	30—193
Portland, "	18—57	Sandusky, "	54—247
Erie, Pa.	35—92	Amherstburg, U. C.	52—299
Ashtabula, Ohio,	39—131	Detroit, Mich.,	18—317
Fairport, "	32—163		

From Detroit to Chicago, Illinois.

	Miles.		Miles.
St. Clair river, Mich.,	40	Mackinaw,	58—329
Palmer,	17—57	Isle Brule,	75—404
Fort Gratiot,	14—71	Fort Howard, Wisconsin Ter.,	100—504
White Rock,	40—111		
Thunder Island,	70—181	Milwaukee, W. T.	310—814
Middle Island,	25—206	Chicago, Ill.,	90—904
Presque Isle,	65—271		

From Cleaveland to Portsmouth via the Ohio Canal.

	Miles.		Miles.
Cuyahoga aqueduct,	22	Irville,	26—158
Old Portage,	12—34	Newark,	13—171
Akron,	4—38	Hebron,	10—181
New Portage,	5—43	Licking Summit,	5—186
Clinton,	11—54	Lancaster Canaan,	11—197
Massillon,	11—65	Columbus, side cut,	18—215
Bethelehem,	6—71	Bloomfield,	8—223
Bolivar,	8—79	Circleville,	9—232
Zoar,	3—82	Chillicothe,	23—255
Dover,	7—89	Piketon,	25—280
New Philadelphia,	4—93	Lucasville,	14—294
Newcomers'town,	22—115	Portsmouth, (Ohio river.)	13—307
Coshocton,	17—132		

APPENDIX. 323

The most expeditious, pleasant and direct route for travelers to the southern parts of Ohio and Indiana; to the Illinois river, as far north as Peoria; to the Upper Mississippi as far as Quincy, Rock island, Galena and Prairie du Chien; to Missouri, and to Kentucky, Tennessee, Arkansas, Natchez and New Orleans, is one of the southern routes. These are,—1. From Philadelphia to Pittsburg, by rail-roads and the Pennsylvania canal; 2. By the Baltimore and Ohio rail-road and stages, to Wheeling; or, 3. For people living to the south of Washington, by stage, by the way of Charlottesville, (Virginia,) Staunton, the Hot, Warm, and White-Sulphur Springs, Lewisburg, Charleston, to Guyandotte, from whence a regular line of steamboats runs three times a week to Cincinnati. Intermediate routes from Washington city to Wheeling, or to Harper's Ferry, to Fredericksburg, and intersect the route through Virginia, at Charlottesville.

From Philadelphia to Pittsburg, by the rail-road and canal.

	Miles.		Miles.
Columbia, on the Susquehanna river, by rail-road, daily,	81	Petersburg,	8—221
		Alexandria,	23—244
		Frankstown and Hollidaysburg,	3—247
By canal packets to		*From thence, by rail-road, across the mountain, to*	
Bainbridge,	11—92		
Middletown,	17—109		
Harrisburg,	10—119	Johnstown	38—285
Juniata river,	15—144	*By canal, to*	
Millerstown,	17—151	Blairsville,	35—320
Mifflin,	17—168	Saltzburg,	18—338
Lewistown,	13—181	Warren,	12—350
Waynesburg,	14—195	Alleghany river	16—366
Hamiltonville,	11—206	Pittsburg,	28—394
Huntingdon,	7—213		

The *Pioneer* line, on this route, is exclusively for passengers, and professes to reach Pittsburg in four days, but is sometimes behind, several hours. Fare through, $10. Passengers pay for meals.

The *Good-Intent* line is also for passengers only, and runs in competition with the Pioneer line.

Leech's line, called the "*Western Transportation line,*" takes both freight and passengers. The packet-boats advertise to go through, to Pittsburg, in five days, for $7.

Midship and steerage passengers in the transportation line, in six and a half days—merchandise delivered in eight days. Generally, however, there is some delay. Emigrants must not expect to carry more than a small trunk or two, on the packet-lines. Those who take goods or furniture, and wish to keep with it, had better take the transportation lines, with more delay. The price of meals on board the boats is about thirty-seven and a half cents.

In all the steam-boats on the Western waters no additional charge is made to cabin passengers for meals;—and the tables are usually profusely supplied. Strict order is observed, and the waiters and officers are attentive.

Steamboat route from Pittsburg to the mouth of the Ohio.

	Miles.		Miles.
Middletown, Pa.	11	*Guyandotte*, Va.,	27—305
Economy, "	8—19	Burlington, Ohio,	10—315
Beaver, "	10—29	Greensburg, Ky.,	19—334
Georgetown, "	13—42	Concord, Ohio,	12—346
Steubenville, Ohio,	27—69	*Portsmouth* (Ohio canal,)	7—353
Wellsburgh, Va.,	7—76		
Warren, Ohio,	6—82	Vanceburg, Ky.,	20—373
Wheeling, Va.,	10—92	Manchester, Ohio,	16—389
Elizabethtown, Va.,	11—103	*Maysville*, Ky.,	11—400
Sistersville "	34—137	Charleston, "	4—404
Newport, Ohio,	27—164	Ripley, Ohio,	6—410
Marietta, "	14—178	Augusta, Ky.,	8—418
Parkersburg, Va.,	11—189	Neville, Ohio,	7—425
Belpre and Blannerhasset Island, O.,	4—193	Moscow, "	7—432
		Point Pleasant, "	4—436
Troy, Ohio,	10—203	New Richmond, "	7—443
Belleville, Va.,	7—210	Columbia, "	15—458
Letart's Rapids, "	37—247	Fulton, "	6—564
Point Pleasant, "	27—274	CINCINNATI, "	2—466
Gallipolis, Ohio,	4—278	North Bend, "	15—481

APPENDIX.

	Miles.
Lawrenceburg, Ind., and mouth of the Miami,	8—489
Aurora, Ind.,	2—491
Petersburg, Ky.,	2—493
Bellevue, "	8—501
Rising Sun, Ind.,	2—503
Fredericksburg, Ky.,	18—521
Vevay, Ind., and Ghent, Ky.,	11—532
Port William, Ky.,	8—540
Madison Ind.,	15—555
New London, "	12—567
Bethlehem, "	8—575
Westport, Ky.,	7—582
Transylvania, "	15—595
LOUISVILLE, "	12—609
Shippingport, through the canal,	2½—611½
New Albany, Ind.,	1½—613
Salt River, Ky.,	23—636
Northampton, Ind.,	18—654
Leavenworth, "	17—671
Fredonia, "	2—673

	Miles.
Rome, Ind.,	32—705
Troy, "	25—730
Rockport, "	16—746
Owenburg, Ky.,	12—758
Evansville, Ind.,	36—794
Henderson, Ky.,	12—806
Mount Vernon, Ind.,	28—834
Carthage, Ky.,	12—846
Wabash river, "	7—853
Shawneetown, Ill.,	11—864
Mouth of Saline, "	12—876
Cave in Rock, "	10—886
Golconda, "	19—905
Smithland, mouth of the Cumberland river, Ky.,	10—915
Paducah, mouth of the Tennessee river, Ky.,	13—928
Caledonia, Ill.,	31—959
Trinity, mouth of Cash river, Ill.,	10—969
MOUTH OF THE OHIO RIVER,	6—975

Persons who wish to visit Indianopolis will stop at Madison, Indiana, and take the stage conveyance. From Louisville, by the way of Vincennes, to St. Louis by stage, every alternate day, two hundred and seventy-three miles, through in three days and a half. Fare, seventeen dollars. Stages run from Vincennes to Terre Haute and other towns up the Wabash river. At *Evansville*, Indiana, stage lines are connected with Vincennes and Terre Haute; and at *Shawneetown* twice a week to Carlyle, Illinois, where it intersects the line from Louisville to St. Louis. From Louisville to Nashville by steamboats, passengers land at Smithland at the mouth of Cumberland river, unless they embark direct for Nashville.

In the *winter*, both stage and steamboat lines are uncertain and irregular. Ice in the rivers frequently obstructs navigation, and high waters and bad roads sometimes prevent stages from running regularly.

Farmers who remove to the West from the Northern and Middle States, will find it advantageous, in many instances, to remove with their own teams and wagons. These they will need on their arrival. Autumn, or from September till November, is the favorable season for this mode of emigration. The roads are then in good order, the weather usually favorable, and feed plenty. People of all classes, from the States south of the Ohio river, remove with large wagons, carry and cook their own provisions, purchase their feed by the bushel, and invariably *encamp out at night.*

Individuals who wish to travel through the interior of Michigan, Indiana, Illinois, Missouri, &c., will find that the most convenient, sure, economical and independent mode is on horseback. Their expenses will be from seventy-five cents to one dollar fifty cents per day, and they can always consult their own convenience and pleasure as to time and place.

Stage fare is usually six cents per mile, in the West. Meals, at stage-houses, are thirty-seven and a half cents.

Steam Boat Fare, including Meals.

From Pittsburg to Cincinnati,	$ 10
" Cincinnati to Louisville,	4
" Louisville to St. Louis,	12

And frequently the same from Cincinnatti to St. Louis,—varying a little, however.

A *deck* passage, as it is called, may be rated as follows:—

From Pittsburg to Cincinnati,	$ 3
" Cincinnati to Louisville,	1
" Louisville to St. Louis,	4

The deck for such passengers is usually in the midship, forward of the engine, and is protected from the weather. Passengers furnish their own provisions and bedding. They often take their meals at the cabin table, with the boat hands, and pay twenty-five cents a meal. Thousands pass up and down the rivers as deck passengers, especially emigrating families, who have their bedding, provisions and cooking utensils on board.

The whole expense of a single person from New York to St. Louis, by the way of Philadelphia and Pittsburg, with cabin passage on the river, will range between $40 and $45;—time from twelve to fifteen days.

Taking the transportation lines on the Pennsylvania canal, and a deck passage in the steam-boat, and the expenses will range between $20 and $25, supposing the person buys his meals at twenty-five cents, and eats twice a day. If he carry his own provisions, the passage, &c., will be from $15 to $18.

The following is from an advertisement of the Western Transportation, or Leech's line, from Philadelphia:—

	Miles.	Days.	Fare.
Fare to Pittsburg,	400	6½	$ 6 00
" Cincinnati,	900	8½	8 50
" Louisville,	1050	9½	9 00
" Nashville,	1650	13½	13 00
" St. Louis,	1750	14	13 00

The above does not include meals.

Packet-boats for Cabin Passengers, (same line.)

	Miles.	Days.	Fare.
Fare to Pittsburg,	400	5	$ 7 00
" Cincinnati,	900	8	17 00
" Louisville,	1050	9	19 00
" Nashville,	1650	13	27 00
" St. Louis,	1750	13	27 00

Emigrants and travellers will find it to their interest always to be a little skeptical relative to statements of stage, steam and canal-boat agents; to make some allowance in their own calculations for delays, difficulties and expenses; and above all, to *feel* perfectly patient and in good humor with themselves, the officers, company, and the world, even if they do not move quite as rapidly, and fare quite as well as they desire.

EMIGRATION.

While on this subject, we would say, for the benefit of those who have determined on coming to the West, that the *State of Illinois* offers every possible inducement to *emigrants*. This State is advancing rapidly in population, and when her public works, which are progressing with all possible speed, are completed, and in successful operation, she will be the admiration of the " far West." It being by far the richest State in soil in the Union, of course it holds out the greatest prospect of advantage to farmers. Here, too, there is plenty of room for farmers, there being vast quantities of first rate land lying in every direction uncultivated, which may be had very cheap, and one acre of it will produce at least three times as much as the same amount of land in most of the eastern States!

If rural occupations are pleasant and profitable any where in our country, they must be peculiarly so in Illinois, for here the produce of the farmer springs up almost spontaneously, less than one-third of the labour being necessary on the farms here that is required on the farms in the east. Indeed, Illinois may with propriety be called the " Canaan" of America!

Industrious mechanics, more particularly brickmakers, bricklayers and carpenters, are much wanted in the various towns in Illinois. We know of no better place west for a permanent location; and we hope that some of those who have been so unfortunate at the east, will come on, and mend their broken fortunes in a state where enterprise and industry meet with a sure reward.

INDEX

ADAM'S, Branch 110 Creek 191
    Fork 145
ADAMS, County 6 46 81 91 92 107
    126 133 151 154 161 163 177
    178 181 184 185 188 199 206
    211 215 238 240 250 254 263
    271 272 277 281 292 294 303
    305 309 313 John 32
AIKIN'S GROVE, 150
ALABAMA SETTLEMENT, 145
ALBION, 29 60 88 101 145 163
    166 168 243 253 308
ALEXANDER COUNTY, 45 46 92
    111 137 150 151 158 164 170
    175 182 210 221 222 253 272
    289 290 304
ALFRED, 132
ALLEN, Capt 247 Daniel 246
ALLEN'S PRAIRIE, 146 263
ALLISON'S PRAIRIE, 146 181
ALTON, 5 17 32 60 61 63 72 106
    117 146-149 152 164 165 172
    180 182 194 200 209 219 220
    226 240 246 253 254 278 294
    FEMALE SEMINARY, 254
    THEOLOGICAL SEMINARY, 71
AMERICA, 92 150 170 210 222
    272
AMERICAN BOTTOM, 26 37 63
    116 121 156 162 168 169 171
    182 183 253 275 276 292 293
ANDOVER SETTLEMENT, 311
APAKEESHEEK GROVE, 145

APPANOOCE, 150
APPLE, Creek 105 111 123 150
    154 157 161 162 173 184 199
    211 218 223 243 259 261 273
    276 284 288 299 311 Creek
    Prairie 150 280 River 150 309
    Head of 216 217
ARMSTRONG, 151
ARROWSMITH'S SETTLEMENT, 151
ASHTON, 151
ATHENS, 133 151
ATHERTON'S SETTLEMENT, 151
ATLAS, 126 151 219 294
AU KAS, 263
AU SABLE, 112 114
AUBUCHON, 151
AUBURN, 152
AUGUSTA, 43 63 151
AUSABLE, 152 Grove 152 243
AUSAUBLE GROVE, 254
AUX PLAINES, 190
AVISTON, 152
BACHELDER'S GROVE, 152
BACK BONE, 212
BAGBY'S FORK, 230
BAILEY'S, Island 241 Point 152
BAKER'S GROVE, 152
BALDWIN, Theron 70 73
BANKSTONE'S FORK, 152
BANNING'S SETTLEMENT, 153
BARBEE'S SETTLEMENT, 153
BARNEY'S PRAIRIE, 153

BARTLETT'S SETTLEMENT, 153
BARTON, Charles B 72
BATCHELDORS-VILLE, 153
BATH, 153
BAY CREEK, 94 126 153
BEAN RIVER, 200
BEAR, Creek 91 107 154 161 174
    185 199 206 215 245 271 281
    292 305 313 Prairie 155
BEARDSTOWN, 95 133 153 154
    174 182 183 186 224 246 259
    260 262 285 288 292 299
    Canal 222
BEAUCOUP, 155 284 Creek 155
    196 301 309 River 140 Settle-
    ment 155 Stream 160
BEAVER, Creek 108 155 191 234
    261 297 298 Fork 291
BECK, 149 204 256 269 Dr 41
BECK'S CREEK, 102 155
BEECHER, Edward 70
BEGG'S SETTLEMENT, 155
BELLEFOUNTAINE, 156
BELLEVIEW PRAIRIE, 94 156
BELLEVILLE, 60 135 152 156 158
    168 178 182 183 199 200 207
    219 229 237 252-254 256 263
    275 277 278 280 281 283 291
    294 303
BELVIDERE, 157 274 College 72
BEMAN'S MILL, 157
BENNINGTON, 157
BENTON COUNTY, 46
BERGEN, John G 70

BERLIN, 157
BERNADOTTE, 157
BERRY'S SETTLEMENT, 157
BETHANY, 158
BETHEL, 158 161
BETHESDA, 161
BIENVILLE, M 86
BIG, Barren Grove 158 Bay 13 Bay
    Creek 112 127 158 175 177
    208 254 275 311 Beaucoup
    125 155 158 184 185 205 239
    258 272 Blue Creek 126
    Bottom 158 Clear Creek 100
    Creek 96 102 103 158 159 212
    221 242 243 303 Grove 95 108
    159 160 168 234 279 305 Hill
    204 Mound Prairie 160 Muddy
    35 Muddy River 103 110 137
    155 158 160 165 177 185 204
    212 234 238 240 243 252
    Muddy Salines 165 Neck 161
    Prairie 141 161 184 Rock
    Creek 161 Stream 163 Vermil-
    ion River 114 138 Wabash
    River 115 141 161 184 196
    197 206 213 241 Woods 112
    161 205 236 241 308
BIRBECK, Morris 206 Mr 88 101
    145
BIRCH CREEK, 161
BLACK, Creek 126 161 Oak Ridge
    158 Partridge Creek 161
BLACKBERRY CREEK, 112 144
    161

BLACKBURN, Gideon 70
BLAKEMAN, Capt 247
BLOCK HOUSE, 162
BLOOD, Charles E 72
BLOOMFIELD, 162 165
BLOOMING GROVE, 162 300
BLOOMINGDALE, 162
BLOOMINGTON, 60 61 120 160
    162 166 178 189 192 207 216
    221 238 279 290 299 305 307
    310
BLUE, Creek 136 162 Mounds 38
    267 Point 163 River 126 163
BLUFFDALE, 37 162 163 280
BOISMENU, Louis 63
BOLIVE, 163 201
BOLTENHOUSE PRAIRIE, 101
BOLTINGHOUSE PRAIRIE, 163
BON PAS, 101 138 163 Creek 139
    163 213 230 Prairie 101 163
    Settlement 163
BOND, County 45 46 92 93 97 102
    116 122 155 191 192 194 202
    209 213 219 222 226 249 252
    259 261 263 267 284 291 292
    294 299 305 308 Gov 52
BONE'S SETTLEMENT, 247
BOONE COUNTY, 46 93 108 111
    112 119 143 144 155 157 175
    234 262 263 266 273 297
BOOZ CREEK, 278
BOSTON, 163 Bay 155 177 Stream
    163

BOSTWICK'S SETTLEMENT, 164
BOTTOM, Prairie 135 Settlement
    164
BOYD'S, Grove 187 Settlement 187
BRADLEY'S SETTLEMENT, 164
BRATTLEVILLE, 164
BRIDGE'S SETTLEMENT, 164
BRIER FORK, 248
BRIGHAM, Mr 38
BRIGHTON, 164
BROAD RUN, 164
BROCKET'S SETTLEMENT, 164
BROCKETT'S SETTLEMENT, 159
    207
BROOKLYN, 164
BROOKS, John F 70
BROWN CREEK, 103
BROWN'S, Point 164 Prairie 164
    165
BROWNSVILLE, 17 109 155 160
    165 177 185 230 238 248 255
    273 281
BRULETTE'S CREEK, 100 165 298
BRUSH, Creek 130 165 287 Hill
    165 Prairie Creek 165
BRUSHY, Fork 165 166 Prairie 166
BUCK PRAIRIE, 166
BUCK-HEART, Creek 166 Grove
    166 Prairie 166
BUCK-HORN PRAIRIE, 166
BUCKLE'S GROVE, 166
BUCKMASTER CREEK, 103
BUDGELY'S SETTLEMENT, 152

BUFFALO GROVE, 290
BUFFALOE, Grove 166 195 196 208 298 Rock 33 167
BUFFALOE-HEART GROVE, 166
BULLARDS PRAIRIE, 167
BULLBONA GROVE, 167
BUMPAU, 163
BUNCOMBE SETTLEMENT, 167
BUNKER HILL, 167
BUREAU, County 46 Creek 167 Grove 128 River 235 312 Settlement 277 Stream 128
BURNSIDE'S SETTLEMENT, 167
BURNT PRAIRIE, 101 141 167 168
BUSH PRAIRIE, 101
BYRON, 168
CACHE MERE, 168
CACHE MERE LAKE, 119
CADWELL CREEK, 197
CADWELL'S BRANCH, 168
CAHOKIA, 6 85 117 168 169 207 211 225 226 276 Creek 116 River 171 184 192 Stream 135 Village 135 169
CAIRO, 60 170
CALAMIC, 53 170
CALEDONIA, 170
CALHOUN COUNTY, 6 46 81 94 105 106 126 153 156 172 209 214 215 223 252 286 293 294
CALUMET, 56 57 170 289 302 River 31 143
CAMDEN, 170

CAMERON'S SETTLEMENT, 170
CAMP, Creek 107 139 170 171 280 Fork 171 219
CAMPBELL'S ISLAND, 170
CANAAN, 171 Settlement 163
CANAWAGA, 227
CANTEEN, Creek 171 Settlement 171
CANTON, 61 159 171 184 199 228 242 252 277 College 72 Prairie 166 171
CANTRILL'S CREEK, 130 171 287
CAOQUIAS, 168
CAPE AU GRIS, 172
CAPE GIRARDEAU, 290
CAPE of GRIT, 172
CARLINVILLE, 117 154 172 191 192 193 247
CARLYLE, 60 97 155 157 167 172 173 202 209 213 222 230 233 246 249 257 265 281 292 293 309
CARMI, 141 173 187 234 247 290 294
CAROLUS, 173
CARROLLTON, 106 146 150 157 162 172-174 182 184 189 199 210 213 216 219 220 229 231 246 262 273 276 280 299 311
CARTER'S SETTLEMENT, 164 174
CARTHAGE, 61 107 150 151 174 184 205 298 309
CASEY'S, Grove 174 Prairie 110 257

CASH RIVER, 92 111 112 137 156
174 175 193 198 208 210 221
222 257 275 288 289 298 302
304 307 Stream 13
CASS, County 94 122 123 130 153
185 229 262 292 Post Office
174
CAT TAIL SWAMP, 142 175
CATFISH STREAM, 283
CATO, 175
CAVE IN ROCK, 33 175
CAVE SPRING BRANCH, 240
CEDAR, Creek 91 158 177 181 249
Fork 177 217
CENTERVILLE, 177 178
CHAMPAIGN COUNTY, 46 95 98
116 120 137 138 159 168 196
211 219 232 244 286 287 292
303 305 306
CHANDLER, S B 63
CHARLESTON, 61 98 151 153 161
166 178 188 189 192 196 197
215 218 220 226 263 266 275
CHARLEVOIX, 168 232 246
CHARTER'S GROVE, 178
CHENAIL-ECARTE, 294
CHERRY GROVE, 178
CHESTER, 178
CHEYNEY'S GROVE, 178
CHICAGO, 32 53-59 62 63 65 79
99 138 152 157 165 173 174
179-181 191 195 201 205 214
215 226 231 237 238 242 244
274 279 282 286 289 301 308

CHICAGO (Cont.)
309 Bay 180 River 55 56 119
Stream 180
CHILLICOTHE, 181
CHIPPEWA, 181
CHOTEAU'S ISLAND, 181
CHRISTIAN SETTLEMENT, 181
CHRISTY'S PRAIRIE, 181
CHURCH CREEK, 126
CLARK, County 46 63 96 98-100
102 159 181 188 191 212 242
247 248 251 252 262 266 300
303 309 313 Mr 168
CLARKE, Gen 87 George Rogers 86
CLARY'S, Creek 130 181 287 288
Grove 181 282
CLAY COUNTY, 46 96 97 101-103
109 114 118 140 175 196 206
241 243 248 258 303 308
Creek 174 181 Lick 181 Prairie
181
CLAYTON, 60 181
CLEAR, Creek 92 130 137 158 181
182 193 222 251 262 305 Lake
182 211
CLENDENING'S SETTLEMENT,
182
CLERMONT'S VILLAGE, 38
CLIFTON, 182
CLINTON, 93 182 185 County 45
46 97 102 116 118 135 139
152 155 157 167 172 182 193
202 213 222 230 232 246 249
265 281 291-293 300 308

CLIO, 183
COAL, Banks 183 Creek 183
COCHRAN'S GROVE, 183
COFFEE, County 46 144 Creek 139 183
COFFIN, Nathaniel 70
COLBY, Lewis 71
COLD, Prairie 183 Spring Settlement 183
COLES, 96 County 46 63 95 98 100 101 109 116 134 137 151 153 161 164 166 175 178 188 189 192 196 197 211 213 215 218 220 226 232 241 258 262 266 274 308 313 Edward 268
COLLEGE HILL, 312
COLLINS, Frederick 70
COLLINSVILLE, 183
COLUMBIA, 235
COLUMBO CREEK, 184
COLUMBUS, 184 290
COMMERCE, 150 184 292
COMPTON'S PRAIRIE, 184
CONANT PRAIRIE, 244
CONCORD, 184
COOK COUNTY, 46 47 99 112 119 142-144 152 165 174 179 192 201 205 218 226 237 250 256 259 289 301-303 309 313
COON CREEK, 184
COONSVILLE, 184
COOP'S CREEK, 184
COPPERAS CREEK, 104 124 184 305

COTTON HILL PRAIRIE, 185
COTTONBERGER'S SETTLEMENT, 185
COURT CREEK, 185
COVINGTON, 185 187
COWNOVER'S BRANCH, 185
COX'S, Grove 185 Prairie 185 248
CRAB ORCHARD, 185 191 213
CRAB ORCHARD CREEK, 271
CRAIG, Capt 269
CRANE CREEK, 130 133 183 185 186 236 287
CRAWFISH CREEK, 139 185
CRAWFORD, 96 193
CRAWFORD COUNTY 13 46 74 96 99 100 102 109 114 115 153 159 196 212 219 222 236 261 262 266 267 278 310
CRAWFORD'S CREEK, 185
CREEK PRAIRIE, 130
CREVE-COEUR, 85
CROOKED CREEK, 97 107 118 133 134 140 153 154 157 171 177 178 186 187 191 209 211 214 229 230 239 240 243 246 249 264 271 280 284 303 305 312
CROSAT, 86 M 85
CROW CREEK, 114 187 Grove 187 Meadow 187 Stream 128
CRYSTAL LAKE, 119 188
CUMBERLAND, 187 River 238
CURRAN, 187
CUTLER'S SETTLEMENT, 188

CYPRESS, 188
DAD JOE'S GROVE, 188
DANVILLE, 17 60 79 138 173 178
    180 188 189 191 201 209 216
    285 292 303 306 307
DARWIN, 96 181 188 242 251
DAVIESS, Joseph H 111 Mr 225
DAVIS, S M 270
DAVISTON, 178 Post Office 188
DAWSON'S GROVE, 188 234 263
DELASALLE, M 83
DE PRU PRAIRIE, 218
DEAD MAN'S GROVE, 189
DEATON'S MILL, 189
DEAUSIX, 189
DECATUR, 60 116 182 185 189
    204 207 209 225 245 251 253
    263 281 286 292 298 309
DECKER'S PRAIRIE, 189
DEKALB COUNTY, 144
DELHI, 189
DELONG NECK PRAIRIE, 121
DEMONBRUN, Timothy 87
DENNIS CREEK, 142
DESMOINES, 61 Rapids 279 River
    203
DESPLAINES, 17 34 38 53-56 63
    99 143 152 180 190-192 201
    237 242 248 255 286 Creek
    142 River 31 119 189 218 223
    226 231 232 244 256
DEVIL'S, Anvil 33 190 Oven 190
    Tea Table 212

DIAMOND, Grove 190 Grove Prairie
    190 Island 75
DICKEN'S FORK, 230
DICKERSON'S LAKE, 190 278 312
DILLARD'S, 190
DILLON'S, 190 Creek 274 Post
    Office 190
DIXON'S FERRY, 166 186 191 196
    233 263 283 290 301
DIXONVILLE, 150 191 208 210
    226 264 303
DOLSON PRAIRIE, 96 191
DONOHUE'S SETTLEMENT, 191
DOUGLASS, 191
DOWNING'S SETTLEMENT, 191
DRESDEN, 191
DREWRY'S CREEK, 191
DRIFTWOOD, 191
DROWNING FORK, 171 191 249
DRY FORK, 192 295 Creek 245
DRY, Grove 192 Point 192
DUBUQUE, 15
DUCK GROVE, 192
DUDLEY'S SETTLEMENT, 192
DUNCAN, Joseph 70
DUNCANTON, 192 247
DUNWOODY'S MILL, 192
DUPAGE, 99 192 201 286 309
    County 205 Creek 142 River
    144 152 205 259 273
DUPONT PRAIRIE, 135
DUTCH, Church Creek 193 Creek
    126 Hill 193 Settlement 193

DUTCHMAN'S CREEK, 193
EAGLE CREEK, 121 193 Point 193
    River 204
EAST FORK, 118 200 202 233 of
    Shoal Creek 194 213 267 of
    Silver Creek 194 of Cash River
    193 of the Kaskaskia River 193
    211
EAST STREAM, 110
EATON PRAIRIE, 244
EATON'S MILL, 193
EDGAR COUNTY, 46 96 98 100
    137 159 162 165 166 181 195
    201 212 252 262 264 266 274
    298 300 309
EDINBURG, 194
EDMONSON'S PRAIRIE, 194
EDWARD'S, River 275 Settlement
    194
EDWARDS, County 32 46 88 96
    101 102 110 114 138-141 145
    163 166 168 206 241 243 253
    308 Ninian 87 River 107 108
    121 139 171 195 260 292 300
    313
EDWARDSVILLE, 38 60 78 117
    171 172 192 194 209 219 221
    226 239 246 247 265 278 279
    281 294 301 303
EFFINGHAM, 96-98 County 46 63
    101-103 109 134 159 163 164
    198 205 207 211 241 286 303
    312
EIGHT MILE PRAIRIE, 195

ELBRIDGE POST OFFICE, 195
ELGIN, 195 206
ELK PRAIRIE, 196
ELK-HEART GROVE, 167 195
ELKHORN, Creek 140 196 242
    Grove 195 196 Stream 195
ELLICOTT, 204
ELLISON, 195 221 229 Creek 139
    295
ELLISON'S PRAIRIE, 146
ELLISVILLE, 195
ELM RIVER, 140 196 248 302
ELVIRA SETTLEMENT, 198
EMBARRAS, River 98 100 109 110
    115 151 159 165 166 178 188
    196 197 212 213 215 218 225
    226 231 237 258 261 275 294
    299 Settlement 197 Stream 96
EMBARRASS RIVER, 13
EMBROY RIVER, 196
EMINENCE, 197
EMMETTSBURG, 197
ENGLISH SETTLEMENT, 197
EQUALITY, 60 105 152 154 187
    188 190 197 201 209 214 216
    226 234 240 280 285 286 295
ERIE CANAL, 57
ESSEX'S SETTLEMENT, 198 202
ESTES'S PRAIRIE, 198
EVAN'S SETTLEMENT, 198
EWINGTON, 102 163 164 198 205
    286
EXETER, 198
EYMAN'S SETTLEMENT, 199

FAIR MOUNT, 199
FAIRFIELD, 60 141 155 160 166 199 216 218 219 226 238 240 248 259 291 302 303
FALL CREEK, 91 199
FALLS of ST ANTHONY, 12 85
FANCY CREEK, 130 199 287
FANNING'S CREEK, 199
FARM CREEK, 136 220
FARMER, Major 86
FARMINGTON, 199
FAYETTE, 93 96 97 155 200 280
FAYETTE COUNTY, 46 96 101-103 118 122 132 134 159 193 211 218 219 222 232 289 306
FAYETTEVILLE, 200
FEVER RIVER, 111 200 208 293
FIEHRER, Elaine 13
FINCH'S SETTLEMENT, 201
FINDLEY'S FORK, 159
FISHING CREEK, 211
FIVE MILE GROVE, 201
FLAG CREEK, 144 201
FLAT, Branch 201 Prairie 184 201
FLINT, Mr 38
FLORA, 201
FLORIA, 201
FLOWER, George 29
FLOWERS, Mr 88 101 145
FONTI, Chevalier 83
FORD'S FERRY, 201
FORK, Prairie 202 263 Settlement 202

FORKED CREEK, 142 201
FORT, Chartres 35 86 87 202 276 Clark 268 269 Dearborn 180 Edwards 203 309 Massac 203 204 River 112 Winnebago 283
FOSTER'S SETTLEMENT, 204 254
FOUNTAIN, Creek 193 204 Green 205 Green Post Office 271
FOUNTAINDALE, 192 205
FOUR MILE PRAIRIE, 205
FOURTEEN MILE PRAIRIE, 205 286
FOX RIVER, 31 53 56 82 93 112- 115 119 144 161 192 195 205 206 221 223 225 236 240 241 249 254 264 279 282 295 301 308
FRAKER'S SETTLEMENT, 108
FRAKERS, 206
FRANKFORT, 60 103 195 198 199 206 209 235 249 252 271 284 310
FRANKLIN, County 45 46 103 104 106 109 110 111 125 137 165 185 195 198 213 218 235 240 249 252 271 284 285 286 295 310 Grove 206
FRAZIER'S CREEK, 206
FREE'S SETTLEMENT, 207
FRENCH, Grove 183 207 Settlement 207 Village 207 211
FRIENDS CREEK, 207
FRONTENAC, 83

FULFER'S CREEK, 207
FULTON, 72 207 216 County 46 81
    103 104 113 118 124 133 157
    159 166 171 184 195 199 221
    222 228 238 241 247 252 265
    266 275 277 298 299 301 302
    305 309 312 Robert 207
FUNK, 207
FUNK'S GROVE, 207
GAGNIE, 208
GALE, Rev Mr 72
GALENA, 60 63 76 79 111 124 150
    157 166 180 187 191 200 208
    217 233 257 274 276 282 289
    290 293 294 303 308 312
GALENA ROAD, 260
GALESBORO, 72
GALLATIN, 35 101 County 14 17
    45 46 103-106 127 141 152
    154 175 187 188 190 193 197
    201 209 216 226 234 240-243
    260 280 285 295
GAP GROVE, 208
GARDEN PRAIRIE, 208
GARDNER'S PRAIRIE, 167
GAYLORD, Reuben 70
GENEVA, 208
GEORGE'S CREEK, 208
GEORGETOWN, 209
GERMANY, 208
GIDDINGS, Rev Mr 39
GILEAD, 209 214 215 286
GILHAM'S SETTLEMENT, 209
GILMAN, Winthorp S 70

GILMORE'S SETTLEMENT, 209
GIRARD, 209
GODFREY, Benjamin 72
GOLCONDA, 127 158 190 209 221
    227 244 249 254 307 308 311
GOOSE CREEK, 209
GOSHEN, 209
GRABBLE'S SETTLEMENT, 209
GRAFTON, 210 260 278
GRAHAM'S SETTLEMENT, 210
GRAND, Cote 210 301 Detour 31
    152 206 210 264 272 Marais
    211 Passe 211 220 Point 211
    Prairie 102 118 140 159 164
    178 187 211 212 218 222 226
    243 260 (arm of) 110 150
    Rapids 247 Tower 33 190 212
    View 212
GRANGER'S PRAIRIE, 211
GRANT RIVER, 267
GRASSY CREEK, 213
GRAVES, Jeremiah 70
GRAYSVILLE, 213
GREAT, Prairie 301 Wabash 31 60
    301
GREEN, Bay 82 84 180 282
    County 94 146 161 213 Plains
    213 River 9 107 213 283
GREEN'S, Mills 31 Settlement 213
GREENE COUNTY, 32 37 46 105
    106 116 117 122 150 154 157
    162 165 173 182 184 189 199
    200 210 211 216 217 219 220
    229 231 239 243 245 246 260-

GREENE COUNTY (Cont.)
    262 265 272 273 276 280 299
    301 311
GREENE'S SETTLEMENT, 240
GREENFIELD, 133 213
GREENUP, 213
GREENVILLE, 93 191 202 209 213
    219 249 252 261 263 267 284
    299 308
GREGORY'S SETTLEMENT, 213
GRIGGSVILLE, 72 214
GRINDSTONE, 172 Fork 174 214
GRISWOLD'S POST OFFICE, 214
GROS POINT, 214
GROVELAND, 214
GUILFORD, 94 214
GUM'S FORT, 215 217
GUN PRAIRIE, 215
HADLEY, 215 Creek 126
HADLEY'S CREEK, 215
HALEY'S, 103
HALL, Miss 225 Mr 225
HALL'S, 103
HAMBURG, 215
HAMILTON COUNTY, 46 103 106
    110 140 141 160 214 220 227
    235 242 250 252 285 293 301
HAMMET'S SETTLEMENT, 215
HANCOCK COUNTY, 43 46 62 91
    107 118 119 126 133 139 150
    151 154 170 174 184 186 199
    203 205 213 215 236 254 263
    271 279 312 Prairie 107 215
HANOVER, 73 215

HARDEN'S SETTLEMENT, 215
HARGRAVE'S PRAIRIE, 199 216
HARKNESS SETTLEMENT, 124
    216
HARRIFORD, John 246 Paul 246
HARRIS, 177 Thaddeus M 176
HARRIS'S CREEK, 216
HARRISONVILLE, 14 216
HAVANNA, 136 178 216 295
HAW CREEK, 216 235
HAWKINS, Prairie 216 River 142
HAZEL'S SETTLEMENT, 216
HENDERSON, 215 217 County 313
    River 113 121 139 177 195
    217 253 275 Settlement 215
    217
HENDERSON'S, Creek 217 Stand
    246
HENNEPIN, 83 128 182 187 201
    218 223 235 236 265 269 274
    277 299 312 313 Father 85
HENRY COUNTY, 46 81 93 104
    107 108 113 121 127 139 142
    144 158 160 171 195 202 206
    214 226 275 276 280 300 311
    312
HERCULANEUM, 216
HERRINGTON'S PRAIRIE, 218
HERRON'S PRAIRIE, 218
HICKORY, Creek 99 102 142 218
    303 313 Post Office 218 Grove
    171 219 Hill Settlement 219
HIGGINS CREEK, 102 219 Settle-
    ment 219

HIGH PRAIRIE, 219
HIGHLAND, 219
HIGHSMITH'S SETTLEMENT, 219
HILL'S FERRY, 151
HILLSBORO, 61 122 164 220 222 246 252
HINDE, Thomas S 255
HITESVILLE, 220
HITTLE'S GROVE, 220
HODGE'S, Creek 220 245 Warehouse 223
HODGES'S CREEK, 262
HOG PRAIRIE, 220
HOLDERMAN'S GROVE, 145 192 220 239
HOLLAND'S GROVE, 220 221 310
HONEY CREEK, 139 221
HORSE, Creek 121 129 130 165 185 221 287 Prairie 221 Shoe Lake 221 Shoe Prairie, 221
HOUSTON'S FORK, 230
HOWARD'S SETTLEMENT, 221
HOXEY'S SETTLEMENT, 221
HUDSON, 221
HUEY'S SETTLEMENT, 222
HUGH'S SETTLEMENT, 222
HURON, 154 222
HURRICANE, 102 220 222 Fork 93 102 122 222 289 Post Office 222 Settlement 222
HUTCHEN'S, Creek 222 Settlement 222
HUTSON'S CREEK, 100 222
HUTSONVILLE, 222

ILLINOIS & MICHIGAN CANAL, 143 264 271 289
ILLINOIS, Bluffs 280 Bottom 162 190 211 225 Canal 31 32 52-54 59 60 231 College 68 Lake 271 Prairie 94 223 River 3 6 7 12-14 31 52-57 60 63 75 76 79 81 83-86 94 95 98 102-106 108 114 120 122 124 126-128 130 131 133 134 136 138 146 149-153 161-163 167 170-172 176 182-184 186 187 190 199 205 210 211 214 216 218 223 224 227 229 231 234 236 238-242 244-248 250 251 254 256 259 264 265 267-271 274 278 279 283-288 290 295 296 297 299 303 305 307 Territory 246 Town 225 Village 135
ILLIOPOLIS, 225
INDIAN, Big Thunder 157 Black Hawk 225 283 298 Pontiac 297
INDIAN CREEK, 95 112 114 122 130 185 192 205 225 226 233 239 267 Prairie 226
INLET GROVE, 226
IOWA COUNTY, 251
IRISH, Grove 226 252 Settlement 167 227
IROQUOIS, 184 227 City 227 County 46 47 108 113 137 142 155 191 227 238 273 300 306 Creek 108 River 114 155 184

IROQUOIS (Cont.)
227 231 273 300
IRVIN'S SETTLEMENT, 227
ISLAND GROVE, 157 227 228
ITASCA LAKE, 12
JACKSON, County 14 17 45 46
103 109 125 129 137 155 160
164 165 177 184 185 190 191
204 208 211 238 248 255 272
281 Grove 228
JACKSONVILLE, 60 63 68 72 123
150 151 153 157 161 165 166
168 172 174 189 190 192 197
198 200 206 208 217 228 229
244 246 248 251 260-263 274
277 297 311 312 Academy 72
Female Academy 72
JARROT, Vital 63
JARVIS, Franklin 303
JARVIS'S SETTLEMENT, 229
JASPER COUNTY, 46 96 98-101
109 114 115 193 196 206 231
261 262 297
JEFFERSON COUNTY, 18 46 103
106 110 118 125 140 145 150
160 174 211 215 230 240 243
252 254 257 309 311
JENNEY, Elisha 70
JERSEY PRAIRIE, 185 229 233
277 313
JERSEYVILLE, 229
JO DAVIESS COUNTY, 32 46 93
110 121 123 129 130 135 136
142 143 150 166 178 195 196

JO DAVIESS COUNTY (Cont.)
200 208 217 230 233 240 256
267 274 284 289 294 308 309
JOB'S, Creek 229 292 Fork 230
Settlement 229
JOHNSON, Johnson 45 46 103 109
111 112 127 137 158 164 167
174 175 177 193 203 208 249
275 285 289 307 James 15 R
M 15
JOHNSON'S, Creek 230 Settlement
230
JOLIET, 82 83 231 256
JONATHAN'S CREEK, 230
JONES'S CREEK POST OFFICE,
230
JONESBORO, 137 182 193 222
230 256 308
JORDAN CREEK, 139 230
JORDAN'S, Prairie 110 230 Prairie
Post Office 230 Settlement 231
JULIET, 56 143 197 215 228
KANE, County 46 47 93 108 112-
114 119 144 159 161 178 184
234 236 240 241 254 264 267
295 308 Post Office 231 246
KANKAKEE, 17 31 34 232 Creek
108 River 12 142 152 190-192
201 223 227 231 232 248 256
303 312
KASKASKIA, 34 35 47 74 78 85-87
95 102 118 129 232 274 River
5-7 12-14 26 31 60 86 97 98
116 129 134 135 140 151 153

KASKASKIA RIVER (Cont.)
155 159 164 165 170 172 178
184 185 187 189 193 195-197
200-203 218 219 221 222 227
230 232 233 241 243 247 252
258 261 263 274-276 278 280
281 285-288 289-292 298-301
306 311 312 Trace 272
KELLOGG'S GROVE, 233 274 313
KELTNER'S FORK, 233
KEY'S CREEK, 126 233
KICKAPOO, 305 Creek 120 124
160 189 279 287 310 River
234 236 269 Stream 233
KINCAID CREEK, 164 234
KINNEY, William 256
KINSAWL'S SETTLEMENT, 234
KIRBY, William 70
KISHWAUKEE RIVER, 93 112 143
144 155 159 178 184 226 234
235 262 263 273 274 298 301
KITE, Creek 239 311 River 124 235
KNIGHT'S PRAIRIE, 235
KNOB PRAIRIE, 235
KNOX COUNTY, 46 72 81 103 104
107 108 113 124 127 139 144
185 201 215 216 217 226 235
266
KNOX'S, Grove 235 Settlement 128
235
KNOXVILLE, 113 199 217 235 242
252 313
L'AIGLE CREEK, 193 204

LABALLANCE, 225
LACON, 235
LAFOX, 236
LAHARP, 86
LAHARPE, 236
LAKE, Erie 13 138 Fork (Creek),
172 192 209 236 245 262 287
Joliet 236 Michigan 1 2 8 9 14
40 52 54 55 79 84 99 119 170
179 190 206 214 242 279
LAMARCHE STREAM, 236
LAMASTER'S SETTLEMENT, 236
LAMOTTE, Creek 100 236 Prairie
100 236 266
LASALLE, 84 85 168 232 County
46 47 54 99 108 112-115 120
123 127 142-145 152 160 167
187 192 220 233 235 239 243
248 260 263-265 274 288 295
303 307 Prairie 124 236 237
LATRAPPE, 253
LAUGHTON'S, 237 Trading House
244
LAVILLE DE MAILLET, 268
LAW, Mr 86
LAWRENCE COUNTY, 13 46 96 99-
101 109 114 115 138 146 165
181 196 206 207 237 244 248
258 285 299 308
LAWRENCEVILLE, 115 146 163
165 167 181 196 207 226 237
248 258 294 299
LE FEVRE, 200

343

LEAF RIVER, 124 237 262
LEBANON, 60 71 135 237 241 252
　263 301
LEECH, Mr 199
LEESBURGH, 238
LEMARDE PRAIRIE, 238
LESTER'S POINT, 238
LEVERETT, Washington 71
LEWIS'S, Creek 238 Prairie 181
　Settlement 238
LEWISTON, 104
LEWISTOWN, 157 159 166 170
　171 195 221 228 238 247 275
　302 309
LEXINGTON, 238
LIBERTY, 190 238 County 230
LICK, Creek 130 198 213 238 287
　299 Run 239
LIMA, 239
LINCOLN, 239
LINDEN, Bottom 239 Grove 239
LINNEUS, 24
LISBON, 220 239
LITTLE, Bay Creek 158 Beaucoup
　Creek 239 Blue Creek 126
　Blue Stream 163 Bureau
　Creek 167 Canteen Creek 171
　Chain 301 Crooked Creek 239
　260 Detroit 239 259 Elm Creek
　205 Embarras River 100
　French Village 207 Grove 181
　Indian Creek 239 Mackinau
　239 244 Mackinau Creek 244
　Mason River 248 Missouri

LITTLE (Cont.)
　Creek 240 Mount Prairie
　240 Mud Creek 258 Muddy
　River 125 140 196 239 240
　Muddy Stream 160 Nine Mile
　Creek 261 Panther Grove 266
　Piasau 240 Rock Creek 240
　Rock River 142 240 Saline
　River 240 Sandy Creek 240
　Vermilion River 56 114 138
　209 241 284 296 303 307
　Wabash River 13 31 60 96 98
　101 102 106 109 110 140 141
　145 159 161-164 166 173 184
　187 193 196 198 206 207 241
　249 258 260 266 286 293 294
　303 308 Woods 113 241
LIVERPOOL, 241 242
LIVINGSTON COUNTY, 46 114 115
　120 242 258 265 307 310
LOCKPORT, 55-57 242
LOCKWOOD, Samuel D 70 Settle-
　ment 214 242
LOCUST, Creek 242 Grove 242
LOGAN'S SETTLEMENT, 242
LOLLARD'S SETTLEMENT, 242
LONG, Creek 159 174 243 Grove
　243 Prairie 101 110 243 252
LOOKING GLASS PRAIRIE, 135
　219 221 240 243 304
LOOMIS, Hubbel 71
LORTON'S PRAIRIE, 243
LOST, Creek 243 Grove 244 Prairie
　244

LOUIS XV, King of France 86
LOUP CREEK, 244
LOWEL, 307
LOWER, Alton 147 175 272 Rapids 184
LURTON, 189
LUSK'S CREEK, 127 209 244 254
LYNN GROVE, 244
LYNNVILLE, 63 151 244
LYONS, 244
M, Dr 43
M'KEES CREEK, 91
M'LEAN COUNTY, 114
MACKINAN RIVER, 136
MACKINAU, 61 245 302 Creek 245 River 115 221 240 265 282 299 304 308 Stream 244
MACKINAW RIVER, 136
MACOMB, 61 72 119 153 164 174 194 249 285 305 308
MACON COUNTY, 46 95 98 116 120 130 134 159 182 185 189 207 209 243 245 247 253 254 259 263 286 287 295 298 309 311 Prairie 245
MACOUPEN COUNTY, 32 45 46
MACOUPIN, 105 154 162 173 County 116 117 122 130 164 165 167 169 172 184 191-193 200 209 231 239 245 247 272 295 301 313 County Creek 105 Creek 117 236 245 246 295 299 301 Point 236 246 294 Prairie 199 219 246 River

MACOUPIN (Cont.) 172 184 192 214 216 221 239 246 271 280 Settlement 246
MADDUX SETTLEMENT, 246
MADISON, 92 93 105 County 22 32 45 46 97 116 117 122 125 135 165 169 171 181 183 194 209 217 219 221 226 243 247 252 253 265 278 279 281 292 293 300 301 303 313
MAGOOPIN, 245
MAN-I-TEAU, 175
MANCHESTER, 246 301
MANTUA, 247 Settlement 192
MAQUAPIN, 245
MARAIS D'OGEE, 230 247 251 Lake 142 Slough 129 Swamp 142
MARCHANT'S SETTLEMENT, 247
MARINE SETTLEMENT, 247 252
MARION COUNTY, 46 96 97 102 110 118 140 145 187 193 211 285 308 309
MARK'S PRAIRIE, 246
MARKET STREET, 147
MARKHAM'S SETTLEMENT, 247
MARQUETTE, 83 P 82
MARROW BONE CREEK, 247
MARSEILLES, 31 56 247
MARSHALL, 247
MARSHALL'S PRAIRIE, 248
MARTIN'S, Creek 248 Settlement 248
MARTINSVILLE, 248

MASON, 176 248 260 Grove 248 Stream 114
MASON'S PRAIRIE, 248
MASSAC, 204
MATHER, Thomas 70
MAUMEE RIVER, 13
MAUVAISETERRE, 168 189 198 224 228 248 259 261 262 288 Creek 123
MAYSVILLE, 97 248
MCADAM'S SETTLEMENT, 249
MCCORD'S SETTLEMENT, 249
MCCORMACK'S SETTLEMENT, 249
MCCREERY'S SETTLEMENT, 249
MCDONOUGH, College 72 County 46 81 103 107 118 119 133 139 153 164 171 174 186 191 194 204 214 219 229 249 284 285 299 302 303 305 308 313
MCEAVER'S SETTLEMENT, 249
MCFATRIDGE'S SETTLEMENT, 249
MCHENRY COUNTY, 31 46 47 93 99 112 119 144 168 188 195 206 221 226 234 249 308
MCKEE'S, Branch 250 Creek 126 133 178 250 271 292 310
MCKENDREEAN COLLEGE, 71
MCLEAN COUNTY, 46 74 95 115 116 120 136 160 162 166 178 187 189 192 207 221 234 238 244 260 262 265 279 287 290 299 300 304 307 310

MCLEANSBORO, 106 220 235 250 285
MCRANEY'S CREEK, 194 250
MEACHAM'S GROVE, 250
MEAD, Dr 43 S B 43
MECHANICSBURG, 182 251
MELROSE, 251
MENOMONE, 251
MERCER COUNTY, 46 81 107 111 113 121 129 130 139 171 195 253 260 275 280 292 313
MEREDOSIA, 60 224 251 294 Bay 251
MESSENGER, John 182
MICHIGAN CANAL, 31 32 52-54 59 60 231 242 County 144
MICHILIMACINAC RIVER, 244
MIDDLE FORK, of Big Muddy River 198 252 of Shoal Creek 252 of Silver Creek 252 Settlement 252 Stream 160
MIDDLE, Grove 252 Stream 110
MIDDLETON'S FERRY, 252 263
MIDDLETOWN, 252
MIER'S SETTLEMENT, 252
MILAN, 252
MILL CREEK, 91 96 112 222 252
MILLER'S, Ferry 186 222 Settlement 252 253
MILLS PRAIRIE, 101 253
MILTON, 132 253
MILWAUKEE RIVER, 206
MINERAL POINT, 267

MISSISSIPPI RIVER, 2 3 5 8 12 13
15 17 26 31-33 57 60-63 75
76 78 79 81 82 85-87 91 92 94
105-111 116 121 124 126 129
130 134 137 139 142 146 147
149-151 154 160 163-165 168
169 170 172 174 175 178 181
182 184 190 195 199 200 202-
204 208 210-212 214-217 221
223 224 230 232 238 240 245
247 250-252 254 257 258 260
265 268 269 272-278 279 281
282 284 286 289 290 292-294
298 302 303 305 309 312 313
MISSOURI RIVER, 12 40 63 83 86
87 223
MITCHELL'S SETTLEMENT, 253
MOCABELLA, 227
MON-E-TO, 175
MON-IT-TO, 175
MONK HILL, 38 253
MONMOUTH, 139 177 253 292
297
MONROE COUNTY, 14 45 46 117
121 122 129 135 156 193 197
204 216 221 254 260 275 278
280 292 301 310 311
MONTEBELLO, 254
MONTECELLO, 254
MONTEZUMA, 254
MONTGOMERY COUNTY, 46 93
102 116 117 122 130 134 154
164 194 220 222 227 228 236
238 246 252 254 278 287 291

MONTGOMERY COUNTY (Cont.)
292 294
MONTICELLO, 72
MOORE'S, Prairie 110 254 Settlement 254
MORGAN, County 46 88 94 95 105
117 122 123 130 133 150 161
165 166 181 182 185 189 190
192 197-199 206 208 217 218
225 228 229 233 239 240 244
246 251 259-263 266 274 277
278 280 288 294 295 301 303
312 313 River 144
MORGAN'S CREEK, 254
MOSS'S SETTLEMENT, 254
MOUNSE'S CREEK, 204 254
MOUNT, Carbon 254 Carmel 33 60
139 151 153 178 183-185 189
230 243 255 272 284 302 313
Charles 38 Flat Head 236 255
Joliet 33 38 218 236 255
Pleasant 256 Pulaski 256 Saint
Charles 256 Sterling 60 256
293 Vernon 110 150 174 191
215 230 231 243 252 254 257
309
MUD, Creek 207 258 298 Prairie
258 259
MUDDY, Creek 258 Fork 109 115
258 Point 258 River 13 14 17
109 165 177 241 254 301
Stream 258 Settlement 311
MULBERRY GROVE, 259 Post
Office 259

MUSCOOTEN BAY, 259
MUSICK'S STATION, 252
MUSKEETO CREEK, 259
NAPIERSVILLE, 191
NAPIERVILLE, 259 309
NAPLES, 63 223 224 248 251 259 293
NARROWS, 259 260 270
NASHVILLE, 60 140 185 195 239 242 260 263 278 302
NATIONAL ROAD, 187 213
NETTLE CREEK, 248 260
NEW, Boston 121 260 292 Castle 260 Design 121 260 Settlement 204 Harmony 18 Haven 260 Hope 229 Lexington 261 Nashville 155 211 Salem 133 261 Virginia 261
NEWBERN, 260
NEWLIN'S SETTLEMENT, 261
NEWMAN, Zenas B 71
NEWMAN'S BRANCH, 261
NEWPORT, 261
NEWTON, 110 261
NINE MILE, Creek 261 Prairie 261
NORRIS'S SETTLEMENT, 262
NORTH, Branch 180 181 Fork River 110 Grove 237 262 Prairie 262
NORTH ARM, Prairie 262 Settlement 262
NORTH FORK, 95 96 116 130 154 182 184 199 201 248 262 of Bear Creek 215 216 of Salt

NORTH FORK (Cont.) Creek 262 of the Embarras 193 262 of the Kishwaukee 266 of the Macoupin 220 262 of the Sangamon 159 166 189 207 209 259
NORWEGIAN, Grove 234 Settlement 262
O'GEE'S FERRY, 191
O'NEAL'S CREEK, 264
O'PLANE, 190
OAKLAND, 262
OGLE COUNTY, 46 111 112 119 123 124 127 136 142-144 150 152 191 206 208 210 214 226 234 235 237 239 262 264 271 272 290 298 310-312
OGLE'S, Creek 135 263 Prairie 135 263 280
OHIO, Grove 234 263 River 3 10 12 13 22 33 92 104 111 112 127 150 158 170 175 176 201 203 207-209 216 227 232 240 244 258 285 290 302 Settlement 263
OKAU, 263 Post Office 263 Settlement 263
OLD DAD, 188
OLD TOWN TIMBER, 188 263
OLDMAN'S CREEK, 263
OLIVER'S PRAIRIE, 263
OLMSTED'S MOUND, 263
ONO, 264
OREGON, 235 City 150 152 264

OREGON (Cont.)
271
ORENDORFF'S MILL, 264
OSAGE COUNTY, 38
OTTAWA, 31 53 56 57 114 160 167
174 187 191 195 205 215 220
223 225 233 239 247 248 264
269 274 303 305
OTTER Creek, 104 220 239 258
262 265 Fork 115
OUT HOUSE SETTLEMENT, 265
OX BOW PRAIRIE, 128 265
PADDOCK'S SETTLEMENT, 265
PADFIELD'S SETTLEMENT, 304
PADUCAH, 203
PAINE'S GROVE, 239
PALESTINE, 78 79 100 153 197
219 220 222 236 261 266 267
310
PALMER'S SETTLEMENT, 266
PANKY'S SETTLEMENT, 265
PANTHER, Creek 244 265 266
Grove 266
PAPPOOSE CREEK, 234 266
PARADISE, 266
PARIS, 61 100 162 181 195 201
212 262-264 266
PARKER'S, Prairie 96 266 Settlement, 267
PARR'S SETTLEMENT, 267
PATTOWATOMIE, 305
PAUL, Col 52
PAUPAU GROVE, 234 235 267

PE-CUM-SAUGAN, 56
PECUMSAUKIN, 241
PEEKATONAKEE, 15
PEEKATONOKEE, 267 283 300
313 River 136 143 150
PEKIN, 61 136 189 244 245 267
269 274 289
PEORIA, 61 103 125 144 150 181
187 191 195 199 216 226 234
259 267-270 277 290 301 309
312 Lake 124 181 221 236 239
259 268 270 284 301 County
46 81 113 124 125 127 128
136 207 236 268 284 289
PERKIN'S SETTLEMENT, 271
PERRY, County 45 46 103 110 125
129 140 158 184 196 211 222
239 244 258 261 271 272 284
293 301 309 G B 72
PERU, 271
PETERSBURG, 271
PETTIGREW, Mr 225
PHELPS'S GROVE, 271 Prairie 271
PHIGLEY'S SETTLEMENT, 271
PHIL'S CREEK, 271
PHILL'S CREEK, 245
PHILLIP'S Ferry, 214 274 Settlement, 272
PIANKESHAU BEND, 272
PIASAU, 117 272 Creek 149 River
165 246 271 278
PICKAMINCK, 227
PIGEON CREEK, 91 126 272

349

PIKE COUNTY, 6 46 81 91 92 94
103 105 107 118 122 124-127
133 139 151 153 161 163 183
193 194 214 215 219 233 250
254 271-273 280 282 293 294
PIKETOLEKA, 267
PILOT KNOB, 272
PIN CREEK, 272
PINATAWEE LAKE, 271
PINCKNEYVILLE, 60 125 205 223
244 258 261 272 284 293
PINE, Creek 237 311 River 124
PINUS, 272
PIPER'S POINT, 273
PISKASAU, Creek 234 297 River 273
PITTSFIELD, 126 151 183 214 219
254 273 274
PLAINFIELD, 201 273
PLATO, 273
PLATTE MOUNDS, 200
PLEASANT GROVE, 137 273 274 302
PLEASANT VALE, 126
PLUM CREEK, 15 111 186 197 227
274 284 289 308 Prairie, 274
PLUM RIVER, 136 230 274
POINT of Oaks, 55 301
POINT REPUBLIC, 274
POLECAT CREEK, 274
POND SLOUGH, 175 275
POOR PRAIRIE, 271
POPE, County 45 46 104 111 112
127 158 175 203 216 221 227

POPE COUNTY (Cont.)
238 244 249 254 265 295 303
311 313 River 121 139 275
PORTAGE, 82
POSEY, William C 70
POST, Col 52
POSTVILLE, 275
POTATOE CREEK, 221 275
PRAIRIE, Creek 275 287 De Long
Creek 135 197 275 Du Long
Creek 280 Du Po 275 Du Pont
275 Du Pont Sream 135 Du
Rocher, 6 202 276
PRATHER'S SETTLEMENT, 276
PRATT'S PRAIRIE, 220 276
PRESTON, 276
PRINCE'S SETTLEMENT, 124 277
PRINCETON, 72 150 191 277 312
PROPHET'S VILLAGE, 276
PROSPECT HILL, 277
PUGH, Mr 54
PULLIAM'S FERRY, 200
PUNCHEON CAMP, 277
PUTNAM COUNTY, 46 72 81 107
113 114 124 125 127 128 136
142 144 158 167 182 183 187
188 198 201 207 213 218 235
236 265 277 288 296 299-301
312
PUTNAM CREEK, 277
QUAKER SETTLEMENT, 278
QUINCY, 60 72 76 79 81 91 151
155 163 188 199 239 251 256
271 277 278 299 305 309

R. Mr 37
RACOON CREEK, 100 115 196 278
RADCLIFF'S POINT, 278
RAMSEY'S Creek, 102 Settlement, 278
RANDLEMAN'S SETTLEMENT, 278
RANDOLPH COUNTY, 15 22 32 45 46 73 87 109 111 121 125 129 135 140 170 178 184 201 202 208-210 221 227 230 232 234 238 252 261 274 276 278 290 298
RANDOLPH'S GROVE, 279
RASHVILLE, 188
RATTAN'S PRAIRIE, 279
RAY'S SETTLEMENT, 279
READFIELD, 280
RECTOR'S FORK, 280
RED OAK GROVE, 196
REDBUD CREEK, 269
REED, Col 86
REYNOLDS, John 63
RHOADES SETTLEMENT, 280
RICHLAND, 133 280 Creek 130 135 208 217 275 280 282 286 287 Grove 171 280 Prairie 135
RICHWOOD, 192
RICHWOODS, 239 280
RIDGE Prairie 281 Settlement 281
RIVER DESPLAINES, 236
RIVIERE Au Feve 200 Au Vase 160 Au Vaseaux 160 Des Iroquois 227 Des Plaines 189 Du Page 192

ROBINSON'S CREEK, 281
ROCHESTER, 133 281
ROCK, Creek 112 130 142 208 244 281 282 287 Port 282 River 2 12-15 31 60 76 107 112 123 124 129 130 143 150 152 157 171 175 186 191 196 210 214 215 230 234 235 237 240 247 263 267 271 272 276 282 283 290 298 300 301 303 313 Spring 15 41 60 71 283 292 293
ROCK ISLAND, 62 76 107 130 170 171 279 282 289 298 305 County 46 107 111 121 129 142 247 289 298
ROCKFORD, 31 282
ROCKPORT, 282
ROCKWELL, 283
ROCKY BLUFFS, 276
RODGER'S CREEK, 284
ROLLIN'S PRAIRIE, 284
ROME, 284
ROUND, Grove 284 Prairie 284
RUSH CREEK, 111 274 284
RUSHVILLE, 134 159 164 174 178 236 240 250 256 264 276 284 285 293 298 303 305
RUSSELL, John 36 37 Mr 37
RUSSELL'S GROVE, 285
RUSSELVILLE, 285
SADORUS, 285
SAGANASKEE SWAMP, 180

SAINT, Clair County 5 14 17 19 21
23 32 35 45 46 63 71 87 97
116 117 121 129 134 135 139
140 151 152 156 158 162 164
168 169 171 178 182 183 189
193 199 200 207 211 219 225
229 232 237 241 243 244 253
254 256 258 263 274 275 277
278 280 281 283 291 292 294
301 303 304 308 Joseph River
180 231 Louis Road 155 172
175 237 283 285 292 Marion
166 298 Mary's 298 Mary's
Creek 129
SALEM, 60 118 187 219 250 285
SALINE, 285 Creek 103 104 106
152 154 188 193 197 216 240
280 286 Stream 13
SALISBURY, 133 286
SALT CREEK, 116 120 130 144
166 182 185 189 209 226 227
234 245 250 252 275 286 287
300 Settlement 286
SALT, Fork 95 159 171 292 306
307 Prairie 94 209 286 Slough
286 Works 306
SAND CREEK, 288 Settlement 288
SAND PRAIRIE, 289
SANDY, 288 Creek 123 303 River
228 235
SANGAMON, 31 95 225 288
County 22 46 94 116 117 120
122 130-134 136 150-152 157
158 166 171 178 181 182 185

SANGAMON (Cont.)
186 194 195 208-210 213 217
222 225 226 227 234 236 238
248 252 256 259 261 265 271
275 281 282 284 286 287 296
297 300 River 8 12 34 94 95
201 130-132 136 151 154 163
165 166 171 178 181 182 185
194-196 199 201 222 223 226
229 232 236 245 254 259 261
262 266 271 275 277 280 281
284 286-288 296 299 306
Valley of 132
SAUGA-NAS-KE, 56
SAUGANASKEE RIVER, 313
SAUGANASKEE SWAMP, 289
SAUK VILLAGE, 130 289
SAVANNA, 60 289
SCAMET'S PRAIRIE, 254
SCATTERS of CASH, 175 193 289
SCHOOLCRAFT, Mr 12 34
SCHUYLER COUNTY, 46 81 91 95
103 118 122 126 133 134 177
178 183 185 186 188 236 240
250 256 263 264 284 285 293
298 303 305 312
SCOTT, William 303
SCYAMORE RIVER, 112
SEMINARY TOWNSHIP, 103
SENATCHWINE, 124 289
SENATCHWINE RIVER, 124
SENEX, 290
SETTLEMENT UNDER THE
BLUFF, 204

SEVEN MILE CREEK, 290 Prairie 141 290
SEXTON'S CREEK, 92 272 290
SHANNON'S STORE, 184 290
SHAW, John 215
SHAWNEETOWN, 62 78 87 110 140 188 190 192 198 201 209 242 243 257 285 290 291 298
SHELBY COUNTY, 46 98 101 102 116 134 153 155 163 165 171 183 201 222 230 232 242 247 278 280 287 288 291 308 311
SHELBYVILLE, 60 61 134 153 158 164 171 183 197 220 266 281 288 291 311
SHILOH, 291
SHIPLEY'S PRAIRIE, 291
SHOAL CREEK, 93 97 154 155 192 202 220 226 236 249 252 291 294 299 305 308 Bridge 292 Prairie 219 292 Settlement 292
SHOCKOKON, 292
SHONT'S SETTLEMENT, 292
SHOOK, Samuel 303
SHOOK'S SETTLEMENT, 292
SHREVE, Capt 12
SHUEY'S SETTLEMENT, 292
SHURTLEFF, Benjamin 71 College 71 College of Alton 70
SIDNEY, 244 292
SILVAN GROVE, 239 292
SILVER CREEK, 15 116 135 221 237 240 243 244 247 263 292 304 Head of 217

SINSINAWAY STREAM, 293
SINSINEWA, 38
SITGREAVE'S SETTLEMENT, 293
SIX MILE, Creek 126 293 Prairie 293
SIX'S PRAIRIE, 256 293
SKILLET FORK, 110 118 145 219 293 294 River 241 Settlement 293
SKILLET RIVER, 140
SLAB POINT, 294
SLOCUMB'S SETTLEMENT, 184
SMALL POX, Creek 200 River 294
SMALL'S SETTLEMENT, 294
SMALLSBURG, 294
SMART'S MILL, 185
SMITH, Joe 36 Joseph 188
SMITH'S, Lake 294 Settlement 294
SMOOTH PRAIRIE, 294
SNIDER'S SETTLEMENT, 295
SNYCARTEE, 193 River 126 161 293 294 Slough 126 151 215 233 250 272 282
SOLDIER CREEK, 142
SOMONAUK CREEK, 112 295
SOUTH, America 295 Branch 180 181 Fork 122 130 152 154 182 185 199 201 217 248 Fork Creek 161 Fork of the Henderson 217 Fork of Spoon River 201 Greene Prairie 246 Prairie 295
SPANISH NEEDLE, 295

SPOON RIVER, 104 107 113 124
    128 144 157 158-160 171 177
    185 195 198 201 206 207 215
    216 223 226 233 238 241 242
    266 275 277 295 313 Settle-
    ment 128
SPRIGFIELD, 60
SPRING, Bay 84 162 295 Creek
    108 130 273 275 280 287 296
    Grove 297 Island Grove 297
    Point 297
SPRINGFIELD, 33 72 78 79 131-
    133 149 151 152 157 158 163
    166 167 172 178 180-182 185
    192 194 195 201 208-210 213
    215 217 220 222 225 226 228
    239 246 251 260 263 271 281
    284 285-288 292 294 296 297
    300 310
SPRINGFIELE ROAD, 265
SQUAW PRAIRIE, 157 297
STARVED ROCK 33 297
STEAM POINT, 298
STEEL'S MILL, 298
STEELE'S MILL, 209
STEPHENSON, 130 171 282 298
STEPHENSON COUNTY, 46 111
    135 143
STERLING, Capt 86
STEVEN'S CREEK, 298
STILLMAN, Isaiah 298
STILLMAN'S RUN, 237 298
STINKING CREEK, 155 298
STODDARD, 204

STOKES'S SETTLEMENT, 256 298
STONE'S SETTLEMENT, 299
STOUT'S GROVE, 299
STRAWN'S SETTLEMENT, 128 299
STRING PRAIRIE, 154 173 213 273
    299
STRING TOWN, 299
STUBBLEFIELD'S BRANCH, 299
STURTEVANT, J M 70
SUGAR, Creek 97 100 108 120 130
    133 134 136 152 174 182 192
    197 204 207 208 220 227 230
    238 239 243 246 250 264 265
    278 284 287 299 300 Creek
    Settlement 300 Grove 300 Tree
    Grove 300
SUMMIT, 301
SWANWICK'S CREEK, 301
SWEET'S, Prairie 240 301 Settle-
    ment 260
SWETT'S PRAIRIE, 301
SWIGART'S SETTLEMENT, 301
SWINNINGTON'S POINT, 301
SYCAMORE, Creek 301 River 234
    283
SYDNEY, 60
TABLE GROVE, 275 301
TALON, M 82
TAMARAWA, 301
TARAPIN RIDGE, 301
TAUMARWAUS, 303
TAYLOR'S CREEK, 247 301
TAZEWELL COUNTY, 46 73 74 84
    120 124 127 130 136 137 161

TAZEWELL COUNTY (Cont.)
162 190 197 199 214 215 220
221 239 244 245 264 268 274
282 286 289 296 300 302 308-
310
TECUMSEH, 301
TEGARDEN'S MILL, 301
TEN MILE CREEK, 136 301
TENNESSEE RIVER, 203
TERRE HAUTE, 8 58 195 242 263
TERRE TREMBLANT, 283
THEAKIKI RIVER, 231
THORN CREEK, 302
THORNTON, 302
THREE MILE PRAIRIE, 302
TILLSON, John 70
TIMBERED SETTLEMENT, 302
TIPPECANOE, 111
TOM'S PRAIRIE, 302
TOMAHAWK, 241 Stream 114
TOTTEN'S PRAIRIE, 302
TOWN FORK, 249 302
TREMONT, 61 137 215 302 310
TRINITY, 92 175 302
TROUBLESOME CREEK, 302 303
TROY, 281 303 Grove 191 303
TURKEY, Creek 303 Fork 284 Hill 303
TURNER, Asa 70 Jonathan Baldwin 70
TURNEY, Mr 199
TURNEY'S PRAIRIE, 303
TURTLE RIVER, 283 303

TWELVE MILE, Grove 303 Prairie 135 196 243 248 301
TWITCHELL'S MILL, 303
TYRER CREEK, 91 303
UNION, County 45 46 92 103 109 111 137 145 155 156 164 174 175 177 181 182 191 193 198 222 230 256 281 298 303 305 Grove 304 Prairie 96 181 303
UNITY, 92 151 304
UPPER, Alton 61 70 304 Mackinau Settlement 304 Yellow Banks 195
URBANNA, 95 168 219 305
URSA, 305
UTICA, 305
VALENTINE'S SETTLEMENT, 305
VANBUREN, 305
VANCE'S SETTLEMENT, 284 305
VANCIL'S SETTLEMENT, 305
VANDALIA, 48 49 60 63 78 102 103 132 155 159 172 173 183 187 197 198 212 218-222 257 259 261 266 278 290 293 306
VANDEWENTER'S SETTLEMENT, 305
VERMILION, 54 95 100 154 223 258 County 17 46 95 108 115 137 138 173 188 209 212 262 307 River 120 159 188 196 232 258 265 274 286 287 292 306 310
VERMILIONVILLE, 307

VERMILLION, River 12 13
VIENNA, 112 164 167 198 216 249 256 307
VIGINIA CENTERVILLE, 177
VILLAGE PRAIRIE, 101 308
VINCENNES, 2 13 60 62 87 114 145 152 163 172 173 180 193 196 197 211 231 237 249 266 272 283 285 292 303 River 155 Road 175 258 308 Trace 197
VINCENT PORT, 87
VINEGAR HILL, 308
VIRGINIA, Grove 248 Settlement 221 308
WABASH, 18 23 98 101 Canal 57 County 46 114 138 141 151 153 163 178 183 184 185 189 230 243 255 272 284 302 313 Grove 308 Point 308 River 2 3 7 12 13 58 95 96 99 100 104 114 115 138 146 154 159 163 165 178 182 183 188 211 212 222 232 236 252 255 266 272 278 285 287 290 300 306-309 313
WABONSIC, Creek 112 River 144
WABONSIE, 308
WAIT'S SETTLEMENT, 308
WAKEFIELD CREEK, 103
WAKEFIELD'S SETTLEMENT, 183 308
WALKER, George E 63

WALKER'S GROVE, 192 273 308 309
WALNUT, Creek 197 244 262 295 303 308 309 Grove 219 309 Hill 309 Hill Prairie 110 309 Point 309 Prairie 96 188 309
WAPELO, 309
WARD'S SETTLEMENT, 309
WARREN COUNTY, 46 81 103 107 108 113 118 121 139 170 177 186 195 215 217 221 229 242 253 276 284 292 295 297 313
WARSAW, 61 203 213 309
WASHINGTON, 221 309 310 City 1 County 45 46 97 110 125 129 135 139 140 155 158 160 185 195 211 239 240 242 258 260 263 272 278 302
WASHINGTON'S GROVE, 310
WATERLOO, 121 122 156 254 260 275 310 312
WATT'S SETTLEMENT, 310
WAVERLEY, 73 150
WAYNE COUNTY, 46 96 101 106 110 118 139 140 141 145 155 160 166 167 196 199 216 218 219 226 238 240 241 243 248 259 291 302 303
WAYNESVILLE, 310
WEBB'S PRAIRIE, 310
WEBSTER, 310
WEED'S SETTLEMENT, 258 310
WEIGLE'S SETTLEMENT, 238 310

WEST FORK, 200 202 233 295
    Grove 311 Washington 277
WEST'S SETTLEMENT, 311
WET GROVE, 311
WHITAKER'S CREEK, 311
WHITE, County 46 103 104 106
    110 140 141 161 163 167 173
    184 187 192 206 213 241 247
    260 290 293 301 Hall 311 Oak
    Grove 272 311 River 13
WHITESIDE, 107 County 46 111
    127 142 175 186 240 247 305
WHITESIDE'S, Settlement 311
    Station 311
WHITLEY'S, Creek 311 Point 311
    Settlement 311
WHITMAN, S S 157
WIGGIN'S FERRY, 168 312
WILCOXEN'S SETTLEMENT, 312
WILKINS, Lt Col 86
WILKINSON, John P 70
WILL COUNTY, 46 47 99 108 114
    119 142-144 201 215 228 231
    236 273 302 309 313
WILLIAM'S CREEK, 312
WILLIS'S SETTLEMENT, 312
WILSON'S GROVE, 312
WINCHESTER, 63 151 244 260
    288 312
WINDSOR, 191 312
WINNEBAGO, 206 213 226 County
    46 72 93 111 135 136 143 234
    263 282 313 Inlet 312 Swamp
    107 108 123 158 312

WISCONSIN, River 15 76 Territory
    111 119 136 143 189 205 234
    251 264 267 283 293 300 303
WOLF, Creek 130 287 312 Prairie
    223 Run 312
WOOD RIVER, 116 117 165 217
    239 253 313
WOOD'S PRAIRIE, 313
WOODBURY, 313
WORCESTER, 313
WORKMAN POST OFFICE, 277 313
WORLEY'S CREEK, 313
WRIGHT'S PRAIRIE, 271
WYOMING, 198 313
YANKEE SETTLEMENT, 313
YELLOW BANKS, 313
YORK, 252 313

www.ingramcontent.com/pod-product-compliance
Lightning Source LLC
Chambersburg PA
CBHW071952220426
43662CB00009B/1098